MISKOLC ●

DEBRECEN ●

Y

R

A

River Tisza

River Tisza

SZEGED ●

R O M A N I A

U.S.S.R.

The Paper Bridge

Monica Porter

The Paper Bridge

A Return to Budapest

Quartet Books
London Melbourne New York

First published by Quartet Books Limited 1981
A member of the Namara Group
27 Goodge Street, London W1P 1FD

ISBN 0 7043 2296 X

British Library Cataloguing in Publication Data
Porter, Monica

The paper bridge.
1. Hungary - Description and travel
I. Title
914. 39'0453   DB917

ISBN 0-7043-2296-X

'Reunion', poem by George Szirtes, first appeared in *Outposts*. 'Budapest 51', also by Szirtes, first appeared in *The Iron Clouds* (Dodman Press 1975)

Excerpts from 'Born of the Shock', an article by Paul Neuburg which appeared in *The Listener*, 2 January 1964, reproduced by kind permission of the author

Excerpt from 'That day in Budapest when the Russians fled', by Gabriel Ronay, published in *The Times*, 23 October 1976

Excerpt from 'I am a Magyar' and 'Alföld' by Sándor Petőfi, from *Petőfi*, English translation by Anton N. Nyerges, published by the Hungarian Cultural Foundation, 1973

Excerpt from Carl Sandburg's 'Timesweep', published in *Honey and Salt*, ©1963, reproduced by kind permission of Harcourt Brace Jovanovich Inc.

Typeset by AGP (Typesetting) Ltd, London
Printed and bound in Great Britain by
Mackays of Chatham Ltd

For Adam

Acknowledgements

First of all I thank my parents for their invaluable advice, and for helping to make their memories my memories.

In Hungary there are many relatives and friends to whom I am deeply indebted for their kindness· and helpfulness. I won't mention them by name.

In England I am very grateful for the co-operation of George Szirtes, Paul Neuburg and Gabriel Ronay. There are also others whom I thank for their encouragement, patience and great assistance, not least of all my husband.

I am more than a traveller out of Nowhere.
Sea and land, sky and air, begot me Somewhere.
Where I go from here and now, or if I go at all
   again, the Maker of sea and land, of sky and
   air, can tell.

From 'Timesweep' by Carl Sandburg

Introduction

In my mother's sitting-room in Budapest was a huge pale green armchair. One day in 1952, my father was relaxing in it when his lighter slipped from his pocket. Searching, he reached deep down inside the chair. He felt something metallic and pulled out a large army revolver. Pointing it downwards, my father pulled the trigger. It went off, blasting a hole into the floor.

My family were terrified. Under the Stalinist régime anyone found with firearms was in the gravest trouble. To this day no one knows how it had got there, or when. It could have been in 1944 when the house was overrun by Nazis several times. Or it could have been in 1945 during the seige of Budapest when the house was used by the Red Army as a billet.

Late that night my father slipped out with the revolver and dropped it into a nearby sewer. Everyone was relieved and that was the end of the matter.

The incident now seems symbolic to me, for one could say that the entire Hungarian nation had been sitting unknowingly on a loaded revolver throughout the decade after the war: a revolver which finally went off on 23 October 1956. The Hungarian Revolution was victorious for less than a fortnight. It was crushed by Soviet tanks and troops on 4 November.

At the end of November my father, mother, brother and I fled to Austria. I was only four at the time so all I can remember is riding inside a dark caravan full of people in the dead of night. In December we began new lives as refugees in the United States. Altogether 200,000 Hungarians fled just after the revolution.

Today the world is full of refugees. Wars and disasters have thrown them up by the million. Two hundred thousand Hungarians, in the light of today's numbers, might not seem many, but being one of them the number can never seem insignificant to me. Someone who was born on top of a loaded revolver, blasted into the air and deposited far from home will always remain scorched.

As a youngster, I never really thought about my life's dramatic start. More than anything else, I wanted to be like my schoolmates, a real American kid. I even dreamed up suitable names for myself to use instead of my own, Gail Brown or Sharon Smith for instance. Who wanted a funny foreign name and parents who answered the telephone with heavy accents?

When we moved for two years to West Germany in the mid-1960s, I was intensely homesick for the Mickey Mouse Club, 'Twinkies' cupcakes and saddle shoes. I yearned for America as if it were my own.

But when I was seventeen, the pendulum swung. I became intensely non-conformist. I developed an avid interest in my own colourful origin. I soon learned that a great many people who had never escaped from anything so dramatic as a national uprising were fascinated by such a story. For others, all things Hungarian could be summed up in a single-worded banality: goulash. Or perhaps in three words: Zsa Zsa Gábor. I came to accept that a great many people in the West didn't even know where Hungary was and that by virtue of their oral similarity Budapest could be used interchangeably with Bucharest.

In my twenties and living in London, my roots became the subject of repetitive conversations at dinner parties:

'So you're from America?'

'Yes.'

'Funny, you don't sound very American.'

'Well, my family is actually Hungarian.'

'Oh, how splendid. When did you leave Hungary?'

'1956.'

'Ah, yes. I remember. I was quite young at the time but it made a great impression. . .all those Molotov cocktails and tanks. . .Saw it on telly. . .'

Such dialogues occurred so often that they seemed to merge into one. In the end I wanted, if not to forget these facts, at least to relegate them to the back of my mind, while I threw myself into a new life in London. I married and started a career as a professional journalist. I hoped that London was and always would be my home. Hungary and 1956 no longer seemed relevant.

Then, in 1978, my son was born. He had black hair, black eyes and olive skin. Anyone could see he wasn't exactly Anglo-Saxon. But I wasn't expecting the hospital paediatrician's reaction when she examined him.

'Ah, so you're from Hungarian stock?'

'Yes. How do you know?'

'Look here,' she said, 'on his right buttock. See that faintly blue patch? It's called the Mongolian Blue Spot, a birthmark which only appears in male babies from that part of the world. These babies can be traced right back to Genghis Khan, so they say.' She leaned closer and fixed me with a beady eye, 'He sired a *great many* children.'

I smiled politely. Afterwards my husband and I laughed together over the story. But later I looked in some medical books and the Mongolian Blue Spot was there, as the doctor had described it. So she was in earnest.

That was how my background and heritage boomeranged back at me, unbidden. A thousand miles from the Carpathians in a Hampstead hospital, feeling myself by now to be a true Londoner, I had given birth to a seven-and-a-half-pound Magyar with a blue spot on his buttock indicating a direct line back 800 years to Genghis Khan. I pondered upon this.

At last I decided to face up to certain questions which had pestered me over the years. Have I any affinity now with Hungary after so many years in the West? Do I still have compassion for the country of my birth and its people? I never really knew that country; is it too late? Am I still a *Hungarian*, despite everything?

Twenty-five years ago I left my country forever, aged four. Since then a new generation has emerged — my generation. I know that if I have doubts about these matters, my own child will be even more confused. After a quarter of a century, with Adam almost the age I was during that decisive revolution, it seemed the right time to return to search for a few answers.

So on a fine autumn day, Adam and I stood before the entrance to the passport control section at Terminal One, Heathrow Airport. My husband embraced us both, said a few last words and looked at us with some sadness and some scepticism. We'd be apart for a month, a long time in the life of a small family.

'Bye-bye!' Adam chirped, the way he does every morning when his father goes off to work. I lifted up my bag with one hand, took Adam by the other, and walked through the barrier.

I was soon to learn more about the nature of barriers and the strange phenomenon of crossing them.

One

I had only visited Hungary briefly once since my family emigrated. That was in 1971, when I was nineteen. I think I was rather a late developer in some ways, for I remember behaving naively and immaturely during that distant summer holiday. Sitting on the British Airways plane bound for Budapest for the second time in my life, I hoped that all the people I had met there when I was nineteen wouldn't remember me for the child I was.

I had been full of enthusiasm for life, but with little experience in handling it. Perhaps that wasn't surprising, for my parents had brought me up with unusual strictness and had generally made all my decisions for me. So at nineteen, on my first independent journey, I had sometimes put my unaccustomed freedom to careless use by proclaiming openly and with heady idealism the virtues of free enterprise. This habit of mine had led me into some tricky situations, and more than once I found myself confronted by the horrified faces of relatives and acquaintances.

This time I resolved to follow Polonius's shrewd advice, and take each man's censure while reserving my own judgement. The totalitarian régime might not have changed, but I sincerely hoped that I had. As the plane neared its destination a voice hit my ear.

'Can't stand these commie places,' it rasped. 'I try to get my butt out of them as quickly as I can.'

To my surprise I grew angry at the flippant remark. Then I wondered why I should feel defensive about Hungary. After all, I've been a refugee from it nearly all my life. For a moment I felt like a divorced woman who couldn't stand her husband but won't abide others making rude comments about him.

I thought of many things during that flight. How would Adam get on with his Hungarian cousins? Would it be too cold to swim in Lake Balaton? Perhaps I should have brought my husband's expensive camera. No, I'd never had the patience to read the

1

handbook, anyway. And I thought about my mother, who was waiting for me in her house in Budapest. She had arranged to come over from Germany where my parents now lived, so that she could show Hungary to Adam and me, and take us under her wing for a while. It would be the first time since 1956 that my mother and I would be together in her old house. My mother can get very sentimental, and I imagined her sitting there tearfully, waiting for us to drive through the old iron gate. This made me shake my head. Luckily, I thought, I have never been prone to sentimentality. I'm detached, logical, sensible. And I'm *never* tearful.

Ten minutes later the plane dipped down onto the sunny tarmac at Ferihegy Airport. At the very instant the tyres made contact, I felt my throat grow tighter and tighter, as if some phantom hand had got a grip on it and was starting to squeeze. Then my lungs seemed to close. I couldn't swallow and I couldn't breathe. At the same time the runway and airport buildings which had flashed into view became suddenly obscured by a strange mist before my eyes. I put my hands over my face in desperation. My face was hot and wet. Next to me, Adam slept underneath a little purple British Airways blanket. Your mother's a great fraud, I told him silently. I blew my nose. But the phantom hand didn't let go of my throat until the plane had come to a halt at last and everyone was rising and squeezing into the aisle.

Adam woke up at the sound of this commotion. 'This is Hungary,' I said. 'We're home.' He peered up at my drenched, sentimental face and nodded sleepily. *Home* didn't mean anything very much to Adam James Porter. It could mean Hampstead, where he was born, or Asia, where his Mongolian Spot came from. For a child of three, his mother is still his only real home. But what if the mother concerned isn't quite sure where *her* home is?

On the roof of the terminal was an observation deck from where friends and relatives could watch the planes landing. The newly-arrived passengers were then deposited by bus at the terminal entrance, directly below this waving crowd. I looked up, trying to find two eager faces I knew would be there watching out for me: my mother's cousin Mári and her husband Dódi.

I couldn't recognize anyone. Yet all of these strangers belonged in some way to one or another of my fellow passengers, for there was a great amount of name-calling, whistling, jumping, hallo-ing. In the excitement, a child's shoe dropped through the railing on the roof and landed lightly on the pavement. Then a man nearly lost the hat he was waving in his hand. I wondered whether every

2

plane from London was met with such hullabaloo.

I had a long time to consider this idea, for by the time Adam and I arrived at the end of the queue for passport control, it seemed to stretch for miles. As each passenger reached the desk his documents received thorough and lengthy perusal. The queue didn't seem to move at all, which was bewildering for someone accustomed to a quick glance at the passport photo, a little rubber stamping and a pleasant nod.

After half an hour on this queue, standing behind a red-nosed peasant in a ludicrous hat and his fat wife, my mood had altered from sentimentality and jubilation to silent fury. After one hour, I reached the young but morose official behind the desk. We exchanged unfriendly glances and I felt my heart sink to think that my very first encounter with a native in my native country had to be with such a dud.

I won't go into the subsequent unpleasantness with the customs official. Finally I reached the throng in the main part of the building where a mass of Hungarians waited impatiently, craning their necks. My spirits picked up again. Adam was propped on top of our suitcases, which I had loaded onto a trolley. He loves such epic scenes, and sat on the cases like a great Eastern potentate.

I was suddenly kissed and pressed tightly into a plump, buxom body. Adam was swept into the air. We had been found by Mári and Dódi. A moment later we were standing together outside in the sunlight. Mári was tearful. I always pictured her with her eyes on the edge of overflowing, so I was not surprised. Dódi still had a moustache and the same beaming round face.

'We were so worried, it took you so long!' Mári said. 'We asked everyone whether they'd seen an English lady with a child.'

I smiled at this, for I think I could only be described as English by those who aren't English. Americans have been mistaking me for an Englishwoman for years, while the British themselves think of me as a Yank, or at least as Mid-Atlantic. What would I be taken for in Hungary? I wondered. The one place in the world where I can call myself a native, they'll probably think I'm a foreigner who has somehow learnt to speak Hungarian with a strange accent. Emigrating at the age of four, then again at eighteen had made a zigzag out of the natural, straight line of my life. But perhaps that wasn't really so disastrous. After all, they say it becomes a woman to be mysterious.

Adam and I were bundled into the back of Dódi's forest green Zsiguli, quite an ordinary Russian car, considered a moderately

3

luxurious item in Hungary. It's Spartan and hard, but as I was to find out, most Hungarians (especially the middle-aged ones who can afford to buy a Zsiguli) have sufficiently well-upholstered bottoms for this not to matter too much.

So we thumped and bumped our way along the outskirts of the city. To be fair, the Zsiguli could not be blamed for the thuds, the roads had all the inevitable cracks and creases of old age.

Thirstily I drank in all that I could see; I didn't want to miss a house, a car, a tree, anything that we passed. I felt an underlying haste as if, from the moment of my arrival, a huge hour-glass was mercilessly measuring my time, reminding me that it was limited.

There was a great deal of road construction going on, judging by the trenches, the piles of rubble, the naked pipes and cables that could be seen. Once in a while we were all jolted into the air as the Zsiguli fell into a rut. I looked at Mári and Dódi, two quite ordinary heads bobbing up and down with the bumps in the road. A married couple in a strange car on a strange city landscape. Yet the thought came to me that we all belonged to each other. And this made me feel that a dormant part of myself might be called into play during my stay in Hungary: the part which belongs to all this strangeness. They had recently returned from a month's camping holiday in Switzerland and West Germany. They spoke disparagingly about coming back to Hungary, which, they said, was dirty, poor and discontented by comparison.

'That's funny,' I said, 'I get the same impression when I get back from Switzerland to England. That's how the Swiss *want* people to feel.' We laughed. But I knew what they were talking about.

When we entered the centre of the city I sensed an old familiarity. There wasn't a single building that I could specifically remember, but the overall aura stirred up a half-forgotten taste in my mouth. The dusty little neon signs clinging to sombre grey buildings, the fancy trappings of the West peeking indignantly through the holes in the Iron Curtain. These I vaguely recollected. Last time I was here I looked, this time I wanted to see; it is easy to do one without the other.

We reached the Chain Bridge, and as we swept across the Danube in a steady stream of traffic, Budapest opened itself. How could I forget how unbelievably, almost painfully beautiful this city was? It was a torture to be across the bridge in a minute and inside a tunnel on the other side. It was like having an exquisite box of jewels opened in front of you, and then slammed shut before you could take it all in. I felt like stopping and taking the whole place into my arms, then examining it, like a great work of art, from three paces back.

On the Buda side of the city, it wasn't long before we reached the hilly residential part where my mother's house was on Budakeszi Avenue, which has gradually, over the past several years, become a busy thoroughfare. Buses and lorries use this route to get into town. But it is lined with tall trees, so it still seems a refreshing place to live, especially with those green hills in the near distance. There is János Hill, with its look-out tower, and Freedom Hill (so named after the Russians ended the Nazi occupation of Hungary).

The Zsiguli stopped in front of the house where I was born. I have seen hundreds of photographs of that house, from the outside and the inside; pictures with my parents, my grandparents, my brother, our friends, our relatives or our pets. Pictures taken in all seasons. Black and white, and colour pictures. And still I didn't recognize the place.

'Why are we stopping here?' I mumbled. Dódi turned towards me and I read the answer in his eyes. He chuckled like an embarrassed schoolboy asking a girl for a date. Then he got out to unlock the creaky old iron gate and swing it open.

We drove through and stopped a few feet before the weather-beaten doors of the garage. To the left was the plain, dense lawn. Beyond it was a wild tangle of flowers and weeds. There was the house — simple, square, covered in ivy. Guarding this domain were three giant pines and two great chestnuts which my grandfather had planted forty years before. Now they stood upright like silent sentries, shielding the house from the road. Perhaps he had been able to envisage this screen and that is why he had put those saplings into the ground.

Adam ran immediately to a wooden swing at one end of the lawn. I made my way down a narrow path along the side of the house, and then to the main door around the corner. It was dark, cool and quiet inside. I stepped into the large central reception room, and slowly looked around. I could hear Adam laughing in the garden and Dódi shutting the car door. But inside, in the half-light, there were no voices and no movement. Time had spun an invisible web over everything, the baby grand before the window, the carved oak dining table, the faded Turkish carpet. The whole room seemed captured by its own past. I hastened towards the staircase. My mother would be upstairs waiting for me.

5

She was in her bedroom. As I went to kiss her, I got another shock. One of her legs was in a plaster cast, from ankle to thigh. I stood in the middle of the room, spluttering, 'Why didn't anyone tell me?' She burst into sobs.

'An accident — in the street — so terrible. I can't do anything.'

By now Mári and Dódi were bringing my suitcases upstairs, and they came into the room, looking helpless and apologetic. My mother had been shopping in a big open-air market two days before, when she had tripped off the curb and gone flying into the street. Her knee was broken. And now she was in great dismay, because she wouldn't be able to show Hungary to her only grandchild.

'I've got to sit here and — ' she blew her nose and spat out with loathing, '*rest.*'

I knew that my mother had never rested in her life. When she was young she had always been occupied with her successful career as a singer and actress. When she was older, after we left Hungary, she had turned into a hardworking housewife. She was hardly likely to learn how to rest now at seventy.

A few years ago my mother gave Mári and Dódi a section of the house, consisting of a downstairs bedroom and bathroom. Their daughter, also called Mári, now lived there with her second husband, Pali, and their little boy, also called Pali. The Hungarians always amaze me when it comes to names. I used to think all Hungarian females were called either Éva or Eszter. Now I know that's not quite true. There's an occasional Gizi and Zsuzsi, as well. Perhaps if people would stop naming their children after themselves, a few new names would slip into use.

Soon my mother's bedroom was filled with relatives — Dódi, Big Mári and Little Mári (a distinction which may apply to age but not to size for both are of ample proportions), Little Pali, and finally Juszti.

Juszti isn't a relative, she's something much more. She has been my mother's housekeeper and cook since 1954. She's short, shaped like a beer barrel, wears very thick glasses, has only one tooth left, and is the most gentle, loyal creature imaginable. When my family left in 1956, she stayed on to look after my mother's parents, who were also living in the house by then. She cared for them until they died, many years ago. Then she continued to stay, looking after the house and living for the brief month or so each year when my mother would return to visit, first from our home in America, then from London, and now from Germany.

Juszti cannot see very well any more, and her feet swell up after each day's work. But her cooking is still tremendous. She still calls my mother the *művésznő*, the *lady artist*. Her devotion is unmatchable. During my stay, she eventually revealed her own story to me, a colourful one. But most of the time she looked after us, tending to all our needs. I had to come to a communist country, it seems, to discover what it is like to have live-in domestic staff.

We were in the middle of eating Juszti's superb dinner that evening, when Big Pali arrived home from his university evening class in electrical engineering. I had never met him before. I reached out for a handshake. But the tall young man with dark wavy hair and moustache just ignored my hand. Instead, he bent down, clasped my shoulders and kissed me firmly on both cheeks. That's Hungarian for 'How do you do?'.

My husband was meant to telephone from London that evening. And shortly after we'd finished drinking the last of the homemade redcurrant wine brought over by my mother's cousin Laci, the phone rang. It had a weak little ring, which I should have taken as a bad omen.

I heard Robin's voice at the other end, amid much crackling.

'Hello? It's me. Can you hear me?' I said.

'Just about. How are you and Adam?'

'We arrived safely and. . .' Before I could finish, the line was disconnected and my words dropped heavily into the empty receiver.

A few minutes later the phone rang again. Robin and I exchanged the same few sentences. Then the line was gone. Again the phone rang, and its ring seemed even weaker than before. This time it was an operator. He told me to hold on. Then nothing happened. Finally I heard Robin.

'Is that you?' he shouted.

'Yes!'

'Finally. Now I want to know — '

'My poor mother has broken her knee.' The line was crackling away in our ears like Guy Fawkes night.

'Broken what? What did you — ' The phone was dead and limp in my hand once more. I sat in silence, and everyone looked at me in silence.

'God *damn* it,' I said. I don't like a roomful of silent people.

Big Mári walked over to me and sat down. 'I suppose you didn't know about the telephone system here,' she said. 'Oh, not everywhere in Budapest. Some districts have a good, modern exchange. We're only a few minutes way, but we don't have such problems. Robin could call you up there.' She sighed. 'I'm afraid this number is on the oldest and worst exchange in the city. It's bad even when you try to call Pest.'

Robin and I had agreed to phone each other at least once a week. But now what had seemed simple had turned complicated, and I felt a sense of isolation creeping over me. I replaced the receiver. This telephone had made a mockery of the international telecommunications network, the modern convenience which I had always taken for granted. I looked down on it with scorn, as if it were merely a dummy, a theatrical prop in a bad play.

I sat up until quite late with my relatives, discussing the missing decade that lay between us. Then, some time after midnight, Big Pali lifted my mother up in his arms and carried her upstairs. Mári and Dódi went home. Juszti had long since gone to bed. And I went to the bedroom opposite my mother's, where Adam and I were staying.

Adam stretched and turned over in his sleep. A small light was on and I looked around the room. This used to be my father's bedroom and study, from 1946, when my parents married, until 1956, when we left. There is a door giving onto a large terrace, which is on the roof of the dining alcove and bedroom of Little Mári and her family. This part of the house was an extension, built in 1948 to accommodate my grandparents who moved up that year from the country. Beyond the terrace are the great dark pines.

I stepped outside and looked over the railing. It was very dark. Budakeszi Avenue, like nearly every other street in Budapest, is lit up only on Saturday and Sunday nights. Otherwise the streetlamps remain unused, in order to economize on electricity. So during the week Hungary's nights are black and eerie. There is a sort of canopy over one end of the terrace, supported by ivy-covered pillars. I picked one of the leaves and took it inside. It was thick and strong, but around the edges it had started ever so slightly to turn crimson.

Before I turned out the light I looked at the full-length portrait of my mother on the wall above Adam's bed. It was done, long ago, in pastel coloured chalk by Anna Éber, an artist who is distantly related to us and whom I hoped to meet. My mother is wearing a pale blue evening gown in the portrait, an orange scarf hangs lightly in the background. During one of the numerous floods which had occurred in the house due to the leaky roofs, the portrait had been damaged. Some of the colours had flowed together. This had upset my mother, who was hoping Anna would touch it up and make it look like new again. But I thought the flood had given the picture an added dimension. My mother now appeared not only beautiful and alluring, but she had the quality of a mirage. It was so like my mother to want things to remain as they were thirty-five years ago, I thought. Doesn't she understand that the past can never be anything but a mirage?

This led me to think about Hungary's past. I lay awake for a long time reflecting on the war and the events which led to the revolution in 1956. The forties and fifties had been crucial decades. I wanted to understand what had happened in my country and why things were as they were today. Before I left London I had done some reading on the subject. And now like an inner news-reel I played it back for myself as I lay in the dark.

Before the Second World War Hungary had been a conservative country with a backward, largely agrarian economy ruled by Admiral Nicholas Horthy, former commander of the Austro-Hungarian navy. He had been appointed regent during the 'temporary' suspension of the monarchy.

His régime was moderate, but authoritarian, and his policy towards Nazi Germany was one of acquiescence. In the Hungary of the 1930s there was social and political discontent, and a dangerously wide gulf between the peasants and the middle classes. It was fertile soil for Nazi and fascist ideas. Pent-up resentments found an outlet in anti-Semitism.

During the war Hungary tried several times, unsuccessfully, to disentangle itself from Allied-Axis hostilities. Hitler forced the country to participate in his aggression towards other European nations, most notably Yugoslavia and Russia. In 1942 the government of Miklós Kállay established contacts with the West and declared its readiness to accept unconditional surrender should the Allied forces reach the Hungarian frontier.

When the Germans discovered this they occupied Hungary in a surprise move on 19 March 1944. The immediate result was the deportation of hundreds of thousands of Jews to death camps abroad. An extreme right-wing (Arrow Cross) government was installed by the Germans.

In late 1944 the Red Army advanced into Hungary. By January 1945 it had defeated the German army, following the devastating siege of Budapest during which the Germans made their final stand in the Castle. The Russians declared Hungary to be 'liberated'.

In effect, one occupying force had merely replaced another.

At first Hungary was a multi-party state. Free general elections were held and a Parliament was established comprising members of the Smallholders, Communist, Social Democratic, National Peasant and Civic Democratic parties. The communists polled only seventeen per cent.

In 1947 there was another general election. Once again, the communists failed to win significant support. This angered the Kremlin and the pro-Soviet faction in Hungary. They proceeded to liquidate, one by one, the rival political parties, whose leaders were forced into exile. In mid-1948 Hungary was declared a 'People's Republic'. Even the appearance of parliamentary democracy had been wiped out.

The new Hungarian Communist Party was bolstered by the U.S.S.R. Years of Stalinism followed, under Stalin's arch-disciple in Hungary, Mátyás Rákosi. Then, when Krushchev came to power, it seemed the reign of terror might come to an end. De-Stalinization began. Rákosi was severely criticized by the Kremlin. In July 1953, the premiership was handed to a more moderate communist, Imre Nagy. It was a time of thaw.

Rákosi, however, didn't give up the power struggle. When the tide turned in Moscow in 1955 he was back in favour once again and Nagy was ousted, mainly because of his liberal policies.

Rákosi was back in power, but Nagy was rapidly becoming a cult hero among the hundreds of former political prisoners whom he had freed during his short period as Premier. Among them were many well-known communist writers and other intellectuals who had been arrested and tortured during Rákosi's purges. They were now disillusioned about communism and despised what Rákosi stood for. They wanted everyone to know the truth about his régime: show trials, confessions extorted under torture, senseless executions. These newly freed and reinstated intellectuals opened the eyes of the country (and most significantly, its youth), and set the scene of moral outrage which led to the national explosion of October 1956.

In June 1956 the Poznan Riots in Poland indicated that violent outbreaks within the Soviet bloc were not unthinkable. Perhaps, for Hungary, that was the point of no return.

The revolution was the story of an amazingly fast-moving chain of events spanning thirteen days, from 23 October to 4 November. It began with a student demonstration, demands for reforms and democratization and the return of Nagy. The students attempted to be heard over Budapest Radio. Police opened fire and rioting broke out. The communist government declared martial law and requested Soviet military aid to quell the rioting.

But within twenty-four hours Nagy was installed as the new Premier by the revolutionaries. He appealed for the fighting to stop. By then the uprising had reached other parts of Hungary. János Kádár was appointed First Secretary of the Party — Nagy's right-hand man. Together they announced that negotiations were to begin with the Soviets for their complete withdrawal. They promised to reconvene Parliament.

Nagy formed his government, which included non-communists. Throughout the country revolutionary workers' councils were set up. They demanded, among other things, Soviet withdrawal, the dissolution of the A.V.O.s (Hungarian secret police), withdrawal from the Warsaw Pact, Hungarian neutrality, free elections, free speech and a free press.

Nagy announced the abolition of the one-party system. Political parties were rapidly being reconstituted and publishing their manifestos — the Social Democrats, Smallholders and Peasants. On 1 November Hungarian neutrality was proclaimed and Nagy requested the U.N., as a matter of urgency, to put the 'Hungarian question' on its agenda.

But Soviet tanks and troops had been pouring steadily into the country. The U.N. was sent a second official message, appealing to the great powers to recognize Hungarian neutrality. Ostensibly, the Soviets continued negotiations for their withdrawal. But the Hungarians watched with growing alarm Russian troop movements around Hungary's airports and railways. Budapest was already ringed by Soviet tanks.

On Sunday, 4 November, Nagy informed his country that the Soviets had begun their attack on Budapest.

Yet another puppet government was set up under the auspices of the Kremlin. At its head was János Kádár. It was later discovered that during the apparent success of the revolution, he had been having secret negotiations of his own with the occupying forces.

Nagy was later executed. Kádár has been Premier for the past quarter century.

'You must report to the district police headquarters within twenty-four hours of your arrival,' Pali told me the next morning as I was having breakfast.

11

'Oh, yes, I'd forgotten all about that. I'm going into town today, so I'll stop in on the way.'

Pali was putting on a leather jacket. He has a job doing some sort of scientific research for the Department of Agriculture, and he was collecting a few notebooks and papers to take into work with him. But before he could walk through the door, something caught his attention. He came up to me.

'What's that you're drinking?' he asked, pointing to the cup in my hand.

'It's tea, of course. With milk.'

Pali rubbed his moustache. 'What an interesting combination. Is that a custom in England?'

'The greatest custom there is. Try it some time.'

'Yes, perhaps I will. Good bye.' More kisses on both cheeks, and he hurried off. Just then Little Mári came out of her bedroom carrying Little Pali, who looked remarkably like his father except for the moustache.

Adam ran up to him, nearly tripping over my mother's outstretched leg in plaster. At the same moment Juszti walked in from the kitchen carrying three different types of homemade jam, and the telephone rang. There was a voice at the other end, which sounded as if it were coming from Alaska. But in fact it was my cousin Klári from Erzsébet Királyné Street, phoning to say hello. I was quite overcome by all the human activity surrounding me in this house. In London I have a nuclear family which has taught me to behave in a nuclear way. I was not used to being part of this wider field of vision, so at first it was disconcerting.

An hour later I walked into a shabby grey building in a Buda side street. I was directed by a porter to a small office, where a policeman sat behind a bare desk. On his right stood a pleasant-faced young policewoman. On his left hung a framed drawing of Lenin, not very pleasant-faced.

I filled in a visitor's entry form, we all signed it, my visa was stamped. It was over quickly and I was much relieved. For some reason I felt like a patient at the dentist, who had arrived expecting to have a tooth pulled and was happy to find that the diagnosis did not require it. I walked off scot free into the sunshine.

I took a bus across the Danube into Pest. I thought of the Blue Danube Waltz, and wondered whether the river had ever really been blue. For now it appeared to be completely colourless, not blue, or green, or even grey. Just translucent, and oily, like a big undulating fish.

12

The city centre bustled with the vibrant life and commotion that exists in any capital, and which I adore. Poets and painters have praised the tranquillity of the countryside, the beauty of a sunset or the magic of the rose. But that unclean urban froth, the mixture of concrete and mankind, has always been the stuff of my inspiration. I take it in gulps, and never seem to have enough.

But something was odd here. Something was wrong. What could it be? Then it dawned on me. Everyone in this place was speaking *Hungarian*.

This observation might sound silly. What could be more natural than for Hungarians in Hungary to be speaking Hungarian? But for me, this language had always been a secret tongue which only a chosen few could understand. In America and England, wherever I happened to be, I knew I could transmit my little secrets, be as rude as I wanted or share a private joke, in Hungarian. It was better than Pig Latin or Esperanto.

If I heard some stranger using my secret language, it was grounds for eavesdropping. It was a real event. So now that I heard my private code being used indiscriminately I was taken aback.

Toddlers were speaking Hungarian, and kids and long-haired hippies, and builders on construction sites. Young lovers were whispering in this once-secret code. Married couples were arguing in it, cab drivers shouting in it. In Hungary everyone speaks Hungarian, and I'll never get over that fact.

I looked more closely at the people around me and they were unfamiliar. There were a lot of squat women with hairy legs. And the men. Their faces seemed to be carved out of a far huskier material than those of Western men. Young and old alike, the men were callous physically, and I thought it unlikely that their spirits could be finer or more sensitive.

I already knew the reason. Since the war and the victory of the proletariat, the peasantry has been moving into the capital in great numbers. The peasants realized long ago that working with the soil is damned hard and that life is more congenial in the city. And as they now ruled the roost, why not get off the tractor and onto the tram instead? So up they trudged in droves, and eventually, this mass movement changed the entire appearance of the city's population. The minority of genuine cosmopolitan folk find this a source of much bitterness. They often talk sadly about the passing of the elegant and the urbane.

Someone really well dressed sticks out of the crowd there in an almost embarrassing way. And once or twice seeing certain peasant types dressed in city clothes made me think of the wolf wearing the nightie belonging to Little Red Riding Hood's grandmother. It wasn't that I had anything against the peasantry. I just felt that they should be manning the fields instead of the city streets. They seemed to be impostors, going through the superficial motions of urban life, but not fitting in. I like the right people to be in the right place. And the juxtaposition of crusty country faces with the divinely elegant backdrop of Budapest confused me. Had Cecil B. De Mille got the extras mixed up for this scene?

There was another visual handicap which struck me: the sheer number of soldiers to be seen everywhere. On buses, streetcars, in restaurants, shops, cafés, being carted around in lorries and digging up the pavements to lay pipes and cables. Soldiers, soldiers everywhere, khaki-clad and hard at it. Few men aged eighteen to twenty can escape conscription in Hungary, so perhaps this isn't surprising.

But not all the soldiers are Hungarian. There are many Russians, as well. The two can be distinguished by the letters sewn on their sleeves: M.N. is for Hungarian Army, C.A. for Soviet Army (although according to a recent rumour these letters really stand for Camping Afghanistan). Another way of telling the difference is that Soviet officers have caps shaped like perfect frying pans, whereas the Hungarian officer's cap is more like a slightly squashed ping-pong bat. But whatever the rank or nationality, whenever I saw a soldier I asked myself nervously: what is the Warsaw Pact up to now?

I also had the strange impression on that first wander around Budapest that the whole city was being dug up. Nearly every street had some sort of building work going on, repairs, renovation, rejigging of the public transport system, the reconstruction of some old edifice or other. But despite all this work, it was obvious from close up that the city was in neglect. It was a city of peeling plaster and crumbling stucco, yet with a perennial pride. It was once 'the Paris of the East', a former capital of the Austro-Hungarian Empire, now it was just a small satellite, like a dowager countess fallen on hard times. But I was soon to learn something about old dowagers: they may have bad teeth, but they can still bite.

That evening Mári and Dódi came to the house to collect me for a drive into the city and a cup of coffee at the regal old café which used to be called the Zserbó, and still is, by the older generation. I had heard that name mentioned countless times in conversations between Hungarian emigreś, and I began to understand that it was more than just a popular meeting place which served strong espresso and fancy cakes. It was the symbol of a lost era.

The Zsiguli rumbled down black, unlit Budakeszi Avenue. The rows of tall chestnut trees threw their shadows down on us. We reached the wide street called the Szilágyi Erzsébet Fasor, and in the moonlight I could just make out the peeling porticoes of the large villas which lined one side of it. These were once the homes of wealthy burghers, but they have long since been divided into small state-owned flats.

This street led into Moscow Square, a medley of bus, tram and underground termini, Soviet memorials and newly dug trenches. It was impossible to walk from one end of the square to the other without constant checks to see whether a tram might be merrily speeding towards you. Then we crossed the river which kept a low profile on unlit nights, but even so had an understated beauty, like an attractive woman without her make-up and jewels. On the other side, in flat, business and commercial-orientated Pest, there was an abundance of nocturnal activity. There were traffic bottlenecks and busy restaurants and cafés and sold-out theatre performances. There were a few youths about selling the evening paper, and a few staggering drunks.

The Zserbó was in Vörösmarty Square, the main showpiece of the city. Here tourists stand in the middle, eye the fine buildings and pleasant greenery in the centre, and think how prosperous things must be under the latest Five Year Plan.

It was in this splendid *fin de siècle* cafè that my brother and I used to romp mischievously among the marble-topped tables and green velvet seats when we were small. Not unlike Adam's behaviour when I have taken him for a treat to Fortnum & Mason's. But the Zserbó has crystal chandeliers and grand old paintings on the walls, instead of Fortnum's Riviera mural, and the Hungarians drink black espresso coffee out of dainty china cups instead of Earl Grey tea. But the air of formal sophistication is the same.

The three of us sat at a table in a quiet corner. Mári dipped a spoon into the dish of whipped cream in front of us and dropped a blob of it into her coffee. She stirred and then looked up at me with that particularly emphatic expression which often came over her big round face.

'Why, actually, did you decide to come home just now?' she asked. 'It's been so long since your last visit. Is there any special reason?' Dódi, too, looked at me questioningly.

'Do I have to have a reason to come home?' I took a gulp of my coffee. It dropped down my throat like a torch. Drinking Nescafé just doesn't prepare you for the stuff.

Dódi knocked his espresso back in one quick gulp, replaced the cup and smiled. 'No, no. Of course not.' He leaned closer to me, arms folded on the table. 'But you are. . .looking, searching for something? Your own childhood, your background?' Mári nodded her head, then tilted it to one side and waited for my answer.

I paused a moment, then lit a cigarette. I let my words ride out gently on the smoke. 'It's true I know very little about my feelings on the subject. I'd like to know more. The problem is, I don't know where to look or how to search for such things.'

Before my arrival I had imagined that from the first moment of my visit I would be on top of the situation. My itinerary would be organized for weeks ahead, with each hour directed at some purposeful activity. I would know just what to do, where to go, whom to go to, I had thought. Had I expected some omnipotent hand to guide me?

But the reverse had happened. Since I had arrived at Budakeszi Avenue I had been trying without success to orientate myself. I had been wandering around the house, upstairs, downstairs, in the cellar and in the garden. I would stroke the faded old tapestry on the wall of the sitting-room, or pick out a book from the shelves. I would brush aimlessly past the wild flowers on the overgrown path to the front gate. They had all been tentative gestures. I had felt I was reaching out, trying to discover something without knowing how to go about it. I was like a light aircraft searching in a vast darkness for the runway. When would the first lights appear? When would I be able to land?

The lights in the Zserbó were gradually being turned off. It was after nine o'clock; the café would soon be empty and closed. Mári spoke again.

'Perhaps it would be a good idea if, before you try to discover your own place here, you learned a little more about your mother and father. That might be the key.' She wore that emphatic expression again, combined with a rapid flutter of the eyelids.

I knew she was right. I smiled at both of them. 'Will you help?' I asked.

They told me they'd be delighted.

Later in the evening we walked along the calm, dark riverfront.

Large Western cars were parked in a row outside the Duna Inter-continental. I was already getting used to the little, funny-shaped vehicles that are so common in Budapest. Compared to these a Mercedes is wickedly luxurious. The East-German-made Trabant is the most popular and sought-after car in Hungary. It is small, with an abruptly sawn-off front and rear and a body made of plastic. It has a two-stroke engine that makes a noise similar to an old washing machine struggling through the final spin. But it's cheap to run and the cheapest car to buy. Unfortunately everyone wants a Trabant, so there's a six-year waiting list.

After admiring a few B.M.W.s and a Jaguar, we moved on. Mári and Dódi stopped in front of an imposing building with Grecian columns and lined with statues.

'That's the Vigadó,' said Dódi. 'It has a beautiful concert hall. Your mother sang there sometimes. Béla Bartók gave his farewell piano recital there, just before he left Hungary forever in 1941.'

Opposite the Vigadó, facing the river, was a small open space covered with grass. In the middle was an obelisk with the inscription: *1945*. It was erected by the Red Army.

'Has your mother ever told you about the Hangli Kiosk?' Mári asked. She took my arm and turned me towards the patch of grass with its Soviet memorial. 'That's where it used to stand. It was destroyed at the end of the war.'

Had my mother ever told me about it? It was like asking whether she'd ever cooked me dinner. I can't remember when I first started to hear stories about the Hangli Kiosk, I always seem to have known about this popular, fashionable night-spot where my mother had sung almost every night from 1939 until 1944. That was her heyday, those were her most glorious years. Every night the Hangli would be packed with the wealthy and the famous. They would send flowers to her dressing-room, and messages of admiration. Her songs became well known throughout the city. Everyone bought her records.

I even knew many of the songs that she had sung there. One of them came to my mind just then, a song about a lonely but proud woman who had never been in love: *I have never been heartbroken on an autumn night. . .my blue eyes never shine with tears. . .*

On that particular autumn night, as Mári, Dódi and I stood before the obelisk, there was no music, no flowers, no cheering admirers. All that ended thirty-seven years ago. There were only the three of us in an empty square, and after a moment or two we walked on, because the night was turning cold.

I wanted to be taken to the great neo-Gothic Parliament, further up the river. One side of it faces the Danube, and the other side overlooks a large square. It was in this square, on 25 October 1956, that my father almost lost his life.

The square had just been washed down. When we reached it, it was still wet and glistening in the moonlight.

'Were you here, too, on 25 October?' I asked Dódi.

'No. I was making my way here, but got held up in another part of the city. By the time I arrived it was all over.' We stared at the shiny, black square. It was empty.

What had happened on that site twenty-five years earlier was probably the single most tragic episode of the 1956 revolution. And my father had taken part in the historic event. There had been a massive demonstration outside Parliament. The square was filled with men, women and children. A column of Soviet tanks appeared at one end of the square, but the Russian soldiers behaved in a surprisingly friendly way towards the Hungarians. This remarkable fraternization delighted my father, who felt that the situation must surely be getting a lot better. He decided on an impulse to phone my mother and let her know of these developments. He happened to have a token in his pocket, which in those days was necessary in order to use a public phone booth. He made his way out of the crowd and across the square to a phone booth by a corner of the Ministry of Agriculture, a neo-classical building directly opposite Parliament.

Neither the demonstrators nor the Russians were aware that on the roof of this Ministry were stationed several A.V.O.s, Hungarian secret policemen. Without warning, and in order to disperse the crowd and put an end to the fraternization, the A.V.O.s opened fire. In an instant the bewildered Russians were inside their tanks and firing into the crowd. My father saw it all from the phone booth; he hadn't had time to dial.

He managed to escape into a side street. But several hundred people were killed. No one ever knew exactly how many died, but it must have been a great number, for the dead were carted away from the square by the busload.

Several years ago, when I was living with my parents in a Bayswater flat, I used to enjoy watching the many demonstrations that passed by our building on their way to the embassies of Kensington Palace Gardens. Sometimes I tagged along. The Ukrainians had especially exciting demos. So did the Israelis. I liked the sense of action and adventure, the chanting and the banner-waving.

On one such occasion my father took me aside before I had a chance to run out. 'Take my advice,' he said. 'Keep out of large, emotional crowds. They can be dangerous.' I didn't know what he was talking about, so I ran out onto the street all the same. Now I understand.

I took one more look at Parliament, with its spikes and huge green dome. On the very top of it, as on the tops of so many buildings in Hungary, is a luminous red star. It seemed as superfluous as the glacé cherry on top of a fruitcake. Then I looked around for the phone booth. But it had long since disappeared.

In the morning the autumn sun shone brilliantly onto the terrace outside my bedroom. When I pulled open the curtains it poured in, flooding the whole room with warm yellow light. The hills in the background seemed to be swaying ever so slightly in a gentle breeze. And it occurred to me that at that precise moment there couldn't be a more lovely sight on earth.

I went downstairs. The contrast made me shiver. It was cold, dark and silent. It wasn't the first time that I tried to stop myself comparing it with a mausoleum. I preferred to see it as part-museum, part-church. And it did have the sort of sombre respectability required by those places. But whenever I entered it from the sunshine, it always struck me as a rather grand tomb. And so it was. For there were more memories buried there than I could ever hope to exhume.

I heard a sound from behind me and turned to find Adam. He had followed me downstairs in his Mothercare dressing-gown and slippers, mumbling something about a cup of tea. Suddenly the mausoleum was no longer. We were in a sitting-room, that's all.

Juszti was in the kitchen getting things ready for the *müvésznö's* and my breakfast. Little Mári was there, too, feeding Little Pali, who is younger than Adam and couldn't yet feed himself. They were sitting at the tiny kitchen table. Pali and Adam were very pleased to see each other. Adam cried, 'Hello!' and Pali cried, 'Ha!' (he couldn't speak yet, either).

The evening before, Adam had been taken for a walk with Little Pali by Pali's parents. The two children had sat in their pushchairs, and all down Budakeszi Avenue and around the wide block, Adam had done all the talking. Neither Mári nor Pali spoke English, so they merely nodded and smiled at Adam's lengthy monologue about London, his grandparents and his nursery school. Adam only stopped chattering when he saw a yellow tram clanging by.

Mári had given them a piece of chocolate each. But Adam ate faster than Pali, so when he'd finished his piece, he made a grab for Pali's. But his little cousin was quick. He stuffed it into his mouth before Adam could reach it. Then they both burst out laughing. Some things just don't require verbal communication.

Adam and Pali liked to imitate each other. When one tripped over a carpet, the other did too. When one laughed, so did the other. The reason for the laughter didn't matter; it was an end in itself. Pali began to pick up one or two words of English. Adam adopted Pali's primitive grunts and groans. Every once in a while Adam would knock Pali down, because he was bigger. Then Pali would cry out and enlist the sympathy of whomever happened to be nearby. In short, they developed the major characteristics of modern international relations.

I left them in the kitchen and wandered out into the dining alcove. I ran my fingers along some of the old volumes on the shelves which covered the walls. In between Browning's *Collected Poems* and János Arany's translations of Shakespeare's plays was an owl which my grandfather had stuffed. It was losing its feathers.

Then I sat down on one of the dining chairs. It was upholstered with the sort of ancient cushion which immediately collapses into nothing when sat upon and makes the sitter feel he is about to fall straight through. From there I had a good view of the strange carvings in the antique oak table which my mother had bought from Count Széchenyi before the war. There was a figure of a naked woman with one breast amazingly larger than the other. I was just contemplating this phenomenon when the telephone rang.

Ever since Robin's abortive attempts to phone me from London, I was always pleasantly surprised when there was actually someone at the other end of the line with whom a conversation could be carried out. It seemed a minor miracle, another small achievement under the Five Year Plan.

'Hello?' said a woman's voice. 'Hello, is that Monica?'

'Yes, it's me. Who is that?'

'Klári *néni*.' (A Hungarian custom: when older people speak to younger people, they refer themselves as *néni* (aunt) or *bácsi* (uncle). It doesn't matter whether the people concerned are related or not. Being a Hungarian brought up in the West, I could disregard with impunity this silly business.)

20

'Hello, Klári,' I said. 'How are you and Laci?'

'Fine. I understand you've already spoken to Little Klári.' (Klári *néni* is Big Klári, her daughter is my cousin Little Klári. But in fact Little Klári is an enormous girl who towers above her mother and everyone else. The only big thing about Big Klári is her bust. But still, conventions must be maintained.)

'Yes. She mentioned something about a concert she is playing in soon. I've been invited to it. Shall I see you there?'

'You'll see us before then. Come to lunch on Sunday. I'm making fried chicken. It's my speciality.'

'That'll be lovely, thanks.' An image of Colonel Sanders flashed briefly into my mind.

'And,' she continued with a big sigh, 'I suppose you ought to meet *him*.'

'Him?'

'Csaba. Klári's fiancé,' she said wearily. 'He'll be at lunch, too.' There was a disparaging note in her voice.

I remembered now that I had heard about Csaba. I didn't know much about him except that he was in some way involved in music. Klári had met him at the conservatoire, where she had studied the oboe.

'I'm looking forward to lunch, then. Love to Laci *bácsi*.' That *bácsi* had slipped out before I could prevent it. I was embarrassed about it, but instinctively I knew that Klári *néni* would prefer it so. And who am I to displease the older generation?

I hung up. Why did Big Klári sound so unhappy about Csaba? I wondered. I'd heard that the girls in Hungary were all bursting to get married.

Meanwhile the table had been laid for breakfast. Juszti looked at me inquiringly. 'Would the *művésznő* like to come and eat now?' she asked.

I drank my tea out in the garden. There was a wobbly wooden bench facing the lawn and I sat on it and studied the wild flowers that grew all around the pine trees. I am bad at botanical names, but somehow those flowers didn't need names, they were better without them. They were simply tall purple flowers, and yellow ones with thick black centres, and delicate pale pink ones. There were small blue buds and wispy white blossoms, too. I liked them all because they just appeared wherever they wanted to, without help or permission. It must be nice to be so free.

I wanted to get to know my surroundings, so I spent the day at home. I watched Juszti preparing a huge jar of pickled cucumbers on a table out in the garden. Then Adam and I collected conkers in a straw basket, and went exploring around the back of the house.

As we were going inside for lunch, I heard someone calling to me from the front gate. A young man and woman were standing there, looking somewhat dishevelled. They had rucksacks on their backs. The man told me they were Polish. I realized they needed some kind of help, but, as we couldn't communicate very well, I fetched Little Mári.

Through a few basic words and some sign language, we understood that they needed a place to bed down for the night. They couldn't afford the fee at the nearest camping site.

Mári paused for a moment and bit her lip. She looked at me, then threw a glance at my mother's bedroom window. Then she shrugged, opened the gate and beckoned the two Poles in. Marcel Marceau couldn't have said more with those few silent gestures. She started to lead them towards the house. The young couple were so shy that they stood rooted to the spot. Mári pressed her two chubby hands tightly together and held them out. 'Poland and Hungary,' she said quietly, nodding her head. She didn't have to say more.

Juszti gave the Poles lunch, and then they were given a note to take to a friend nearby, who might have a vacant room for the night. I saw them leaving from the upstairs terrace. They took a good long look at the house from outside the gate, hoisted up their rucksacks, waved to me and walked away.

That evening my cousin Géza dropped in. When I had last been in Hungary a decade before, I had been closer to Géza than to any of the others. He had seemed then to be a lonely, quiet young man. He had looked upon me as an exotic creature, brought up in New York and living in London — distant, exciting places. He had worn cheap, old-fashioned shoes. When I had been with him, I had felt a little uncomfortable in my Western clothes. But he had been kind and gentle.

Now Géza had a wife and small daughter. His wife was a doctor in a working-class suburb in Budapest. He no longer had to live with his mother and stepfather in their neglected house opposite a knitting factory. He wore a suit now, and decent shoes.

We embraced each other. He smiled. Many things had changed in his life. But the loneliness, the *silence* in his eyes was still there. We sat opposite each other, talking, exchanging news. Gradually I began to feel that I, too, was somehow the same as I had been when we were last together. Many things had happened to me, the whole world had altered around me. But to Géza I was still the magic vision, his cousin from abroad. The years peeled away, leaving only what was unchanged.

'Shall we go out for a coffee?' he asked suddenly.

A few minutes later we were in his battered old Mercedes, rumbling underneath the black trees and unlit streetlamps which were fast becoming familiar. Even in the darkness I could see his face clearly, I suppose because of his very light blond hair, fair skin, and nearly white eyebrows and lashes. Géza has more German blood than Hungarian.

'Are you happy?' I asked.   He didn't reply right away. Then he said, 'I don't complain too often.'

'That's not the same thing at all.'

He glanced at me. 'Shall we go to your favourite spot?'

Frankly I couldn't remember which my favourite spot had been, or even that I'd had one. But I didn't admit it. 'All right,' I answered.

He turned sharply to the right and drove up a steep narrow hill. We reached a part of the city where the roads were cobbled and the houses were large, chalky monuments from the seventeenth and eighteenth centuries. It was the district surrounding the Castle which overlooks the city from one of the Buda hills. Now I knew where he was going.

A minute later he stopped beside the Fishermen's Bastion. Now I could recall that evening when I had been nineteen and had stood for a long time up in one of the look-out towers, drunk with the view of the Danube and, beyond it, the lights of Pest.

'I've often thought about the evening I brought you here. We talked a lot then, do you remember? You said you'd never forget this view, that you'd take it with you wherever you went.' Géza spoke quickly but softly. The Statue of St Stephen cast a shadow over the bonnet of his car. What a fickle thing the human heart can be.

For a while we looked at the view, standing in the chilly wind. Then we went to the Hilton, just opposite the Bastion, where three Americans were drinking gin and tonics at an outdoor table. We went inside. The decor was bright orange and there were more potted plants than people. I don't like empty cafés.

I knocked back a black espresso (I was acquiring the technique) while Géza sipped a soft drink.

'Do you really remember all that?' I asked him.

He nodded. 'You were such a sweet little thing. I've thought about you a lot over the years.'

I looked at my hands, folded primly on the table. I couldn't look into his eyes. How quickly I had abandoned my thoughts about him and my Hungarian summer. When I went back to London, I had lived only for London. This is the sin of being young and full of expectation.

Géza had wanted to be a dentist, like his father. But when he applied for a university place in the mid-1960s, he was turned down in favour of more suitable candidates, such as the offspring of workers and peasants. This policy is still largely maintained in Hungarian universities, although I've heard it said that things have really improved: nowadays anyone can get in provided they have the right connections.

So, thwarted in his ambition, Géza became a mechanic instead. Now he was not only a first-rate one, but he had his own thriving car repair business. Quite an accomplishment in a country which for thirty years has viewed private enterprise the way Hitler viewed the Jews. There is a growing number of self-employed businessmen in Hungary. They even have their own 'union' of sorts. But in a communist country, such people will always remain more or less outside the mainstream of society.

'Are *you* happy?' he threw my own question back at me.

'I have most of what I hoped for, and much to look forward to.'

He nodded, looked at me and finished his drink. 'That's good,' he said.

'But,' I added, 'I don't believe in being *too* happy. A little discontent makes you try harder. Like the Avis people.'

'Like who?' he laughed. 'Come on, I'd better take you home, or your mother will give me a thrashing.'

Yes, maybe I had never really grown up after all. Perhaps I was still the nineteen-year-old who had to be home early or turn into a pumpkin. I picked up my handbag with an air of resignation which Cinderella could never muster, and we walked back to his car.

On the way home he talked about his wife, Gizi, and their daughter, called Mercedes. 'We're planning a little trip to Sopron next week. Would you like to come? Gizi is attending a medical conference there, but that'll only take a couple of hours. The rest of the time we can go sightseeing, or do whatever you want. We could stay overnight.'

I had never seen that old town by the Austrian border. 'Yes, I'd like to go with you.'

When we got back to the house, the downstairs rooms were

dark. It looked as if everyone had already gone to bed. But I noticed as I walked up the uneven stones of the pathway leading to the front door that my mother's light was still on. She'll never get out of the habit of waiting up for me.

I fiddled for a while with my key. Finally I got in and crept past Juszti's bedroom door. I could hear my mother upstairs, limping around on her crutches. I pulled aside the heavy curtain which hung across the bottom of the staircase, and hurried up to see her.

Two

The following Saturday was Big Mári's 'free Saturday'. In Hungary part of the population works on Saturday one week, while the other part is off-duty, and the next week it's reversed. So, as Mári wasn't working, she decided to go shopping with Little Mári and I asked whether I could join them.

We took one of the big blue buses that stop near the house on Budakeszi Avenue. It was a warm and sunny day towards the end of September; what the Hungarians call an 'old women's summer'. We three old women certainly enjoyed it. We wore light dresses and let the sun warm our faces through the windows of the bus.

The bus drivers in Hungary all seem to be frustrated Formula One racers. The passengers are generally juggled, tossed about and pitched high out of their seats. That's why most people don't mind putting on a bit of exta fat around the bottom: you can bounce better that way.

We got off at Moscow Square. There were untidy queues in front of bus stops and tram stops and there was an ebb and flow by the doors of the underground terminus where the gypsies stood selling roses, carnations and sunflower seeds. Dark girls and women and a few children were trying to tempt passers-by with a few meagre bouquets. One woman flashed a gold tooth at me while she kicked a cat out of the way with her bare foot. 'Fine sunflower seeds,' she called out, sticking a fistful of them under my chin.

From the square we took a tram to the big, open marketplace where each week Little Mári did her main food shopping. The market was on two storeys and was stuffed fit to bust with food.

On the ground floor there were butchers' counters piled with joints of pork and mutton. 'Beef is the only thing that we can't always get,' Big Mári explained. 'Let's buy some rabbits' liver for the kids.'

We went to another stall overhung with pale, plucked chickens with sunken eyes and outspread toes. Next to them were pigs' trotters and even great bristly snouts. Little Mári noticed the look of unconcealed disgust on my face and giggled. 'Those are delicious in aspic,' she said. 'Oh, we shave off the hairs first, of course.'

We passed chunks of fatty bacon, spicy Gyulai sausages and long rods of 'winter salami' and paprika salami. There were tubs full of pickled cabbage, pickled stuffed peppers and tomatoes. We bought a bagful of pickled cucumbers. Hungarians love pickling things.

Before we went upstairs we stopped at a stall where a man was selling fresh, hot *lángos*: lumps of dough that are fried until they're crisp. Most people serve them salted and doused with garlic juice. It all sounds slightly primitive, but it makes a tasty snack. A nice change from the Big Mac.

We went upstairs eating our *lángos*. When I reached the upper level I couldn't believe what I saw. Everywhere I looked there were tables sagging under mounds of bright-coloured fruit and vegetables. It seemed as if all the country markets had been poured together into one bulging bazaar. All the traditional things were there — green peppers and red peppers and the aromatic yellow 'butter peppers', cricket-ball-sized tomatoes so red that you think they must surely stain, a dozen different types of beans of all sizes and colours, red cabbages, white and green cabbages, more sorts of mushrooms than I could count, outsized water melons and apples and peaches whose combined fragrances almost made me drunk.

I walked along between rows of stalls, slowly examining the goods. Behind each stall stood a peasant woman with a scarf around her head. Most of these women were old and toothless. They were dumpy, and wearing dark skirts and aprons. As I walked past, they cajoled and pleaded with me to taste their fine produce.

'I have a colleague,' Big Mári whispered, 'who often comes here at lunchtime. When the old peasants offer him samples of their juicy fruit, or their walnuts and almonds, he accepts. "Yes, yes, it's lovely," he tells them. He tastes his way around the whole market. But he never buys anything. Then he returns to the office no longer hungry. If someone has just come back after a three-course meal in a restaurant, he berates them: "You should always have a light lunch. Like me." '

I leaned back against a wall to get a better view of the array. 'I never knew you could grow so many different things,' I said.

'Do you know what all this is?' she asked, with a wide sweep of the arm to indicate the whole market. 'This is our wealth. This is to us what oil is to the Arabs. Each peasant woman who comes up to town once a week to sell her produce is like a little oil well. You know we can't import any fresh fruit or vegetables. We can't afford to. All this is our own. There is no soil in the world richer than ours.'

By now the sight and the aromas had quite gone to my head. The three of us staggered out of the market under the weight of several shopping bags filled with the raw material of Juszti's future gastronomic miracles. But our work was not yet over. Further up the street we stopped at a state bakery to buy the week's bread.

'This place is very popular,' Little Mári told me, quite unnecessarily, as that was obvious from the long queue which stretched out of the bakery door and halfway down the block.

We put our bags down and waited. Several minutes later we were still at the same spot. After ten more motionless minutes vague tremors of discontent ran along the line of long-suffering shoppers. Being an impatient person, I left the queue and went inside the bakery. The counter was empty, devoid of sales assistants and devoid of bread.

'But there's nothing going on in there,' I said, when I returned to our place in the queue.

'Of course not,' Little Mári answered. 'They're at the back, baking.'

It wasn't long afterwards that we noticed some movement and heard voices coming from inside. The line of shoppers sprang to life.

'Orders, orders, please!' said the voice from within the bakery.

Soon we were at the door and I looked in to see long trays of fresh bread being wheeled in rapidly like patients in an emergency ward.

There were four saleswomen at the counter, dressed in white coats like doctors. They were expertly popping the loaves into the customers' bags, sometimes three or four loaves per customer. There was a delicious smell.

We bought our bread, as well as a few buns and pretzels, and turned to leave. Just then a storm blew up at the other end of the counter. One of the 'doctors' glared at a man hurrying out of the door.

'Who was that person? Does anyone know that impossible man?' she cried.

One of the customers called out, 'That's the third time I've seen him jumping the queue in here.'

'I know who he is,' said a woman, 'he's a hairdresser at the beauty salon a few doors down.'

'Oh, is he?' yelled the 'doctor'. 'What a nerve! Do I go bursting in there and ask him to do my hair? He'd better not dare come in here again. That's all I can say.' She smoothed down her white coat.

The shoppers grunted in agreement and the rapid popping of loaves into bags continued as before.

We made our way back to the tram stop. Shopping always tires me terribly. Not so much physically, as mentally: it's the strain of knowing that I shall have to go on heaving those shopping bags around for years, for decades, until the end of my days. Sometimes it seems to me that the one Great Truth in life is the reality of the shopping syndrome, and that God has turned into an omnipotent plastic shopping bag.

I turned to study Big and Little Mári. They are alike in many ways. Most obviously in appearance, both being rather short, rotund, with plump faces and alligator legs.

Their outlook is also similar. They combine the practical with the philosophical, and want merely to enjoy the simple (not too expensive) pleasures in life, do a decent day's work and be left in peace. Politics and officialdom have little to do with them: very suitable for living in Budapest.

Perhaps their attitude could be summed up in one of Big Mári's throw-away lines. The other evening during our tour of the city, I asked about the statue on top of Gellért Hill, overlooking the river from the Buda side.

'Oh, that?' she said. 'That's the Liberation Monument. The Russians erected it in memory of the Red Army having liberated us from the fascists.'

'But what is it a statue of?' I asked, for it was difficult to see.

'Just a woman waving a palm above her head.' She looked up at it with a wan smile and shrugged. 'Most of us don't really notice it any more. But, what-the-hell, there's room enough for it up on that hill, isn't there?'

For Big Mári there will always be room enough for everything. Her own desires don't demand a lot of space.

When we arrived back home I found my mother downstairs, sitting in the big green armchair with her leg propped up on a stool. She was reading a letter, trying hard to concentrate on it while Adam was chasing Little Pali around the dining table.

'Who is that from?' I asked out of a rather meagre curiosity.

She looked up, her face strained. 'From Dunci.' Her expression

29

seemed to soften slightly. 'Do you remember her? She looked after you and your brother for a while, in 1955.'

'Really? Well, I'm afraid I don't remember her, as I was only three at the time, and my memory is not too great even about last year — '

'All right, never mind. She's had an accident. Broken her hip.' My mother folded the letter.

'How old is she now? Must be very old.' I slipped into a chair. Adam climbed onto my lap.

'She's eighty-four.' Now the letter was back in its envelope. I could tell there was something else on my mother's mind.

'What's the matter?' I asked.

She shook her head. 'Dunci says she has nothing to live for any more. She wants to die.'

'How terrible. Poor woman.' What is there to say in such a situation? When you want desperately to live, and live fully, it's inconceivable that anyone should want to die.

'She was always so brave, so hopeful. I always wondered at her incredible strength. Now. . .' My mother held the letter out towards me as if it were a candle which would light up my face. 'Now, she's given up at last.'

I stared at the envelope in her hand. 'What can we do?'

'She's very poor. And has nobody, really.' My mother seemed to be talking to herself more than to me.

'Let's give her some money,' I suggested. For some reason, after saying that I felt ashamed of myself. It was the same sort of guilt that I feel when I look at my bank statement and realize that my standing order to Oxfam has bought me peace of mind rather cheaply for another few months. 'No,' I said. 'I'll phone her up and. . .'

My mother cut me off impatiently. 'She hasn't got a phone.'

'Well then, I'll write to her. I'll send her a card saying that I'm in Budapest and that I'd like to see her. Perhaps her memory is better than mine and she'll know who I am.' Adam was still sitting on my lap, and I pressed my mouth against the back of his head. 'Do you think she would want to see me?' I asked my mother.

'She'd be thrilled. She thought she'd never see you again.'

'Good. Then it's settled. Where does she live?'

'Just outside the city boundary. Of course she hasn't lived in Budapest since she and her husband were forced to move out during the *kitelepités*.' It was the first time I had heard that word. I was to hear it again, often. And to learn its meaning.

'Perhaps Géza could drive me there one day. I'll take her some food, perhaps a book or two, and photographs.'

'Hold
at it. 'It sa

'I'll see her
upstairs to get a p
this old woman fron
past I had never welcor
comfortable. But I found
fancied that because of me sh
Perhaps I was only flattering
decidedly worth exploring.

At noon on Sunday Laci came to pick us up
back seat was covered with a striped cloth and l
was a fat grey poodle.

'This is Fleur,' Laci told us as we got into the car. A
either side of the poodle, which refused to move, an
manoeuvred herself into the front seat with her broken leg
cushion.

Laci is one of those slow, cautious drivers who bowls along in a
sensible way until someone in another car does something silly an
then he bites their head off like an angry bulldog. So we growled our
way slowly across the city, from the west to the City Park in the east,
where Laci and Klári have a flat.

When we arrived Big Klári insisted on taking us into the kitchen to
inspect the pieces of chicken, smothered in breadcrumbs, which were
waiting to be fried. Laci then poured us each a glass of his homemade
redcurrant wine. Afterwards he showed us a great tub in the bathroom
where last summer's pickings were already merrily fermenting away.

'You must come up with us one day to the bungalow at Bánk and
see the garden. We're there every weekend until mid-October.
You'll be charmed, simply charmed,' he assured me.

'I think Bánk has become far more chic than the Balaton,' called Klári from the kitchen.

'Now, now, beloved, let's not exaggerate,' Laci answered,
squirming a little uneasily beside the tub of next year's wine.

'When is Little Klári coming home?' I asked.

'Her woodwind quintet had a rehearsal this morning. She and
Csaba will be along in half an hour,' said Laci.

'Did I hear you mention Csaba?' Klári yelled from the kitchen.
'My God, we'd better warn you about him.'

I strolled in to where Klári was patting the chicken pieces,

on a minute.' My mother took the letter out again and looked

ys she's leaving hospital in two days.'

next week.' I eased Adam onto the floor and went

en and postcard. To my surprise, I was anxious to see

my childhood, and even excited about it. In the

ned meetings with people which might be un-

myself welcoming this one with open arms. I

e might have less reason to want to die.

myself. But the possibility seemed

in a bright red Lada. The

ng majestically on top

dam and I sat on

d my mother

sting on a

uiet,

d

through the park. 'Because dogs aren't allowed in that part.

I glanced down at Fleur, swaggering along at the end of her leash. Adam complained as I held him back. Triumphantly, Fleur wagged the pom-pom which hovered above her fat bottom.

As we moved along together, we passed several people who looked down, smiled warmly and whispered words of admiration. 'Sweet!' and 'Charming!' and 'How lovely!'

I felt proud of Adam. He has always been much admired. I felt especially pleased with him that day because he looked quite startling in his Western clothes, blue jeans overalls and trendy shoes, with a little red cap perched cockily on his head. He was an unusual sight here in Hungary, I thought.

Then Adam ran off to inspect a pair of lovers who were smooching in a car parked on the side of the road. We passed another small group of people. They looked down, smiled and uttered the same words of admiration. That was how I found out that a French poodle is more exotic than an English boy, to the eyes of strollers in Budapest's City Park.

Laci went after Adam, to pull him away from the open car window into which he was peering with great interest. Inside, the lovers had stopped their steamy activity, and were exchanging pleasantries with the intruder.

Further on we came to a grey castle brooding in the middle of a dried-out lake. It could be reached by a narrow causeway and we started along it, looking at the carpet of muddy leaves where the water should have been.

'This is the Vajdahunyad Castle,' Laci explained. 'It's a nineteenth-century replica of the Hunyadi family's castle in Transylvania, which was built in the thirteenth century. Nice, isn't it?'

We studied a few gargoyles, then Laci decided it was time we turned back, for the chicken would be nearly fried by now.

Soon after we reached the flat and settled ourselves comfortably in the small but opulent sitting-room, the door bell rang.

The next minute Little Klári was coming towards me, her big peachy face beaming. She was even larger than I had remembered her. I barely noticed that there was someone following in her wake, a short, curly-haired fellow with eyes that drooped a little at the corners. He was wearing a thick pullover which he must have long outgrown because the sleeves stopped halfway down his arms. His wrists hung vulnerably at his sides.

'Csaba, this is my cousin,' said Little Klári, 'Monica, this is my fiancé.'

It was a most unHungarian first meeting. There was neither kissing nor embracing nor hearty camaraderie. Just a spongy handshake and the merest nod. Csaba then sat down in a corner of the room and stared gloomily out of the window.

During the meal Csaba sat in between Laci and Big Klári. He grew visibly smaller with each course. He seemed such a nonentity, and I wasn't sure whether I liked him much, but I felt rather sorry for him. He looked like a goldfish in a bowl, peering out myopically at a load of cats.

As I munched the chicken and tasted a funny pink sauce which was served with it (which turned out to be made of mashed rhubarb), I eyed the flat. Despite the crystal chandelier and smooth reproduction furniture, it was a sort of do-it-yourself place. And the person who did it was Big Klári. The puce-coloured tapestry on one wall was her handiwork, as were the small rugs on

33

the floor. She even sewed the traditional Hungarian tablecloth we were eating off, or rather, the one underneath the see-through plastic protective cover we were eating off. (Understandable enough: the red, white and green cloth mustn't get rhubarb-coloured as well.)

The place was spotless. She had a great many plants by the window and not one of them dared droop. There was a Victorian sense of order and discipline in everything. Poor Csaba was the only item which didn't conform. You had to admire him for that, at least.

I watched Adam nervously as he walked around, pulling the net curtain off its railing and picking up dainty porcelain figurines. He took Fleur's ball away from her and threw it up into the crystal chandelier. He tapped my mother's plaster cast for a while. I was immensely relieved when, as soon as we finished eating and left the table, Adam turned his attentions to Csaba instead.

'What's your name?' Adam asked him.

He seemed startled at being addressed, and didn't say anything. Probably because he didn't speak English.

'I like you,' said Adam. My son says that to practically everybody. I think he just likes to hear himself saying it. He also likes to hear himself say 'dear God' and 'don't forget me'.

I had a feeling that Csaba did understand him then, for he looked at Adam and smiled ever so slightly. I hadn't seen him smile before.

Adam ran to the upright piano and clambered onto the stool. He immediately began to make up a song, accompanying himself energetically. It was a silly song, about his Mummy doing the shopping and his Daddy going to the office — the sort of 'sexual role-playing' stuff the women's liberationists would love to have heard. But it didn't matter what it was about, because no one understood it but me. What did matter was that it was the first untethered outburst of pleasure we had heard that afternoon. And within seconds it seemed to raise the temperature in the room by several degrees.

My mother, naturally, began to sing with Adam. An ex-singer can never resist such an opportunity. But because of her leg she couldn't play the piano as well. So Little Klári offered to play. She was used to giving children piano lessons, so felt at ease with the assignment. She pulled up a chair, got out some sheet music, and started to play a lively tune.

Adam jumped off the stool and started to dance. He was like

34

one of those contestants in an amateur talent show, who tries to demonstrate how many different things he can do, until he collapses into an exhausted heap at the footlights. Everyone started to laugh. Even Csaba. I was the first to notice this, but soon Big Klári did, too. The expression on her face was guarded, but there was no doubt about it. She was utterly amazed.

Adam whirled around the room, then tripped and landed by Csaba's feet. He bent down to lift him up, and as he did so, Adam grabbed his arm and nearly pulled Csaba off his chair.

'You play the pinano,' said Adam, still pulling Csaba's arm.

'Yes, let's both play something for him,' called Little Klári enthusiastically. She beckoned to Csaba. 'Come on, a duet!'

Her fiancé was reluctant. He had already smiled and laughed. Did he have to perform as well? His face was flushed. Then Adam gave his hand another mighty yank and Csaba staggered in the direction of the piano.

The two of them sat side by side. Klári shifted her enormous frame a little away from Csaba. 'Hey, you're taking up all the room!' she teased, and we all laughed.

They began to play. Adam sang, danced and gesticulated grandly like David Garrick. As the music went on, the playing acquired more and more panache. I glanced at Klári's parents. It was obvious that they'd never heard Csaba playing before. He wasn't at all bad. And every time he turned around to see what Adam was doing, he chuckled to himself, and his performance got even better.

When it was over there was a great round of applause. Laci even gave a standing ovation. This embarrassed Csaba somewhat. He left the piano and went back to his seat by the window. But Adam still had no intention of leaving him alone. He climbed up onto Csaba's lap. And there he stayed.

When I looked back a few minutes later I saw that they were leafing through a colour magazine together, bilingually discussing the pictures. Adam's head lay heavily on Csaba's shoulder.

'Monkey,' said Adam, pointing to a page.

'*Majom,*' Csaba agreed.

Big Klári gazed at the scene, shook her head slightly in wonderment, and smiled. 'I'm going to get my cake from the kitchen,' she said. 'And, Laci, let's have some more of your excellent wine!'

There was more music later. Csaba waltzed Adam around the room while Klári played some Strauss, all of them giggling. We had cake and coffee. Outside the light had changed to a dusty blue hue.

At last Csaba rose to leave. He shook hands firmly with Adam. He nodded good-bye to my mother and me, and gave Little Klári a hurried peck on the cheek. He gave Laci a wave. He moved towards the door but just before he got there he stopped, turned around and looked hesitantly back into the room. For an instant he seemed as small and out of place as when he first entered, a few hours before. But then he straightened his back a bit, strolled quickly over to where Big Klári was sitting on the sofa, and kissed her on both cheeks. 'Thank you, Klári *néni*,' he said. 'Good-bye.' And he was gone.

She sat there for a moment without moving. I could see her mind was at work. And her daughter was watching her with apprehension. 'Well,' she sighed at last, looking around at us all, 'perhaps our Csaba won't be so bad in this *duet,* after all.'

'Let's celebrate. Let's have more redcurrant wine! And more cake!' cried Laci. His wife rose to get them. 'And Mother,' he called after her, 'this time, don't forget a piece for Fleur!'

That evening, Mári, Dódi and I were sitting together at a table in the old New York Café where my father, when he was a young writer, used to meet his friends and colleagues. It isn't called the New York any more, but the Hungária. We were drinking espressos and talking about the old days.

'Your father actually used to work in this building,' Dódi told me. 'He wrote for a weekly paper called *Hétföi Hirlap* which had its offices upstairs above the café. Of course the place was badly damaged during the revolution, because of all the fighting going on outside on the Nagy Körut. It remained closed for years. When it opened up again it had a new name, but it still looks just the way it used to inside.'

I looked around. There was a marble floor, elaborately gilded walls and ceiling, neo-classical paintings and carved figures, huge mirrors and globe lights. But I was disappointed. There were no animated groups of writers huddled over black coffee and *pálinka,* blowing smoke rings high up to the painted cherubs.

If everyone carries with them a spiritual home, a movable feast which they store away inside to warm them in the cold, then mine is the continental café. I have dreamed about such places. I get a pang whenever I have to pass one by without going in. This is hopelessly European. Or perhaps it's just hopeless, full stop. Because the sort of café I transport around inside my mind doesn't exist any more. The clientele has changed.

Like everyone else, I'd read those books about Paris in the twenties. The things that went on in the the Dôme, the Cupole, the Deux Magots. Writing, drinking, smoking, reading. Hemingway, Fitzgerald and Pound. A few years ago I went to Paris to write a story about it. I went to one of those grand old cafés on the Boulevard Saint Michel, sat down, ordered *café noir*, took out my pen and papers and started to write. Then someone at a neighbouring table said, 'Hey, look! It's Françoise Sagan!' And everyone sniggered. I packed up and left. It serves you right, I told myself, for pretending to like *café noir*.

'Do you know,' Dódi was saying, 'at one time the waitresses here brought pencils and paper along with the coffee. This was where all the writers, the newspapermen, theatrical directors and producers used to meet. Famous people.'

I answered with a grunt. The place was empty now except for a tableful of Arabs and two spotty youths trying to feel the waitress's bottom. God, was I born after my time.

Suddenly the New York was filled with loud music. We had been sitting in a corner near the door and until then I hadn't even realized that in the middle of the café was a deep pit with a restaurant and a group of gypsy musicians. I got up and leaned over the balustrade. Down below there were several tables with diners. Standing in front of the musicians was a hefty lady singing in a deep voice. It was one of those old folk tunes which I remembered hearing at countless Hungarian restaurants on Second Avenue.

'Yes, that style of life,' Dódi went on, 'always suited us Hungarians. Even in the nineteenth century, when we were part of the Austro-Hungarian Empire, our inclinations were much more bohemian, more French than Teutonic. We were never straight-laced, rigid people. The Hungarians always liked to live it up.'

I had heard about the golden age, after the 1867 pact with Austria until the outbreak of the First World War, a half century of peace during which the arts flourished. Great national artists, like Munkácsy, and poets like Endre Ady went to live in Paris. And when they returned, they brought Paris back with them.

'What have you lined up for yourself this week?' Mári asked me.

'On Monday and Tuesday I'm on a trip to Sopron with Géza and his family. On Wednesday I'm going to visit Dunci. And after that, I shall have to play it by ear. There are so many things I want to do.'

'Have you thought about visiting Gölle?' Mári asked.

Gölle is another name, like the Hangli, which I have been hearing for as long as I can remember. It is the name of the small village where my mother was born. I had never been there. I knew that my grandfather was the headmaster of the village school there until he retired, and that every Sunday he had led the singing in the village church. But that was all.

'How far away is it?' I asked.

'About three hours,' said Dódi. 'Well, it takes that long in my car, anyway,' he laughed.

It was hard to believe that a place which had always existed for me purely as a fantasy could be reached in a mere three hours. One morning session at Adam's nursery school. The length of a West End play. And I could be in that village which I had tried so often to imagine, seeing the old school, the church, the house where my grandparents once lived. Suddenly it became important to me.

'Could you take me there?'

Mári and Dódi looked at each other. 'Next Saturday we must work,' Mári began, 'but the Saturday after that we're free again. Would you like to go then?'

'I'll put it in my diary,' I said. 'The pages are starting to fill up.'

Dódi ordered glasses of white wine for Mári and me. He never drinks before driving. Few people in Hungary do. It's the one law that seems to be unquestioningly obeyed, because the penalties are so severe. So I wonder why there are so many car accidents?

The wine warmed me up and I found myself giggling without knowing why. 'Should we phone anybody up in Gölle to tell them we're coming? You know, my mother's relatives. There must be a few peasants down there that we can visit.'

Mári smiled. 'There are, yes. But they haven't got telephones. It's not like going to Zürich, you know. It's just Gölle. One street. Two rows of old peasants' houses with chickens in the front yards. That's all.'

I sipped my wine. 'Of course.'

'And anyway,' she continued, 'it's better not to let anyone know we're coming. That is, if you really want to meet those people as they genuinely are, and not in their best clothes with their houses all clean and tidy.'

'She's right,' said Dódi. 'Let's surprise them.' He winked at me.

I wondered what I would learn in Gölle about my grandparents, my mother and perhaps even myself. I've never really liked villages. Dust, dirt, the smell of pigs and stables. But there comes a time, I thought to myself as I gazed around at the gilded splendour of the New York Café, when you have to get to the root of things. And you can't do that without getting some mud on your feet. For that's where roots are. In the mud. Then I laughed and nearly choked on my wine. The metaphors were killing me.

Mári and Dódi looked at me as though I were mad, then looked with perplexity at each other.

'Sorry, sorry,' I spluttered. 'Just a thought I had.' With that I turned my attention once more to the gypsies in the pit. They were still playing tempestuously, but the singing had stopped. 'What is that lovely music?'

'Liszt,' said Dódi.

'I like it.' I looked down over the balustrade again. The diners weren't paying much attention to the music. They seemed to have finished eating and were now chattering away over coffee. The violinist was wandering around among the tables doing his best to serenade the ladies, but they were oblivious to his attentions. They're not Hungarians, I thought to myself. They've got no romance, no Liszt in their souls. (By now I had drunk a fair amount of wine.)

I sat down again. I was feeling intoxicated. But not from the alcohol. It was a familiar feeling, because I had had it before. I felt as though I were trying desperately to place myself somewhere. My head was spinning, with the Liszt, with the Austro-Hungarian Empire and those poets and artists who leapt over to Paris the way pins fly to a magnet, with the cafés and the coffee, the streets full of great flaking buildings, the bridges over the river, and my own dreams — lost or yet to come. If only I could put a shape to these things, a name. If only this sensation, similar to the one I had the moment my plane landed at Ferihegy, could be bottled and label-led. Then I would know where to put myself. I don't find it easy being a Hungarian, because the question keeps arising: where is Hungary? Is it, for me, the little nation in the middle of the Car-pathian Basin? Or is it part of that bigger continent called emigra-tion, a portable country?

Later, but still with these thoughts, I wandered out into the crisp autumn night with Mári and Dódi. Just outside was a dark empty charabanc, with the name of an East German city written on it.

'Ah,' Dódi commented, 'this must be waiting for the group which just had dinner in the pit.'

So I was right, after all.

Three

We drove from Budapest to Sopron early the next morning across a Hungary that was hiding under a dense white fog. I found this amusing because I remembered that when Adam was born Juszti had said, 'Really, Monica should bring up the child here, and not in England — that damp, foggy place. That island is unhealthy.' And other Hungarians since then (those who have not been to Britain) have made comments which gave me the impression that they still think of the place as being perpetually buried under an oppressive, Dickensian fog. In vain I've explained that the England I have known for the last decade is different from the one which wallowed in darkness, dirt and pea soup during the Industrial Revolution. In vain, because people need to cling to their little illusions. I am no different. My month in Hungary rattled a few of my own illusions about my homeland.

Through the fog I could occasionally make out the form of a huge rectangular haystack by the roadside, or see the misty outlines of little peasant cottages. There were fields of corn, wheat and sunflowers, looking pale and fragile. From time to time farm animals wandered near the roadside, lost, perhaps, in the endless fog.

But all this was only a backdrop to my central activity: getting to know Géza the family man. For in the back seat was his wife, prim but chatty, and little Mercedes, who has the same white complexion and fair hair as her father. Merci, as she is nicknamed, was rather hungry, as she had got up at five o'clock that morning and left home without much breakfast. So Gizi was searching through an enormous pile of things in the back of the car to find the sandwiches and pastries she'd brought along for the trip.

'Ooh, look, I've found something here,' said Gizi, extracting a hand from the bowels of a bulging overnight bag.

'I want it!' cried Merci. In her enthusiasm the little girl upset a case on the seat next to her and a dozen shoes fell out.

'Now look what you've done,' her mother scolded. 'You've knocked my best pair of suede shoes into the doughnuts! They're full of jam!'

'What do you need suede shoes for in Sopron, anyway?' asked Géza. He peered at his wife through the rear-view mirror. 'You'd ruin them on the cobblestones.' Just then a cart full of fat sows loomed up ahead in the fog and he had to swerve suddenly. 'See what you made me do! You and your blasted suede shoes. Throw them out of the window.'

'Are you joking?' Gizi snorted. 'I had to give the salesgirl 100 forints under the counter before I could buy these. The whole country is after them. They're beautiful.' She looked down at the sticky shoes on her lap. 'They *were* beautiful,' she corrected herself, sadly.

'I need a new ring,' piped Merci. She was holding out her small dimpled hands and I saw for the first time that she was wearing three tiny rings with glass stones in them, and that her fingernails were lacquered bright red.

'You've got enough rings,' said Géza, this time without peering into the mirror.

'But I might lose them,' said Merci, not without logic.

'It's true,' her mother added, 'she's always losing her rings, and you know how unbearable she gets when she hasn't got any. We'd better find a shop in Sopron and get her some more. What's a couple of forints, anyway?'

Géza turned a weary face towards me and smiled ironically. 'This is what I get for keeping two women.' He sighed. 'It doesn't matter if they're three years old, or thirty-three. Women are all the same.'

We drove on in silence for a while, the headlights of the Mercedes breaking the fog ahead of us. I strained my eyes to see something of the countryside. What a waste! Here I was, for the first time in my life (no, the second; the first time I had been four and it was 1956) travelling westward across Hungary, and I couldn't see anything except vague forms and outlines. I had so wanted to get a *feel* of the country. But all I felt was the imitation fur seat cover in Géza's car. And although I hate imitation fur, I was glad of its warmth, for outside the fog was cold, and I hate the cold a lot more than I hate imitation fur.

'I don't know. . .' Géza was muttering, almost to himself. 'I have a feeling we're going the wrong way.' He was looking to the left, then to the right. But there were no signposts, and even if there had been, who can read signposts in the fog?

Merci started to giggle. She held her tummy and rolled from side to side on the seat. 'Isn't Daddy dumb!' she said.

'Shh!' said Gizi, slapping her daughter's bottom. 'What's the matter? You're not lost?' she asked Géza, poking her head in between the two front seats.

'We should have been in Győr by now,' he answered vaguely. 'It's you two back there, you've mixed me up, with all that nonsense about shoes and rings.'

'Wait!' Gizi squealed suddenly, and Géza nearly ran off the road.

'What is it?' he yelled.

'I think I recognize where we are. There's going to be a sign soon, I just know it. So go slowly.'

And a moment later, there was indeed a signpost. The Mercedes crawled slowly up to it. And we all sighed with relief. We would be in Győr shortly. We were on the right road.

This was something to celebrate. Gizi passed around the cakes and the soft drinks, the pears and apples. By now the back seat resembled the ladies' department at Harrods during the January sale. There were clothes, shoes, handbags, coats and make-up everywhere. Merci sat in the middle of it, applying lipstick to her pursed lips. You had to admire her, she had the sort of self-possession most women never manage to acquire. And she was only three. She was a little blonde fairy, with the eyes of the Artful Dodger. Not a bad match for Adam.

'Ah, yes,' Gizi began, 'I remember this road well. I went to a medical summer school at Sopron one year, long ago when I was a student. When Géza and I were courting.' She rested her chin on the imitation fur cover of Géza's seat. 'You used to know this road, too, my little bunny. You drove out to see me every weekend.'

'Mmm, that's right,' Géza mumbled. 'And now look at me.'

Gizi gave him a little jab in the shoulder and leaned back into her seat with a laugh that sounded slightly forced.

I should mention here that in Hungary endearments such as 'my little bunny' are widespread. 'My little squirrel', 'my little pussycat' and 'my little angel' are among the most commonly used. In some cases these endearments are applied only occasionally, but in other cases (usually between older married couples) they are used every single time the dear one is addressed. Thus the country is absolutely seething with bunnies, squirrels, pussycats and angels.

By mid-morning we reached Sopron. The fog had been thinning out, and I had no trouble seeing enough of the town's pretty main street to whet my appetite for more. But first we had to find the hospital where Gizi's conference was being held. We asked for directions and a few minutes later we were parked in front of a large, nondescript building.

I heard some sort of commotion going on in the back seat so I turned around, and got a nasty fright. I thought some strange woman had sneaked into the car.

'It's only me!' laughed Gizi. 'I've put my wig on.' It made her look like one of those trendy rock musicians, with their studied dishevelment.

'Now what are you doing?' asked Géza, eyeing his wife disapprovingly.

'Just changing my skirt.' She was skilfully slipping one off and another on simultaneously. 'And my shoes, of course,' she added.

'Why your shoes?' asked Géza.

'They don't go with this skirt, silly bunny.'

'Oh, I see.' Géza replied laconically, but he didn't really see at all, because he was watching two rather pretty lady doctors walking up the steps of the hospital.

Gizi got out of the car, adjusted her attire and smiled through the window at us all. 'Well, see you later. Have fun. Meet me here at twelve.' She clicked away on her high heels.

We drove around for a bit, then parked the car and walked along the main street. Merci walked in between Géza and me, holding our hands. She moved somewhat stiffly, for she had on a thick coat on top of woollen trousers on top of woollen tights, rubber boots and a furry hat. Gizi said she catches colds easily.

We saw an Ibusz tourist information office and went in to book our rooms for the night. I was a little surprised when I heard that Géza was considering booking one room for us all. He must have seen an odd look come over my face, for he suddenly amended his request.

'Oh, well, two rooms, I suppose. Yes, two rooms, please,' he said. I hoped he wasn't offended. But I didn't much like the thought of everyone seeing me in my green winceyette nightgown with the lacy sleeves. I've got to keep something to myself.

We were assigned two rooms in a private house a few minutes outside the centre of Sopron. It is quite common for families in areas frequented by tourists to let some of their rooms. And, more and more, private individuals are being given permission to build small family pensions with up to ten rooms for guests.

'You can make a very good living that way,' Géza was telling me. 'And it's a much nicer life for these country people than farming the land and raising livestock. Better to tidy up a few tourist's bedrooms than rake the muck out of stables.'

As we rambled along, Géza added, 'Look at all the Austrian cars parked along this main street.' I studied the Mercedes, B.M.W.s, Audis and other Western sports cars, estate cars and convertibles. Most of them bore Austrian licence plates. 'These Austrians come across the border just for the day. They buy up all our inexpensive goods — food, drinks, clothing and whatnot — have a nice lunch in a restaurant and a pleasant walk around town, perhaps use the hairdresser's, then fill up on our cheap petrol and go home.' He shook his head and stroked the bonnet of a flashy coupé. 'Of course,' he added, 'all these things are cheap for them, not for us.'

'The Austrians can cross the border without visas now, can't they?' I asked.

Géza nodded. 'Any time they like. Unfortunately, it doesn't work the other way around.'

'Rather like those one-way mirrors,' I said, 'the sort they use in police stations and certain hospitals. They can look in, but you can't look out.'

Just then Merci spotted a little kiosk on the pavement with an array of children's rings on display. She ran up to it and wouldn't rest until Géza had bought her two, both with tiny red glass centres.

'I love jewellery,' she confessed, quite unnecessarily.

By now the fog had disappeared. And I realized that I was somewhere really quite special. As I looked around I felt that I was drinking an extraordinary historical concoction. Several centuries had spilled together in a myriad of faded, pastel houses, like the chipped and tired sticks of chalk in Adam's toy chest. The streets bespoke a fragile gentility, and away from the cars and shoppers, there was silence in the ancient cobbled courtyards and alleyways.

At noon we fetched Gizi and found her waiting at the curbside, talking animatedly to a man with a hunchback.

She waved excitedly. She and the man came up to the car. 'You remember Professor G, don't you?' she asked Géza. 'He taught me at university.'

'Of course. Good day, Professor.'

'I have an idea,' said Gizi. 'Let's all have lunch together at the Kékfrankos, just across the street.'

The Professor's face lit up. 'I like that idea!' he said. 'We could have a bottle of Sopron wine to go with it.' I began to like the Professor. He smiled and winked at Merci, then looked curiously at me.

It wasn't until we were sitting around a table in the warm, cosy restaurant, surrounded by tables full of soldiers, that I was introduced to the Professor.

'Do you really live in England?' he asked. 'How fascinating. You know I spent some time there. In Birmingham. I was doing research at a hospital there.'

'Did you like Birmingham?' I asked.

'Loved it.'

'You speak fluent English, I presume.'

'Certainly.' He took a sip of wine. 'Of course, that doesn't help a great deal in Birmingham. I used to hide when I saw my landlady coming. I never understood a word she said to me.'

The waiter brought us a bottle of *Soproni Kékfrankos* (the restaurant is named after the local wine) in its devil colours of red and black. I tasted it. It was dry and good.

I turned to Gizi. 'Did you learn anything interesting at the conference?'

'Yes,' she replied. 'A big new department store is opening up in Sopron tomorrow morning. We've got to be there.'

The Professor then spoke for a while about his recent work in biochemistry. He had been making certain discoveries regarding the muscular system and these were being internationally recognized.

'Will you return to England?' I asked.

He shook his head. 'I'm afraid that seems impossible now. It is too difficult to get a state grant for such a project. Science always suffers when money is a little tight. Ah, how I would like to go back to England, though. Just once more. I would even take my wife along.'

The soldiers got up and all left at once and suddenly the Kékfrankos was much more peaceful. We ate our meal and drank our wine. Even Géza indulged in a glass and immediately said it had given him a headache because he wasn't used to alcohol.

The Professor was catching a train back to Budapest that afternoon. So, shortly after we finished eating, he stood up and shook hands with us.

'I have enjoyed myself. It was kind of you to invite me,' he said, grinning. 'The wine has quite gone to my head; the journey home will pass quickly indeed.' He bade us farewell. Then, turning back to me, he added, 'Until we meet again in London!' He waved and I watched him leave. A moment later his crooked form passed by the window of the restaurant.

I thought of the Professor for a long time afterwards. I tried to picture him in his Birmingham boarding house, mixing his chemicals and discovering things. I hoped he was right, and that we would meet again one day.

The rest of us followed a few minutes later. It was still cool outside, so we began to walk as briskly as we could with Merci amongst us, towards the main shopping street.

We stopped in front of a millinery shop. Gizi pointed to a strange mauve hat in the window. 'Oh, I just love that,' she exclaimed.

'You've got nothing to go with it,' said Géza, rather good-naturedly, I thought.

'I can always get a nice mauve dress to match. In fact, there's a little dress shop just down the block.' She hurried us along.

We went into a few shops but nobody bought anything. It tired us out just the same, so we went for some coffee in the restaurant of a big hotel. Here Merci promptly fell asleep. I looked out the window at the cars and pedestrians passing by, and thought sadly of all those museums and galleries in Sopron which it now seemed unlikely I would ever see. I felt my energy slowly sapping away. And then it didn't seem to matter, and I was content just drinking my espresso and watching the sky turn deeper shades of grey.

Gizi spoke about the new department store. 'I hear it has *everything*. And it's terribly modern. And they even carry ladies' nightgowns imported from France!'

'Far too expensive, I'm sure,' said Géza.

'We'll see, we'll see.' Just then she spotted a shop selling fur coats across the street, and she said she just wanted to have a look and asked whether we would mind if she ran over for a minute. She went off at a gallop, and I had to smile and admire her pure, unadulterated relish for all forms of shopping.

Gizi re-emerged a little later, limping. 'The heel has broken off my right shoe. What can I do?'

'For God's sake,' said Géza, 'you've got hundreds of shoes in the car, can't you put on another pair?'

'But how am I to get all the way to the car in this state?'

'Well, I'm not going. I'm getting fed up. . .'

'All right. I've got another idea. I think I saw a shoe repair shop nearby. I'll go and get this fixed. You wait here for me.' She hobbled away with dented pride.

So we waited. At last Gizi returned, Merci woke up, Géza paid the bill and I got up from that chair which by then felt like a natural extension of my anatomy.

We drove off in search of our rooms for the night and eventually, after driving up and down several quiet, residential streets in the outskirts of Sopron, we stopped outside an ordinary-looking house. An ancient man came out to greet us.

We were led upstairs. The house was simple, sparsely furnished, and seemed devoid of any other guests. The rooms were adequate, but cold. By now it was nearly night-time and we were feeling the chill in the air. I looked down at the old and uninspiring contraption in one corner of my room which I guessed was some sort of heater. I beckoned to Géza.

'Does this thing work?' I asked.

'It should do. I'll ask.' He went up to the tall grizzled man who was just showing Gizi the toilet and bathroom. The man scratched his stubbly chin, which sounded like a carpenter filing down some rather tough wood. Then he appeared to be trying to pull his nose off. Then he nodded and said something I didn't hear. Géza came back to me. 'He said he'll get his son to put some fuel in. By the time we return from dinner, the rooms should be fully heated.'

We settled ourselves into the bedrooms and took turns freshening up in the Spartan bathroom. The same vague sensation came over me then as at the end of my honeymoon, when the money was running out and we had to spend a night in a draughty, ramshackle farmhouse in Cornwall. Unlike others, who relish things like camping and caravaning, I've never really enjoyed being uncomfortable. And this time I didn't even have a bridegroom for company.

Gizi put a few more layers of clothing onto Merci and we were ready to go out for dinner. We decided not to go into Sopron, but to eat at the famous Hotel Lővér, in the forest at the foot of the Lővér Hills. Gizi and Géza had come here once or twice during their courting days, and Gizi wanted to return, for old times' sake.

There were a few Austrians and Germans in the hotel's lofty restaurant, paying scant attention to the rather weird little orchestra squeaking away in one corner. The hotel was modern and decorated in a combination of ill-matching styles.

The menu was what is known as 'international'. That means that no one is meant to be particularly enamoured of it, but at least everyone can read what it says. We ordered our international food. I started with a cold cherry soup. It was cold, and I took their word for it that it was in some way connected with cherries. Indeed, when I had finished the thin, pink liquid I found three or four whole cherries, lying heavily on the bottom like submerged mines.

Merci was being fussy and not eating much, so after the three of us ate our international main course, we left. It was cold and dark in the middle of the forest. I was tired and not looking forward to returning to the stubbly old landlord and his chilly house.

But a miracle awaited us. When we stepped into our rooms, we were met with luxurious warmth. The heating contraptions not only worked, they put the modern boiler to shame.

In the morning I opened the curtains on a sunny back garden which wallowed in a sort of pleasant, friendly mess. There were *ad hoc* rows of vegetables, some fruit trees, little wooden sheds, bushes and flowers. A cock and some hens were sauntering around this obstacle course and two cats were asleep in a wheelbarrow. A mangy goat was tethered to a pole. I wanted to paint the lot of them.

It was a warm, clear day. With renewed zest we tackled Sopron again. We breakfasted on light, milky coffee and rolls at the big hotel on the main street, then strolled into the ancient heart of the town, the quiet network of streets, alleys and courtyards.

We soon reached its hub, a cobbled square with a seventeenth-century belfry poised above the old city gate and lined with baroque and renaissance buildings, churches and museums. I saw some people looking down from a gallery high up on the belfry. I wanted to see the view, so I quickly ushered Géza towards it, before Gizi could think of some urgent shopping which had to be done.

Géza and I climbed the steps to the gallery, just ahead of a lively group of young Russian tourists. One of them had a small transistor and was humming to an awful pop song.

From up there Sopron seemed almost unreal, like a town for dolls or children. It was a collection of crooked red tiled roofs and grey brick chimneys. In fact it was all red and grey, a soft, untouchable vision. And just beyond the skyline of steeples were the Lővér Hills, a dark, curving mass of trees.

The Russians were wandering around with their pop songs,

soaking up the view. They seemed to know each other very well, and I thought they might be a student group, or colleagues from an office or factory.

'Are there many Russian tourists in Hungary?' I asked Géza.

'No. It's not easy for them to get visas to come here, and of course they can only come in organized groups. You never see a Russian tourist on his own.' He leaned over the parapet and squinted in the sun. 'It's all quite understandable. After all, compared to the U.S.S.R., Hungary is the South of France, and compared to Moscow, Budapest is as sparkling as Paris.'

'Budapest is a lot more beautiful than Paris,' I said.

Géza put an arm around my shoulder. 'Of course it is,' he breathed in my ear. Then he laughed gently. 'Anyway, what does it matter? We all live where we live. Let's just enjoy the sun while it shines.' He kissed my forehead. 'Let's go back down. I can see Gizi going crazy chasing Merci all over the square.'

I took a last look at the Russians, in particular a tall, lanky fellow standing next to a stocky girl with long, thick hair. I didn't know exactly why, but they inspired my affection. I wanted to pat them on the back. Then the next moment I wondered why I should be so patronizing. For all my life I've thought of Russians as people either to loathe or to pity. But I've never considered any of them to be ordinary human beings.

We reached the ground just as a shiny green Mercedes pulled up outside the town hall, next to the belfry. A chauffeur stepped out. Formally dressed people were starting to emerge from the town hall, a small crowd was gathering by the entrance, and the next minute the bride and groom came out. They were young, good-looking and sombre. No doubt they already knew all about Hungary's divorce rate: fifty per cent. One out of every two marriages flops. That's probably the only thing Hungary has in common with California.

The handsome pair got into the Mercedes. Would they, too, end up in the statistics one day? I wondered. At least the sun was beaming down on them today and they looked splendid. It might all be downhill from now on, but, what-the-hell, they were riding in a shiny green Mercedes and that's a great way to go. The people of Sopron were impressed.

Géza stood looking wistfully at the car as it drove once around the square and disappeared. 'What a beauty,' he said. 'You know, the Mercedes has always been the great love of my life. I was fascinated by it long before I took any notice of women.' We started walking towards the elaborately carved column in the middle of the square.

'That's why you named your daughter after it?' I asked. He nodded. 'In that case, it's lucky your big love wasn't for the Zsiguli. That would have made an awful name for a girl.'

Géza then told me that there were fewer and fewer Mercedes in Hungary now. 'All important state officials used to have them,' he explained, 'until a recent visit by Brezhnev. He was rather put out by our socialist leaders in their flashy West German cars, so he told them all to switch their Mercedes for Ladas.' He sighed. 'The only trouble is, I really did enjoy repairing those beauties once in a while.' He shook his head.

'There you are!' It was Gizi. 'Come on, let's go. The department store is about to open.'

We were soon back on the busy main street. We seemed to be swept along on a tide of people, all heading for this latest temple of the divine Plastic Shopping Bag God.

We turned a corner and there it was — new, clean, light, bright — not unlike one of those modern churches. There were policemen outside the building, keeping the congregation at bay. The doors had not yet been opened. The shoppers were craning their necks to get a better view of the goods on display in the windows. They were clutching their handbags and purses eagerly, just bursting to trade in their forints for a few real bargains.

It was an almost circular, two-storey building. Above the main entrance was a huge sign proclaiming *WELCOME TO OUR NEW DEPARTMENT STORE!* (In Hungary, they use exclamation marks as freely as paprika.)

I looked at Gizi's face. There was sheer excitement and pleasure on it. Merci, too, was in a state of great anticipation. She had been promised a pair of clogs, which are now in fashion in Hungary.

At last the doors were swung open by two uniformed salesgirls. The shoppers surged forth, ignoring the agitated policemen. We were swept up some steps and in front of the windows and through the main door.

Gizi began searching at once for various things. Géza stared around with a mixture of suspicion and awe. Merci got lost among the ladies' clothing. Behind their check-out counters the salesgirls in their crisp uniforms and smart caps were watching the customers, smiling and exchanging glances like satisfied astronauts at their controls after a successful take-off from Cape Canaveral.

It was soon apparent, however, that the new store didn't have quite 'everything' as Gizi had supposed. For she began to look more and more crestfallen. She didn't buy anything downstairs in the clothing department. We went upstairs to the household goods, but, after a lengthy exploration, she emerged clutching only one small package.

'It's a baking tin,' she said apologetically. 'I had to buy *something.*'

After this major disappointment, we retreated from the shopping precinct's chaotic rumblings, which by now had reached seismic proportions. We returned to the quiet old inner town and there stumbled, quite by accident, upon a medieval synagogue which was now a small museum, entered through a cobbled courtyard framed with ripe, dark roses. There was a bench along one high, flowery wall and I sat down there, closing my eyes to the sun. There was silence, but for two little birds quarrelling over a morsel of food. Slowly my senses readjusted to sanity. I couldn't believe my luck in finding this exquisite corner of Sopron. It was almost enough to convert me to Judaism. Anything was preferable to the religion of the shoppers, which I had just left behind.

When I could drag myself away from the roses and the birds in the courtyard, I followed the others into the synagogue. I was most impressed by the deep, square well with wooden steps leading down into it, where centuries ago the Jews cleansed themselves. They dunked themselves underwater in order to become kosher. It occurred to me that we could all do with a bit of spiritual cleansing now and then. I'd love to dunk myself in a well and come up rid of all my unfortunate 'impurities'.

We had already decided that we would return to Budapest via the famous castle at Fertőd, once the home of the Esterhazy family. So, after for a few more glorious minutes in the courtyard, we returned to the car. All too soon, Sopron was behind us. I took one last look at the red roofs and dark green hills. I thought of the new deparment store and the synagogue, the Professor and our ancient landlord. It may be a small town, I thought, but it is nevertheless a junction for all of life's winding railway lines. And I marvelled at such profundity.

This time, as we travelled across the countryside, the picture was unobscured by fog. I could see clearly every peasant village, every cow pulling a cartload of hay and every horse dragging a plough across a field. I gazed at the figures by the roadside, mostly dumpy peasant women wearing black dresses, headscarves and moustaches. The road itself was not too busy. Every once in a while we passed a very old-looking, drab bus, sweeping slowly and dustily down the narrow highway like a leaky vacuum cleaner.

There's a nice story about a young chap who went on a school outing to the Fertőd Castle. At the entrance there was a woman selling tickets for the guided tour, but while all of his classmates lined up to buy a ticket, he refused to do so. The woman rebuked him. The boy didn't flinch. 'Listen,' he said, 'I'm sure *you* don't have to pay whenever you go home.'

He turned out to be one of the youngest in the line of Esterhazys, and not lacking in the style of Hungary's well-known aristocratic family. He was let in for free. Today he is on the national football team, one of the more popular players.

Hungary has a strange love-hate relationship with aristocracy. In the past there have been great aristocrats who did much to bring the country more into line with its Western European neighbours. Count István Széchenyi, for example, founded the Academy of Science in 1832 and imported scientists from all over the world to give lectures there. He travelled a great deal, collecting ideas on how to improve the capital. He went to London to find out about bridge construction. The outcome of the trip was the construction, in 1849, of the Chain Bridge in Budapest, the first permanent bridge over the Danube in Hungary. (The square on the Buda side of it still bears the name of the British engineer who erected it: Adam Clark. In fact it is the duplicate of Hammersmith Bridge and the work of the same designer, William Tierney Clark.)

After 1948, when the Communist Party seized total power in Hungary, being aristocratic was a dodgy business. The aristocracy were forced to flee, or were imprisoned and punished. And now, after three decades of asinine persecution, what have we got in Hungary? Plebeians by the thousands are striving to prove that they've got blue blood in their veins. People whose surnames have for generations ended in *i* are changing the all-important final letter to the aristocratic *y*. They are employing genealogists to trace their family trees and come up with a few aristocratic twigs. They are paying small fortunes to have their own coats of arms designed. Genuine aristocrats are being interviewed on radio and television and asked to recount their favourite little aristocratic anecdotes.

So the love-hate goes on. It's all a bit confusing. But I also find it somehow reassuring. You can't be too angry at a people who make a fashion out of being an 'enemy of the state'. Even hypocrisy has its charms, sometimes.

But all this is meant only as an introduction to my foray into the world of the aristocracy via the Fertőd Castle. The moment we stepped through the great wrought-iron gates I noticed something peculiar going on. There were signs on the weedy lawn saying that it was forbidden to walk on the grass, yet there were several delinquent youths riding their motorcycles back and forth across it. There were more of the same ilk yelling and laughing out of the windows of one wing of the castle. It has apparently been turned into a residential school for wayward boys.

But luckily the castle has enough wings to go around. Opposite the Hell's Angels home is the hotel wing. In the centre of the castle, a sizeable chunk is open to the public for viewing, and each hour a guided tour goes through the grandiose baroque chambers and halls.

Before the tourists are allowed to step onto the shiny parquet floors of the castle, they have to tie felt slippers onto their shoes. When our entire group had put on these amusing slippers we slid off noiselessly behind our guide. There were no slippers small enough for Merci, so she tapped along at our side, delighted at being the only one making a racket.

But Merci's goodwill was not to last long. She obviously wasn't too keen on baroque. She found no particular stimulation in the antique porcelain collection, the ancestral portraits or the violin of the one-time resident composer of the Esterhazys, Franz Joseph Haydn. When she started testing the echo potential of the great gilded stateroom, Gizi decided it was time to remove the child from the bosom of aristocracy.

Géza and I slid through the rest of the rooms, then followed the others down the wide staircase and back to the felt-slipper depot. Outside we found Gizi trying to stop Merci from falling into the water fountain. The delinquents were still riding their motorbikes across the lawn. But inside I had been impressed by the reverential treatment given to all things Esterhazy. Everything was impeccably preserved and documented. Perhaps the indoor-outdoor contradiction just about sums up Hungary's ambiguous feelings towards its high-born citizens.

And so we returned to the car park with its tourist buses and *lángos* stand. It was late afternoon. 'Have you ever seen the Balaton?' Géza asked me.

'Never.'

He shook his head disapprovingly. 'Then let's drive back to Budapest along a different route. We'll go along the northern side of the lake. I'm sure we can reach it before dark.'

It occurred to me after about an hour in the car that I had seen the Balaton, at least once. It must have been when I was two or three. I remembered seeing a photograph of my brother and myself clutching the side of a small motorboat, squinting in the sun. 'That was taken on the Balaton,' I could hear my mother saying, 'we were on an outing with some friends.'

Several times we had to stop in front of level crossings and wait for trains to go by. There were even old steam trains puffing down the line, filled with soldiers, which reminded me of scenes from countless war movies. One such train passed by slowly just a few feet away from us, as Géza's car waited on the other side of the barrier. I looked at the faces of the soldiers on board. Young, patient, relaxed faces. I caught the eye of a bored, good-looking soldier. We studied each other for the brief moment that we could; in the last instant I saw him start to smile. How is it, I wondered, that we can feel such tenderness for a stranger? Of course, I have always found the uniform a particularly alluring façade.

By the time we arrived at the Balaton it was dusk, and the hazy blue light gave the lake a gentle serenity. There was silence on the water. It was empty — no boats, no swimmers, and not many fish (over-fishing has seen to that, followed by the usual pollution). We stopped at Tihany, a popular little resort. It has a steep hill leading up to a Benedictine abbey. While Gizi took Merci off to the toilet, Géza and I walked to the top to see the view of the Balaton.

We stood by the low wall and gazed down. The whole long lake stretched out below us. At what spot had my brother and I been photographed? The lake became time itself, and that moment had long since drifted below the surface into obscurity.

Opposite the abbey was some rough parkland with a walk leading into it, among trees and flowers. 'That's for lovers,' said Géza.

'I thought it was for abbots.'

'No,' he laughed, 'a different sort of praying goes on in this wood.'

Afterwards we drove to Balatonfüred, another resort along the lake. We ate at the Golden Star Restaurant, accompanied by a singer and his harp, performing Hungarian versions of various old Frank Sinatra songs. He wasn't very good and one or two of his higher notes nearly caused me to choke on my paprika chicken.

It was late in the evening when we finally wound our way around the dark and bumpy roads towards Budakeszi Avenue.

The artificial fur seat cover made a soft pillow for my cheek and, by the time we stopped before my mother's house, I was sleeping deeply and having a forgettable dream.

In the morning Géza came for me. He had agreed to drive me to see Dunci, who lived in a suburb of Budapest called Pécel. I was taking her a long rod of salami, a bottle of wine and some other provisions. But I felt she ought to have something slightly more extravagant. I knew she smoked cigarettes.

'Let's go to the Intertourist shop first,' I told Géza, 'so I can buy her a carton of English cigarettes.' In Hungary English and American tobacco is considered a true luxury. A great number of people smoke, but mostly they buy foul-smelling Bulgarian and Russian cigarettes. Even the packets they come in look embarrassingly cheap.

There are several Intertourist shops in Budapest, where luxury goods imported from Western countries can be bought for Western currency. We went to the one in the Duna Intercontinental Hotel. There are soft carpets and sparkling showcases packed with French perfumes, Swiss chocolates, German bath powders and the best booze convertible currency can buy. Here the Trinity is composed of the Dollar, the Deutschmark and the Pound Sterling. Shopping there inevitably makes you feel highly privileged. It's like being a guest at the Queen's garden party. The latest addition to the Intercontinental is a gambling casino strictly for the use of Westerners, where the only acceptable currency is the Deutschmark.

Besides Dunci's cigarettes I bought some presents for my relatives — whisky, cognac, soaps, cassettes, Milky Way bars. These are the most significant commodities in a country such as Hungary. There was a time when the most sought-after item was a pair of blue jeans. The Hungarians call them 'farmer trousers'. They symbolized the West, youth and optimism. Now Budapest is crammed with people wearing farmer trousers. There are denim and corduroy jeans, frayed and patched jeans, and crisply ironed ones. On kids and on adults. Twenty years ago someone in a pair of blue jeans would have received a dozen offers to purchase it before he could walk from one end of a block to the other. Now Hungary manufactures its own Levi's and no one takes any notice. I suppose that's real progress.

Dunci lived in a quiet residential street, in a tiny two-room bungalow which was really more like a shed. It was in the back garden of a doctor's house and I think it used to be some sort of caretaker's residence.

I had sent her a card to say I was in Budapest and would be coming to see her, but I couldn't give a precise day. So I hoped I wouldn't catch her at a bad time. Géza and I walked up to the door of her 'shed'. There was no bell, so I knocked. No answer. I knocked again, more loudly.

I thought I heard a sound from inside. I tried the handle of the door. It was unlocked, so I walked into her dark and musty home. I found myself in a minute hallway which opens onto two rooms. The doors to these rooms had glass panels on the upper parts and through one door I could see a figure moving about.

'Good day. It's Monica,' I said a little uncomfortably as I opened this second door and nearly tripped on a low step dividing it from the hallway. I stood facing a woman who looked inextricably aged. She was wearing a loose nightdress and clutching a walking stick. Her white hair was awry. Her initial look of agitation lasted only for an instant. When she heard my name she repeated it with delight.

'Please forgive us for disturbing you, we'll just stay for a short while,' I started to explain.

She raised her stick in the air and pointed it at Géza, who was still hesitating by the door. 'And who is that young man?' she demanded. I explained. 'Tell him to wait out there while I get dressed. You come in and sit down.' She waved her stick towards an armchair.

'How are you?' I asked.

'Well, as you can see, I'm still alive.' She fumbled with her nightdress. Behind her, the iron bed was unmade. She saw me looking at it. 'I go to bed in the afternoons. I read in bed. It's easier than sleeping.'

She managed to strip down to her woollen underwear, tottering only slightly. Then she got dressed, and her choice of clothes was rather surprising. Over her weak and sagging flesh she put on a dark blue track suit with white stripes down the side. Standing before a washstand mirror she smoothed her hair down, then reached for her false teeth from a plastic box and put them in her mouth.

She sighed. 'Oh, I look terrible,' she said. 'And I feel worse.' She put on a pair of thick glasses and studied me more closely. Then she turned back to the mirror and applied dark red lipstick to

56

her mouth and some powder to her cheeks. 'That's better,' she said, sinking into a chair opposite me. She motioned towards the door. 'You can tell the young man to come in now.'

The three of us sat in that small room which smelled of dust and old bedclothes. There was one big window, overlooking the doctor's garden, but it hadn't been cleaned for so long that it was nearly opaque.

'Do you know what my worst problem is?' she asked, looking from me to Géza. 'The cold.' She pointed her stick at a white iron stove in one corner. 'That's all I have. I'm given some coal for it, but not enough. And it's so much work to keep it going.'

I stood up and began to unpack the things I had brought for her, laying them in the dust on a table before the window.

'What's all this? It's not Christmas,' Dunci declared.

'Nothing at all,' I said. I don't like playing the role of Father Christmas, being the one with all the wealth to distribute.

'I'm not starving, you know,' she said. 'I haven't got anything to my name, but the local council brings me lunch each day. And one meal a day is enough for ancient creatures like me.' She eyed the array of provisions on the table. 'I never drink milk,' she said, 'you can take those two cartons away with you.' Then she noticed the English cigarettes. 'Oh, you angel!' she beamed at me, pouncing on them. She lit one up, drew a deep breath and smiled.

'How do you like living in London?' she asked me.

I went into my 'spiritual home' routine, about London being the only place I would ever want to live, about the city's exciting admixture of people and activities. But she cut me short.

'I know all that. What I want to find out is — what's it like being married to an Englishman?'

'Well,' I was somewhat disconcerted, 'it's not too bad, really. . .'

'It's something that has always intrigued me, the English husband. You see, I had several proposals of marriage from Englishmen when I was young and living in London. I rejected them, of course. Couldn't imagine being married to anything but a Hungarian. 'Yet,' here she pursed her red lips and looked thoughtful, 'I've always wondered what I missed.'

'I never knew you lived in London,' I told her.

'1914, just before the war. Only for about half a year or so. But it was enough to make me realize what extraordinary people the English are. I liked them very much.' Reluctantly, she stubbed out the cigarette she had been smoking, and she kept her eyes on it for a while.

'What did you do in London?' Géza inquired, finally overcoming his shyness.

'I was studying the science of phonetics,' she replied slowly and deliberately. Then she grinned. 'I can't quite remember the reason why. And I was living in a boarding house in Hampstead. It had the most wonderful landlord. When the war broke out and I was no longer able to receive funds from home, he told me I was to continue living there anyway, and repay him when the war was over. And that despite the fact that I was officially classed as an "enemy alien". Now, isn't that an extraordinary thing to do?'

Géza and I nodded.

'Oh,' she continued animatedly, with a wave of the hand which resulted in her picking up another cigarette from the table, 'I could tell you many things about life there in those days.' She seemed to remember something which made her smile. 'I adored all the museums in London. But while I was there the suffragettes kept going into them and smashing things up, so most of the museums had to be kept closed. At the outbreak of war the suffragettes calmed down, I suppose they had other things to think about. And I could see all the museums I wanted.' She turned to the window and stared out for a moment, although I don't think she could have seen much through it. 'Alas, I had to leave London all too soon.'

'So you came back to Budapest and got married?' By now Géza was most intrigued by Dunci's life history.

'Yes. That was my husband.' She glanced at a framed photograph on the wall. 'He died two years ago.'

I went to examine the picture. The man looked large and jovial, but I couldn't make out what sort of clothes he had on. 'What's he wearing?' I asked.

'Oh, one of his hunting outfits. He used to do a lot of hunting and had a special outfit for each different creature he hunted. He enjoyed it so much. My God, even in recent years, long after we'd lost everything, he could talk for hours about those old days to anyone who'd listen.' She pointed to something which was lying on the window sill. 'Take a look at that.'

I picked up a small photo album. It was held together with a rusty paper clip and all its pictures were yellowed and cracked with age. As I turned each sticky page I saw that all the pictures were of her husband, in a variety of places and poses. But in every picture he was wearing the same broad, friendly smile. Except where he was laughing outright. In fact he seemed the most good-humoured man I'd ever seen.

She began to tell us about him. His name was Ádám Fiath, a member of an aristocratic family one of whose greatest ancestors was János Fiath, the patriot who was first to raise the Hungarian flag over the Castle in Budapest, after the Turks were finally defeated.

'There is still a street named after him in the Castle district,' Dunci said.

Ádám had been a wealthy landowner and she the daughter of a banker: altogether the wrong credentials as far as the communists were concerned. So from 1948 to 1956 Ádám was imprisoned, all of their property and valuables were confiscated after the war and in 1950 they were banished from Budapest.

'That was the year of the *kitelepités*,' said Dunci. 'The new decree by which all of us — aristocrats, the wealthy, the ones with the wrong "background", the politically unacceptable — were "deported" out of Budapest into primitive God-forsaken villages in the middle of nowhere. Much later we were allowed to move a little bit closer to the capital . So we ended up here in Pécel.'

She told us how Ádám became a menial worker, then was eventually given a job as a petty administrator. 'But to the very end of his life he was so light-hearted. He laughed so much.' She put a few more pieces of coal into the stove, then clanged its door shut. 'I can hardly believe he's gone.' She turned her eyes upwards. 'I'm not very religious, but I wish they'd make some room for me up there, as well.' Then, grasping her stick, she sunk back into her chair.

She looked at me and smiled. 'I often think about my time in London, you know,' she said. 'I was always good at languages, quite a few of them. But English has always been my favourite. I used to speak it perfectly.' Behind the thick eyeglasses, her eyes were filled with amusement. 'When I lived in London I used to avoid speaking to anyone who didn't have a perfect accent. I didn't want to pick up any of that Cockney business myself. I wanted to keep my English unpolluted. It all makes me laugh now.' She folded her arthritic hands in her lap and studied them for a moment. 'I was the same way with French. Once your mother asked me to write a few extra lines in French to a *chanson* she was singing at the Hangli. So I couldn't have been too bad at it, really.' She smiled at me with mock modesty.

'I'm sorry I'm ignorant about this, ' I said. 'but when did you stay with us at Budakeszi Avenue? I mean, if you were "deported", as you say, out of Budapest in 1950, then when could you have come to look after us? I was only born in 1952.'

She had been shaking her head impatiently during this little speech of mine. 'I was in Budapest illegally, of course. For a few months in 1955. As far as the authorities were concerned, I was somewhere else. Your parents knew it was dangerous to keep me there, but they were always very good to me.'

She reached for another cigarette; they were obviously a success. She smoothed it in her fingers for a little while before lighting it, and this momentary play gave me time to reflect on what she had said. I think for the first time I had a vision of the horrors my country was going through when I was a toddler. No amount of books or documentary films can communicate such things as well as being in the presence of a survivor. 'Those must have been frightening times,' I said, feeling the words to be inadequate.

'Hungary has had a thousand years of frightening times,' was Dunci's reply.

'But you seemed to bear those times very well,' Géza said quietly, 'and to be courageous.'

'There isn't such a thing as "courage". Everyone just does what he feels he must. How else is there to live?' She pointed a finger at me. 'If you want to know about courage, ask your mother. In 1944 when the Jews were in trouble, she hid the Jews. In 1950 when everyone else was in trouble, she helped a different lot of people. I've always thought of her house as a refuge for the persecuted.'

There was a long pause after this, during which I envisaged the house with shadowy figures fleeting in and out of doorways, hiding and whispering like in some Gothic horror movie. When Dunci spoke again it was not about fear or persecution, but about me.

'How I adored you,' she said, 'when you were a little girl. You loved me, too, and I think your grandmother was even a bit jealous. You always preferred *me* to give you a bath. And you were a terrible eater, but would eat just beautifully for me.'

I glanced with embarrassment at Géza.

'And I loved to take you out for walks,' she continued. 'That was one of the best periods of my life. In the evenings we often sat around and talked. I could listen to your father for hours. I always enjoyed our conversations.'

She got up to inspect the stove once more. She shook her head. 'Useless thing,' she said. 'I'd get something better, but I can't afford anything on Ádam's pension. I don't call that "money".'

It was getting late and Géza had to get back to work that afternoon. We stood up.

'Couldn't you come again, and bring your son with you? I'd love to meet him. Is he how you used to be? You looked quite oriental when you were that age.'

'Yes,' I answered, 'I understand he's a descendant of Genghis Khan.' We promised to try to come back, but somehow I knew we wouldn't. I would be swept up by too many other people, and unable to retrace my steps.

Dunci hobbled out to the gate with us. She left a red smudge of lipstick on my right temple. She waved and I saw that she was trying, unsuccessfully, not to cry. Then she turned and started towards her dismal little home.

Four

It was another day of the 'old women's summer'. Clear and warm. On the terrace outside my bedroom the many shades of flame were creeping slowly into the ivy. The hills in the near distance, too, were changing all the time. I thought of those New England autumns I had always loved, which are a feast of colours no artist could ever capture.

I sat down in a wicker chair and drank in the morning. The two scruffy mongrels from next door had gambolled over to the gate which opens onto our driveway, because they had a better view from there of passers-by. They were barking and jumping with excitement. On the other side of the gate, a tall lady was walking a Scottish terrier. To my surprise, the lady looked into our garden, waved and called, 'Good morning!'

She wasn't greeting me. I was probably difficult to spot up there, and she hadn't looked in my direction, anyway. I got up and peered down over the edge of the railing. I saw Juszti directly below me, in her apron and headscarf. She was also waving, and said, 'Good morning, Teréz *néni*!' in return.

I wondered who the woman could be. Just a neighbour, perhaps. Then my eyes followed Juszti. She had now left the narrow stone path that runs along the side of the house and was walking across the overgrown part on the far side of the driveway. There she suddenly stopped, before a wild tangle of bushes in the shade of the two great chestnut trees. With one hand she brushed aside some of this overgrowth. She was blocking my view to some extent, but I could see that there was something behind those bushes. Or rather, that something else was a part of that neglected mass.

I watched Juszti, hoping to discover what was hidden. But, after a moment, she drew away her hand, turned around and crossed back to the path.

It is possible to reach the garden directly from the terrace, without going through the house. On the opposite side from my bedroom there are steps leading down towards the driveway and garage. They are not often used as the railing which once guarded them had long since deteriorated and been pulled down. I now tied my dressing-gown tightly around me and crept down these steps. The garden was quiet and empty. The only noise came from the two dogs next door; they were still excited.

I went to the spot where Juszti had stood, scratching my bare legs on some bramble in the process. I brushed aside branches, leaves and brittle, dying vines. Beyond them was something made of stone. But what was it?

I had hoped, perhaps, to find some mysterious, unmarked grave, or the entry to a secret tunnel. Something to enkindle the Agatha Christie in me. . .or at least the Nancy Drew. Instead there was this bare stone *thing*, without a carving, a sign or any indication as to what it could be. All I knew was that it was shaped vaguely like a renaissance arch with a concave centre.

I went back up the terrace steps. I looked through the window of my mother's bedroom. She was lying in bed, her broken leg propped up on one of those enormous continental pillows, reading a newspaper. The door beside the window was unlocked and I went in.

'Do you know what that old bit of rubble is, under the chestnut trees?' I asked.

She stared up at me, then went back to the paper on her lap. 'Rubble?' She didn't seem to have understood me.

'Beyond the driveway, near the edge of the neighbouring garden. You must have seen it.'

My mother paused, then smiled a little distantly. 'Oh, that. Your grandfather built it a long, long time ago. It's been in ruins for years now.'

'But what was it?' I demanded impatiently.

'A little replica of the cave at Lourdes where the Virgin Mary appeared to St Bernadette.'

I must have seemed sceptical and rather flippant, for my mother continued somewhat defensively, 'He was a very religious man, very devout. He kept a small statue of the Virgin Mary inside the cave and put flowers before it.'

'There's no Virgin Mary there now,' I said.

'No, the head broke off years ago. The statue is in the cellar somewhere, gathering dust.' She wore a look of infinite sadness, which actresses are very good at.

I have never been able to take very seriously any sort of earnest religiosity. Or perhaps that is not strictly true. For I do remember emerging into the sunlight after confession at Our Lady of Mt Carmel in the Bronx, and examining the skin on my arms to see whether it was any lighter or clearer. After all, I had been 'cleansed', according to the Sunday school teacher. I was about eight at the time. By the age of eleven I had already decided that the best method of cleansing was to take a bath every day.

I went back down into the garden, taking Adam with me. I sat on the wobbly bench while he climbed onto the wobbly swing. The strong sun shone luxuriously onto us, giving us a sense of well-being. But my eyes kept going back to the hidden ruins of that stone 'cave' in the shade.

For the first time since I arrived in Hungary I began to reflect on my grandparents, my mother's father and mother. Two people I hadn't known very well, and now it was too late. It suddenly occurred to me, as I sat there that, after my family emigrated, my very first instance of awareness that I was now an emigré directly concerned my grandparents.

It was a dream which I had several times when I was five or six years old. It may have been the sort of dream you have when you are really half-awake and can direct the scenario as you go along. In that dream my grandparents were cowering behind a very large boulder of some sort. There was fighting going on around them. They weren't very well, because besides being in danger of their lives, they were hungry, cold and tired. Then I came along (alone, I think) and led them away from the boulder, away from the fighting and the danger. I took them to a nice warm room, put them each into a comfortable bed, and brought them trays of food. With amazing rapidity they recovered and began to bloom with happiness.

That was the only dream I ever had which I can remember. And the first time I realized that God isn't in His Heaven and all isn't right with the world.

Of course later there were many indications that there had been some kind of mistake, and my family wasn't really where it 'belonged'. At first, my brother and I didn't blend very well into the tough, urban set-up of the neighbourhood playground. (In the late 1950s the Bronx was not like it is today, but it was still a mean hang-out.) Once I was being hounded by a gang of boys. My mother heard my yells from our flat on the third floor and screamed out at them: 'Animals!' Far from being deterred, the boys collapsed with laughter at my mother's accent.

But there were enough Hungarian refugees in the neighbourhood to make us feel a little at home, like Bundzsi and Kari with their two sons who were not much older than me. There was a former star of the Hungarian ballet, Eszter, who opened a dance studio in the next block of flats. I took ballet and tap dancing lessons there. And there was Mrs Monoki who came twice a week from Yonkers to teach me the piano. After a while she gave up in despair and my mother taught me instead (until she gave up, too).

There was a girl of my own age called Naomi whom I was good friends with for a while, until I decided she was depraved and refused to see her again. Later, my mother explained that her parents had just separated under the strain of adapting to a new country, and that was why Naomi had been acting rather strangely.

There was Éva, a year older than me, who lived in a nearby block. Her mother had married well, then divorced well and married well again. So she always had plenty of clothes to hand down, and, as she had no sister, she handed them down to me. She was a plump girl and I was shorter and skinnier. But I was always excited by the heap of garments she presented me with whenever I went to visit her. For years I thought that there was *supposed* to be room for three people inside a dress.

But there were other immigrants to be found besides Hungarians. There was a Greek family called Kalinikos living high above us on the seventeenth floor. They had a son called Gary who became my best friend. Each year his father bought a new convertible Chevrolet. And his mother cooked the most exotic food. Its aroma permeated the whole of the seventeenth floor. She had long black hair and wore bright dresses which reached down to the floor. They all had olive complexions and laughed a great deal. They were not at all like the Hungarians. They didn't have a revolution behind them.

The day came when my father could also afford a car. He bought a used Volkswagen beetle. And not long afterwards came the next big step forward — we moved to the suburbs.

Éva's mother and stepfather had discovered a new development of houses in Hartsdale, Westchester County. It was that land of two-car garages and a television in every room that so many ambitious immigrants dream of. They persuaded my parents to buy a house down the street from theirs. With a car, a house and a mortgage, you would think, we were well on the road to becoming a typical American family.

But the more American we became on the surface, the more those deep ties to the Homeland rebelled against the new, foreign values surrounding us. There was never any chance of genuine assimilation.

There are two categories of immigrant. There is the person who relishes the challenge of succeeding in a new country and throws himself in wholeheartedly. He assumes the characteristics of its natives (sometimes rather overdoing them). Perhaps he also changes his name. The one thing he loathes and fears is to look back at his former life in the old country. So he doesn't. And one day he realizes he's forgotten most of it. That makes him happy.

Then there is the other type of immigrant. He wants to succeed, too. Who doesn't? But he realizes early on in the game that he will never be able detach himself from his previous life. It is too much an integral part of his existence. Without his background and memories, he wouldn't recognize himself. As the years go by, he realizes that, while he has never attempted to become an honest-to-God native and so been rather left out of the mainstream of life in the adopted country, the other life which he has cherished and clung to has also been slowly slipping away. It doesn't exist anymore, except inside his head. He knows if ever he were to return home, it would all be as foreign to him as the moon. And that makes him profoundly sad.

My parents belong to the latter category.

Whether we lived in the Bronx or in Westchester, our Saturdays were much the same. They can be summed up in one word: Yorkville. That is the area of Manhattan known as 'Little Hungary', composed of the stretch of Second Avenue between Seventy-eighth Street and Eighty-second Street. It was a much larger area, originally. At one time it was unusual to hear anything but Hungarian spoken on its pavements. But, by the time my family became a part of it, it had shrunk considerably in size and population.

Nearly every Saturday we paid a lengthy visit to Yorkville. There were two main reasons for this, shopping and meeting people. Even in the 1950s and 1960s there was a staggering number of Hungarian shops, clubs, cafés, restaurants and other businesses.

It was vital for us to go to the delicatessen known as 'Paprikás Weisz'. For it was there that my mother bought the essentials for Hungarian cooking, in which she was a perfectionist. The silver and red bags of paprika imported from Szeged, the salamis and sausages, barley, poppyseed and special noodles, the green and red peppers grown for Yorkville Hungarians on a certain farm across the river in New Jersey. The shop got its name from a Hungarian immigrant called Weisz who, at the turn of the century, used to peddle his bags of paprika from a horse-drawn cart. When the residents of Yorkville saw him coming they'd tell each other, 'The paprikás Weisz is here.' He became a rich man.

The shop also carries cooking utensils used in Hungarian cooking which don't exist in America. And items unheard of by other people, such as 'potato candy', a favourite of mine. And each Christmas we'd buy a box of *szalon cukor*, sweets wrapped in shiny paper to hang on the Christmas tree. There were other marvellous-looking things to eat which I could never convince my father to buy for me.

A woman called Nelly worked in Paprikás Weisz. She was soft-spoken, with large dark eyes and dark hair wrapped in a bun. Her husband, Berci, was a painter. After the war he emigrated to Cuba, then went to Paris for a while before moving into Little Hungary. Sometimes we would visit them in their flat. The walls were decorated with his paintings, large and vivid canvases depicting scenes that always seemed to exist halfway between the real world and his dreams, that curious limbo of emigration.

Often we would have lunch at one of the Hungarian restaurants on Second Avenue. Little Hungary, Zettl, Terhesné. My favourite was called Tik Tak. It was owned by a big fat woman called Márika, and they served the best beef broth with noodles that I ever ate. Márika had a son who also went into the restaurant business. He cooked very well and opened a place called Jacque's. Soon afterwards the local gangsters came to see him, demanding protection money. He kicked them out, and everyone thought he was asking for trouble. But he was tough, shrewd and had definite charisma. He never gave in to the racket, and the mob never touched him. Even in Yorkville, miracles can happen.

There was a café called the Monkey, which I liked because they had a very good pianist there. This was a great meeting place for my parents and their friends and acquaintances, both from before the revolution and afterwards. They sat around for hours, drinking espresso, my father smoking his pipe, talking, exchanging news across the red and white checked tablecloth. Years later the café's owner, a man called Gárdos, was mugged and murdered on his way home.

There were several Hungarian butchers. We usually went to one owned by a man called Nagy. He became a good friend of my parents, and when he grew rich and bought a big house on Long Island, we were all invited to his house-warming party. I can still recall the delicious fragrances of the food at that party, and probably everyone else on the Island can, as well.

There was a Hungarian bookshop named Corvin, after King Matthias Corvinus, Hungary's most scholarly ruler, who owned the finest library of his time. The shop always carried copies of my father's latest book, and we generally paid a visit to see how it was selling.

A central figure in Yorkville was Buchsbaum, the impresario. He knew everybody. He organized elaborate emigré variety shows for which he brought over guest artists from Hungary — singers, actors, comedians. Together with the emigré artists (who were either living in New York or would come over from somewhere else in the U.S. or Canada) they presented a few shows a year, which were always played to an auditorium packed to bursting point with Hungarians.

For these shows Buchsbaum usually hired the auditorium of the Julia Richman High School, between First and Second Avenue. As often as not, my mother would sing in these shows and my father compère. So I always went to them. When I was fifteen I started to perform in them myself, singing popular songs and exchanging 'improvised' humorous dialogue with my father. At that time I was planning a career on the stage and I thought it would all be good experience. After all, if I could entertain Hungarians with a skit about an English schoolgirl misunderstanding the teacher in an American high school history class, I could entertain anyone with anything. (Whenever a joke fell flat, I nearly did, too.)

On one occasion I was all made up to perform and wearing my frilly white 'stage dress', but still had half an hour or so before my cue. So I wandered out of the school building and found myself in the fenced-in concrete playground behind it. I strolled around for a while, reciting my lines. Then I noticed that a group of teenage boys on the other side of the fence were taking an interest in me. I must have been an odd sight, wandering around in broad daylight in a playground, all done up like an aspiring Gertrude Lawrence. And mumbling to myself in addition.

I thought a bit of mild flirtation might put me in the right mood for my rendition of 'If I Fell in Love With You', so I smiled coyly. I wandered slightly nearer to them. I had had my hair done that morning and felt rather sophisticated and glamorous. I hoped they appreciated these little touches. They smiled back and called out a few encouraging words.

Suddenly I heard other words, gruff and not at all encouraging. They came from the opposite side of the playground, but still, fortunately, on the other side of the fence. I turned and saw a group of teenage girls and their faces froze my blood. There was no mistaking the message: I had been flirting with their boyfriends. Suddenly I envisaged a street fight to make the one in *West Side Story* seem like *Playschool*. Surely the punishment for such a crime in the concrete jungle of New York was Death.

I ran as fast as my satin pumps could take me back to the rear door of the school. But it was one of those doors which opens only from the inside. I had my back against the wall. The girls were closing in, slowly making their way around the high fence. It was obvious their boyfriends would be of no earthly use to me. Fickle creeps.

Then I noticed the narrow gate in the fence. It was slightly ajar. If I ran like hell I might just slip through it before the girls could reach it. I took a deep breath and shot through it like a bullet. For an instant the girls were stunned. That gave me all the time I needed. I rounded the corner at a speed which could easily have broken the sound barrier.

I ran through the main entrance to the school, but only had time to crouch down behind the impromptu ticket stand set up for the show, before the girls sped in after me. There was no one around, they were all watching the show. Roars of laughter and applause wafted out from the auditorium. The girls split up, some went down one hallway, the rest down another. And I escaped into the auditorium. The darkness there was a balm. By the time I crept down the aisle to my dressing-room and locked the door behind me, I was feeling rather proud of myself. And I learned my lesson: even in Yorkville, it's not enough to be Hungarian.

For a year my father ran a Hungarian radio station which was on the air every Monday evening from 7 p.m. to 8 p.m. Radio Bartók was a real one-man operation. My father was the writer, broadcaster, producer, editor and technician. Sometimes my mother would join in as announcer or to read out the commercials.

Frequently a live interview was broadcast and one evening I went in to watch this being done. At that time an extremely handsome and equally wealthy young man was running for the office of councilman of Yorkville. His name was Carter Burden, and he was a part of the Kennedy crowd, having once worked for Robert. He was also married to the beautiful daughter of the president of C.B.S.

Burden knew very well that to get anywhere in Yorkville it was necessary to have the support of the Hungarian population. Hearing of my father's position in the Hungarian community, he asked him to handle his campaign to woo these immigrants. As part of this job, my father made a lengthy interview with him on Radio Bartók, so that the Hungarians could learn Burden's views.

Needless to say, Burden won the election. And for years afterwards, each Christmas we received a card from the Burden family, with a photograph of the glamorous couple and their lovely children. Each year until they got divorced.

Another short-lived venture was the Petőfi Theatre, which existed for a couple of years just after the revolution. The little theatrical company rented auditoriums in Yorkville to put on Hungarian plays, many of them dealing with the crisis in Hungary and the subsequent trauma of emigrating and starting life anew. The theatre plays an extremely important part in people's lives in Hungary, so the Petőfi Theatre offered, for a while, a token continuity of this cultural base.

Hungarian emigré newspapers seem to live much longer in the U.S. There are such papers in California, Minneapolis and other states, but the oldest is the *Amerikai-Magyar Népszava* (American-Hungarian People's Voice). It was started a century ago, as a daily. Eventually it became a bi-weekly and now it is a weekly.

Ever since I can remember my father's articles have been appearing in the *Népszava*. And a regular feature of our post in New York was the small brown envelope with a postmark from Cleveland, where the *Népszava* is published, containing the thin, inexpensively produced newspaper. In it my father often wrote about the bewildering experiences of being an emigré in America. There was the story about the canary my parents bought because I wanted a pet and they thought a bird would be the cheapest pet to keep. Just a bird and a cage, so they assumed. But when they learned that a canary in America must also have regular supplies of stamina nutrient, song food, colouring seeds, vitamins, a fruit tree, a compressed fishbone, egg biscuits, parasite killers, minerals for his bath water and stereo records of the *Feathered Stars* series to encourage him to sing, it was decided that, after all, it would have been cheaper to keep a horse, which was what I had really wanted in the first place.

There is an anecdote about the Hungarian who came to

Yorkville with high hopes of building a new life. He had little money and even less English. He made a few friends, emigrés who had already found out some things about living in the 'land of opportunity'. He managed to get a small room somewhere. One of his new friends asked him where he was living. 'Oh,' he replied, 'very nearby. The precise address is No. 225 One Way Street.'

He was not the only emigré in Yorkville to find himself on a one way street. Every ghetto can be described so, by the majority of its inhabitants. And the 'one way' is backwards, or, at best, forwards in isolation from the mainstream.

But ghettos tend to shrink and ghetto-dwellers dissipate, sooner or later. The character of Yorkville has been changing over the last few years. In the late 1950s, following the massive injection of refugees of the revolution, it was a vibrant sector with the aura of a Hungarian provincial town. Emigrés in their tens of thousands created a closely knit community. The common bond was adversity.

But ever since then the influx into this ghetto has been declining, and the oldest generation disappearing. For many Yorkville was merely the first rung on the ladder of emigration, to be followed by the Bronx, perhaps, or Yonkers, or for the more fortunate ones, Bronxville and the suburbs. And so community activities began to shrivel. Shops and restaurants were sold, taken over by Americans or other immigrants. For most of the rest, catering purely for Hungarians was no longer enough, and their commercial approach had to change. The third-generation Weisz now owns the old delicatessen. His grandfather drove a horse and cart around the streets, but this young man went to college, is shrewd and ambitious. Paprikás Weisz is now advertised in *The New Yorker* as a sophisticated shop for international gourmets, importing delicacies not only from Hungary but from all over the world. It has a new face, and it is filled with new faces.

Add to this the constant churning up of New York streets as a matter of routine, anyway, and there is not much left of the original Little Hungary. The old brownstones are being systematically pulled down, and character is being sacrificed for the sake of modernity. In New York, something is always dying.

But there is still something to the old adage which says that whenever a Hungarian goes into a revolving door behind you, he's bound to come out in front. By now it is legendary that that most American phenomenon, Hollywood, was founded by Adolph

Zukor. And everyone knows that the British film industry became internationally recognized only after Alexander Korda took hold of it. But not many are aware that so fundamentally Parisian an institution as the *Folies Bergère* has been directed and shaped for the last forty years by a Hungarian, Michel Gyarmathy. Or that that pillar of New York high life, the Four Seasons Restaurant, has been in the ownership of a Hungarian ex-agriculturalist, Pál Kövi, for over two decades. Time and time again, it seems the Hungarians have a knack for outdoing the Romans in Rome.

Gyarmathy emigrated in the late 1920s which made him a completely different type from the war refugees or the 1956ers. He wasn't forced to leave by hardship or persecution. He left because Hungary was too small to contain him. He had worked there for a while as a set and costume designer, then decided to take his few pennies with him and try his luck in Paris. He must have been influenced by the old artistic, bohemian affinity between Paris and Budapest.

Today he has a mansion on the Right Bank and a butler who always wears white gloves. But I have never seen him in his Paris home. For me he will always be a creature who dwells solely in swanky *haute cuisine* restaurants in Manhattan. Each year Gyarmathy put on a lavish production, an off-shoot of the Paris *Folies*, in Las Vegas. At the same time he came to New York to visit people, among them my parents. He would invite several friends to dinner at one of the best French restaurants where he would hold court, usually wearing a roll-neck pullover with a huge gold medallion swinging across his ample belly. He particularly enjoyed the company of writers and other creative people. He intensely disliked the company of voluptuous young women (which means he didn't mind me being there at all).

These were grand occasions with a variety of people doing some quite odd things, such as reciting Russian poetry or singing obscure songs in a low voice. Gyarmathy usually didn't say much, he liked to listen to the others. But I do recall his telling me once that he'd had to look at so many fabulous female bodies that they meant no more to him than so much meat to a butcher. And he shocked me by saying that the first thing an *artiste* had to do at an audition was to take all her clothes off so that he could get her measurements. That's the dullest part, he told me, yawning. It was then that I decided not to ask him for a job.

Kövi, too, is a man I only ever met at a dinner table. Every so often he would invite my family to the Four Seasons, where once he convinced me that the 'butterfly steak' on the menu was really a fillet of butterfly. Kövi was always suave and cosmopolitan and good-looking. Once his handsome teenage son was home from boarding school and he, too, dined with us. I was so enthralled with him that even when I learned that Sophia Loren and Marcello Mastroianni were eating at the next table, I didn't bat an eyelid. Kövi left Hungary soon after the war. His first restaurant was in Italy. But his story is one of extreme success (even for a Hungarian). He became a king on East Fifty-second Street without ever touching Second Avenue.

Kövi and Gyarmathy are two of emigration's V.I.P. products. But the majority of emigrés that permeated my life in America, and later for a while in London, were neither very successful nor very unlucky. They merely co-existed along with everyone else in a sort of comfortable ordinariness. And sometimes being ordinary and inconspicuous is exactly what a refugee wants.

It was certainly what I wanted most as a teenage Hungarian-American. I wanted to blend in and do all those things that the *real* American teenagers were doing. Having pyjama parties, gossiping for hours on the telephone, staying out late at dances, having dates and 'going steady'. But I was never allowed to do any of those things until I was almost married, and then what was the point?

It would be wrong to suggest that all these delights were forbidden me simply because my parents came from another country where such permissiveness was unknown. It also had to do with there being not one but two generations between my mother and myself. She was forty-one when I was born. In addition, a liberal and flexible approach to life is the last thing to be acquired by a person who was raised with corporal punishment by a devout headmaster father, and educated at provincial convents. But this, too, is an over-simplification. It wasn't until after I had been to Gölle that I began to see a little more clearly beneath the surface of the once-hated régime of my upbringing.

From the age of thirteen I battled valiantly to gain that conformity and ordinariness which I knew would make me happy. I screamed, sulked, wept and sneaked around. I resented everything Hungarian because it kept me from what I wanted, which was to be undeniably American.

I enlisted the support of a few schoolmates in this struggle. My closest ally was Nan, a tall, buxom girl who really had little cause for complaint because her well-heeled Boston-bred family ensured her membership in the coveted school cliques. But for some reason she took up my cause, the way privileged Americans like to sponsor us 'tired, poor huddled masses yearning to breathe free'.

By the age of fifteen Nan had totally mastered the art of nonchalance. Very little could crease her composed demeanour. Around us the world could be going to pot, but Nan's lipstick remained unsmudged and her tights unladdered. She wore immaculately matched skirt and pullover sets from Bonwit Teller's in Manhattan, but wouldn't flinch when I met her in a pair of slacks from the bargain rack at the local Corvette's. That's true friendship.

So together we planned the strategy for our various little skirmishes in the name of liberty and the pursuit of happiness. When we were not doing this, I sat by the window of my bedroom and wrote tragic poetry.

Our efforts culminated in a Master Plan which consisted of taking several boxes of chocolate chip cookies from a cupboard in Nan's kitchen and running away to the nearest town — White Plains. We had about $3.50 between us.

Our first coup was to convince a taxi driver that our cause was worthwhile and that he should drive us into town for nothing. It was already getting dark when we arrived, and the shops were beginning to close. It was a cold November evening. We searched for some friendly establishment where we could warm up.

Nan, being Jewish, suggested we try the synagogue. Its door was open. We crept inside and up a flight of stairs. Moments afterwards we heard the front door being locked and bolted for the night. Lights were turned off downstairs. It was already dark upstairs. We tried the handles of the doors leading off a long corridor. One was open and we nearly stumbled inside. We couldn't quite see what sort of a room it was in the darkness. It had an odd feel about it. We felt the wall for the light switch and finally found it. In the sudden glare of bulbs we realized we were in the men's lavatory. A row of mirrors stared at us accusingly and the white tiles seemed unwelcoming.

As usual, Nan was unruffled. 'This isn't too bad,' she said, camping down on the floor and taking out a box of cookies from her shoulder bag. We had the cookies for dinner, then lay down and covered ourselves with our jackets. 'Don't forget to undo your bra,' I heard Nan say just as I was going off to sleep. 'I read in *Seventeen* that it's bad to keep it on overnight.'

In the morning we were two crumpled bags of aches and cramps. We sneaked downstairs, dreading some kind of confrontation with moralists. But we came across no one. The door was unlocked and we went out into the cold.

We spent most of the day wandering idly around town. This made us hungry, but we decided not to buy any food until we could bear it no longer. We seemed to spend hours in Alexander's, where at least it was warm. But not having money to spend is a torturous state to be in at Alexander's. So at last we left. By now we were slightly downhearted. What started off as a great adventure was becoming a great bore. And what were our parents up to, we wondered. The police had probably been notified by now. Whenever there was some sort of problem with me my parents always threatened to enlist the aid of the police. No one else's parents ever thought of doing that. You would think that having lived in a police state would be enough to put my parents off that idea.

By the time evening came we were famished. The last cookie crumb had been devoured long ago. We were fresh out of ideas. We sat down in one of those narrow diners which look as though they were converted from old caravans, and ordered a portion of French fries each. Nothing had ever tasted so good. Then reluctantly and without a word we got up, paid our bill and headed for home. We didn't have to discuss anything between us, or give each other false assurances. There was nothing to say. We knew we were beaten.

We spent our last few cents on the bus ride home. At the street corner where we always said our good-byes we merely nodded to each other. I turned around to take a last look at Nan just before I rounded the corner into my street. She was putting her fur-lined gloves on, and I thought I could even hear her whistling. But that may have just been the wind in the suburban trees. She didn't turn around to look at me.

I can't say I was severely dealt with on my return home. There was little in the way of punishment. There didn't have to be. The result of our escapade couldn't have pleased my parents more. Nan and I never spoke to each other again (at least not until graduation day two years later). I gave up all ambition to join cliques and fit in with the others. A curious instinctive understanding had passed between Nan and I on the evening of our ignominious return. Somehow we knew that there was nothing else for us to do. We didn't need each other any more. And once you've lost a war completely and decide to acquiesce, it can come as an immense relief.

I turned my attentions to other things. I read a great deal, wrote more poetry, joined the school dramatics club and decided to become an actress. Almost before I knew it, I was on my way to London to study dramatic art.

But long before this happy turn of events, when I was still only fourteen and bobbing about on the turbulent seas of my teenagerhood, a particular incident impressed me. I was secretly shaving my legs in the bathroom when I heard my mother coming up the stairs, sobbing. I quickly finished the job and went out to see her.

'Your grandmother has died,' she said with great difficulty in between her sobs. And there was a telegram from Budapest in her hands.

I made some feeble attempt to placate my mother but I knew it was a hopeless task. So I just lay down on my bed. I felt that I ought to cry, too. But I couldn't. So I returned to the bathroom, this time to pluck my eyebrows.

Sometime in the early hours of the morning I woke up suddenly and started to cry uncontrollably. For the first time in many years I thought about that dream again, about leading my grandparents away from behind the boulder. My grandmother was dead. She had slipped away from me. And I was never able, in the end, to save her from anything.

I tried to remember all I could about her. For a short period, during my family's two year sojourn in Germany, my grandparents came to stay with us. I was about eleven at the time. I thought of her soft, brown tearful eyes, her hair in a bun, her quiet manner. I pictured the dark dresses she wore, usually with some small flowery print on them. And I tried to taste again her pastries, which I always loved — poppyseed cakes, walnut cakes, marzipan rolls.

But none of these images were as clear or as real to me as my dream. That was still as vivid as when I was five, a newly arrived refugee child. And I couldn't help but feel, as I still feel, that if your strongest memory of a loved one is contained in your saddest childhood dream, then Life must have let you down somewhere.

I walked along slowly in between the rows of graves. There were marble and stone slabs with wrought-iron lanterns at one end, carved urns and vases, statues of the Madonna, little monuments with benches in front of them and elaborate tombs. Some graves were alive with roses or geraniums. Others were ensnared in brittle, dead vines.

My grandparents had a joint grave in this cemetery in the Buda hills, covered in foliage, with the small wooden cross hidden behind a strong young fir tree. The cross had a round metal plaque which said that my grandfather died aged eighty-five and my grandmother aged seventy-four, 'Peace upon their dust'.

This simple grave suited them. Their lives were simple and unostentatious. Some of the families of the deceased in that cemetery have obviously pooled together a small fortune, 20,000 forints or so, in order to erect a grand tomb. But smooth, cold marble could say nothing about my grandparents. They were earth-bound country people. And so the fir tree which grew above them was an apt sentinel.

But no matter how fine some of the tombs were, the cemetery itself was sadly neglected. The state had little money to lavish on the dead. (They didn't even pay people to sweep the streets for the living.) So there were many weeds and wayward, untended trees, wild flowers and tall grass. Rough, unpaved paths disappeared into a tangle of wood and marble, dead flowers and churned-up earth. But it was a fine, windy day, and on top of all was a careless layer of yellow autumn leaves, recently descended from above. Every once in a while a gust of wind would catch them up and make them dance in little circles above the dead.

I was with Big Mári, doing the rounds. Her parents were also buried there, in a simple grave with a prickly bush growing on top, and Dódi's father was buried underneath a huge gravestone of grey marble engraved with the one word *Apu* (father). I had heard that Dódi's mother spent her last forint on that slab.

On all these graves Mári put a fresh bunch of dahlias from her garden. She also picked a few weeds and snapped off some dead twigs from overhanging branches. After a moment of respectful silence, broken only by the swirling of the leaves, we turned and walked back up the untidy path. From the other side of the entrance gate came the welcome sound of cars and buses speeding towards Pest.

It doesn't happen very often that a refugee will build up a new life somewhere, do rather well, then towards the end of his life, pack up and go back home. But it has happened. For some people, the deeper they sink into the new country and the new life, the more they are pulled by the Homeland's spiritual magnet. Until one day they can resist it no longer. So they decide to give up the life of ease and comfort and unquestioned freedom they have grown accustomed to in the West. But going back is a tricky affair. They are returning not only to the old country, but the old times. And the old times are gone.

These returnees are not ignorant. They realize that the whole world has changed, even Hungary. Indeed, if things were the same as in 1956, who in their right mind would ever think of going back? But just what *will* things be like? Once the decision is taken, the loose ends are tied and the ticket bought, they must feel like the player in blind man's buff who is blindfolded, spun around a few times and then stumbles around in the darkness trying to orientate himself. That's what happened to Bandi.

Before the revolution, Bandi practised as a dentist in Budapest. He was married to a pretty, blonde ex-operetta singer, Gizi. In 1956 they emigrated to the U.S. Knowing that America was the land where everyone's dreams can come true, he announced that he didn't really want to be a dentist any more. His ambition was to become a psychiatrist. He was already over forty.

All of his past qualifications counted for nothing. He had to start from scratch. For years Bandi sweated it out as the lowest-paid, hardest-working trainee in various hospitals in different states. Gizi also worked hard as a typist and office clerk. They had that double-powered drive which the refugee needs just to reach base one.

One day Bandi made it at last as a fully-fledged, qualified psychiatrist. And America is one big field day for psychiatry. He was offered a position at an asylum in upstate New York. It came with a house, and Bandi and Gizi moved into it and settled down to a comfortable life.

Of course Bandi was very well paid. They began to travel around the world. Every time we visited them in their smart house down the street from the asylum, they showed us their home movies of holidays in Peru or Venezuela or Iceland. And after the movies, Bandi would drink a few more glasses of wine and laugh loudly and tell anecdotes. He'd light one cigarette after another, pop corks and illustrate with vivid gestures his stories about all kinds of people. The more he drank the more he laughed and the longer his stories became. In contrast, Gizi sat quietly looking as pretty as a doll, and got up only to offer everyone more cakes and chocolates. When she smiled, which was often, the room grew brighter.

Later on there was grave trouble in their marriage. They separated and eventually divorced. But after a few years of being lonely and miserable, they decided they just couldn't live without each other. I can still hear Bandi telling my father in his hoarse, smoke-encrusted voice, 'I'm a psychiatrist but I swear I don't understand it. I want to get married again. That's bad enough. But I'm going to marry the same woman twice. That's *crazy*.' He gulped down a Scotch. 'Well,' he added, waving a hand with a cigarette embedded in it and smiling like a conspirator, 'who said crazy people can't be happy?'

A few years ago Bandi retired. And not long afterwards he stunned his friends by announcing that he and Gizi had decided to move back to Budapest. Then everyone, Hungarian and American alike, thought he must be crazy.

He said that his two decades in the U.S. had been marvellous. He'd enjoyed his career, he'd made money, he'd seen the world. But now he was homesick. He felt the urge to return to the atmosphere and the surroundings which, throughout his immigration, he'd quietly hankered after. Suddenly he knew he had to end his days among old friends and old haunts. In America his friends had slowly dispersed, they were too far apart. And Bandi could only be happy where there was gaity and bonhomie.

Bandi and Gizi knew that they could live very well in Hungary on their U.S. pensions. They would be expected to renounce their U.S. citizenship, of course, and become Hungarians again, which meant being subject to all the laws of that land. But being retired and requiring no financial assistance from the state, they didn't expect to have any problems with the authorities. And they didn't. Not for a long time.

They bought a flat in the Castle district of Buda and filled it with many of the beautiful things they'd collected over the years. They brought back the Volvo, and although it wasn't a new model, it seemed like a limousine on the streets of Budapest. And they continued to travel. Once a year they applied for permission to go to the West, and each time they were granted it. They visited the Canary Islands, they went to America and all over Europe.

They found their old friends and made new ones. At last it seemed as if Bandi had all that he could want. His evenings were spent in restaurants and cafés, or at home playing cards with his companions. There was good Hungarian wine, *pálinka*, songs, jokes and stories in abundance. And Gizi couldn't be more content, either. She made frequent pilgrimages to the Zserbó where she took great delight in the famous cakes and pastries. She put on weight, but even that didn't seem to matter. This wasn't America, where you are supposed to be skinny. In Hungary it's nice to be plump.

One afternoon during my stay in Budapest I arrived back from a shopping expedition in Pest and ran upstairs to show my mother what I'd bought. I barged into her room with my bags and parcels only to find that she had a visitor. A man was sitting in an armchair by the window. I didn't recognize him. He turned to me and smiled shyly. I nodded politely.

'Don't be rude,' my mother scolded. 'Let's have a nicer greeting than that for someone you haven't seen in ten years!'

The man stood up apologetically. 'Remember me?' he asked. 'I'm Bandi.'

He seemed smaller than I remembered. Or perhaps I'd only grown taller. But there was no mistaking the fatigue, the age and bad health which was written on his face. And when he came closer to kiss and embrace me, I noticed that his thinning hair was dyed an unnatural shade of auburn.

Juszti came in just then, bearing a tray with espresso and cakes. I was glad of this interruption for it gave me a moment to cover my surprise and discomfort. I sat down at the foot of my mother's bed.

'Please tell me about yourself. And how is Gizi? Do you like living in Budapest?' I said.

He put up his hands and laughed. 'One at a time, please!' he implored. Then he looked at me and I saw in his eyes that something had gone wrong with his dream, with his brave return to the Homeland.

He told me that a year earlier he had suffered a severe stomach haemorrhage. 'It must have been my lifestyle,' he said with a weak laugh. 'Anyway, the doctor told me I mustn't ever drink alcohol again, if I want to stay alive. I can't even have any good strong espresso.' He glanced at the tray Juszti had put down on the table, and I noticed that there was nothing in front of him but a glass of mineral water. 'But you know something? I don't really miss them.' He smiled again and put his hands together on his lap.

He seemed to shrink inside himself. Then he lit a cigarette, turned to my mother and regained some of his old animation as he recounted an anecdote about a mutual friend. I didn't listen. I thought about those visits to the house near the asylum, the laughter and the empty bottles of wine.

He became serious again and lowered his voice. 'This year for

80

the first time we were refused permission to go abroad.' He shrugged. 'Don't know why. No explanations given. We handed in our passports, but they were simply returned, without the usual stamps on them.'

'So you couldn't leave? You had to forget about the trip?' I was even more uncomfortable than before.

'Oh no, we went. We just had to resort to different means. *Protekció*. You understand?' In Hungary everyone understands that word. It means 'connections'. 'Things seem to be tightening up here,' he added with a sigh. 'We'll just have to see what happens.'

He had little else to say after that, and my mother tried unsuccessfully to entice him to stay for dinner. 'Must go now, I'm meeting someone in town. You know I've a busy social life,' he chuckled. 'Don't come downstairs, Juszti will see me out.' With that he buttoned his American jacket and left. He hadn't even finished his mineral water.

Things worked out more fortunately for Sándor. In the forties and early fifties he was Hungary's most acclaimed classical actor. He appeared in many films, but was known best of all for his stage portrayals of Cyrano de Bergerac and Romeo. He not only had a great talent, but the magnetic presence of an Olivier or a Paul Scofield. He was married to an actress called Kató, who was rather lightweight by comparison but was so extraordinarily beautiful that it didn't matter.

It must have taken unusual courage for them to emigrate just after the revolution. They had everything to lose, fame, position, comfort. Someone whose stock-in-trade is a mastery of the Hungarian tongue, such as an actor or writer, forfeits all on leaving Hungary behind. The two great tragedies of the Hungarian race are a totally vulnerable geography and an isolated language.

But despite this, a huge number of actors and writers fled in 1956. Ironically, it was often those who were most firmly bound to Hungarian culture who felt it was no longer possible to remain. Perhaps the creative nature is also less willing to compromise, to accept restrictions on creativity. So many of these people detached themselves from the only country in which they could reasonably hope to flourish. They lost their one true 'public'.

At least Sándor was able to continue working as an actor. He never gave up his profession in favour of earning more money as a salesman or used car dealer. He wasn't offered leading Shakespearean roles, mainly because King Lear and Coriolanus didn't have a Hungarian accent. But for several years he was a member of Tyrone Guthrie's repertory company in Minneapolis, where he played a variety of characters with accents. Who in Minneapolis could tell the difference between a Hungarian accent and an Austrian one? If you're foreign, you're foreign and that's it.

Sometimes Sándor's company toured around. Once we went to see him at the Lincoln Centre in Manhattan in a modern play. He hadn't a big part, but nowadays all the players are treated as equals, they are all important people in one happy company. In any case, no one had ever heard of the actor who played the main part, either.

But while Sándor was doing all right, Kató was suffering. She had a job as hostess in a restaurant. All evening, until late at night, she was on her feet showing guests to their tables. As a girl she had had some trouble with her hip, and this job put a terrible strain on it. Eventually she needed an operation. But something went wrong after the operation and her state deteriorated. She had to give up working and resigned herself to a limp, a walking stick and inevitable pain.

In 1975, when Sándor was sixty and Kató was not much younger, they moved back to Budapest. Like Bandi and Gizi, they were able to buy a desirable little flat and live most comfortably on their U.S. social security. And Sándor was welcomed back as Hungary's 'grand old man of the theatre'. He was showered with offers of parts in plays, films and on television. Once again, when he walked down a street, he was stopped by fans and admirers. And in shops and cafés he heard what must be the sweetest music to an actor's ears: his name being whispered excitedly, followed by 'he's just as handsome as ever' and 'doesn't he look marvellous?'

But, in time, some of the other leading actors in Budapest (those who had never left the country) began to resent Sándor. Who did he think he was, leaving the place for twenty years and then sauntering back as if he'd never even been away and expecting to pick up where he'd left off? What right had he to steal all the best roles from the others? Of course, deep inside they must have known exactly by what right he was doing all that. He was still the best goddamn actor in Hungary, and they knew it.

Inevitably these resentments faded and disappeared. In 1980 Sándor officially retired. He is still able to work, but not more than a few hours a week. Once in a while he accepts a small television part or does two stage performances a week in repertory.

Soon after I arrived in Budapest the new theatrical season opened, and one of its main attractions was the Hungarian version of

Brian Phelan's *The Signalman's Apprentice*. It was being staged by the Pesti Theatre. Sándor was playing the role of Albert, the sham station-master of a rickety disused railway station, who is both tyrannical and paternal towards his weak subordinate, Alfred.

Before the play began I had a note sent up to his dressing-room to let him know I was in the audience and would like to see him if I could. During the interval I was shown upstairs. I knocked on his door.

'Come in!' he boomed.

Among all the theatrical bits and pieces on his long dressing table were two glasses of champagne. After the usual hugging and kissing, we sat down opposite each other and began to drink. He told me about his sons and I told him about my parents. We exchanged addresses.

'You haven't become a famous actress, after all,' he said. 'Why not?'

'I decided I would rather write instead. So I'm a journalist.'

He laughed loudly and banged his fist on the dressing table, causing a few assorted jars of make-up to leap into the air. 'You've got more brains than I thought!' he thundered.

Soon somebody called his name and said the second act was about to begin. We stood up, he clasped my hands and smiled down at me. He didn't seem at all old. He was just as youthful and powerful-looking as I remembered him.

During the second act I realized what an immense physical strain the part of Albert must be on a man of sixty-six. He never left the stage, and the tension continued to mount to an electrifying climax. Sándor appeared to have a great reserve of energy which was finally exhausted.

Playing the part of Alfred was Antal Páger, an actor much older than Sándor. He, too, was a one-time refugee who returned to Hungary. But his story reads like a bad joke. He was born in 1899 and became an actor with strong right-wing tendencies. He was quite content under fascist rule, but when the Soviets took control at the end of 1944, he fled to Argentina.

He worked as a photographer there and occasionally he performed in some play for Hungarian exiles. But he remained poor. He was married to an actress called Julia Komar, by whom he had two daughters. But in 1956, *before the revolution*, he left his family and returned to Hungary. For a while he thought he had made a grave mistake. His old colleagues were reluctant to forgive him his

83

murky past. The government of the day, however, received him warmly. He had been a well-known actor before his emigration, and his return to a communist Hungary was a good advertisement for the cadres.

Then came the revolution. Páger's fate hung in the balance. What would become of him if the moderates, who distrusted him, won the day? But the uprising was crushed and the victors, who had already given him the offical 'okay', ensured his future well-being. No one in Hungary dared challenge his position. That is how he made his way upwards to become, once again, a star of stage and screen.

A few days after seeing the performance, my mother, Adam and I went to visit Sándor and Kató at their flat. It was what in Hungary they called a *garzonlakás*. A sort of bedsit, I suppose. But that calls to mind a sleazy, unheated room in Clapham, and their flat was anything but that.

In fact it was an exquisite place. Bright, warm and decorated in superb style. It had oil paintings and Persian carpets and Kató's collection of antique porcelain, shiny mahogany tables supporting delicate *objets d'art*, and on a platform set in an alcove, a sumptuous white bed. That was the first thing Adam tested.

But more visually striking than anything else was Kató herself. It is amazing how a woman can be ageing and lame and still remain just as attractive as when she was eighteen. She had the same seductive curve of the mouth, luminous eyes and graceful hands. Some of the impact may have been due to good make-up, jewellery and becoming clothes. But when the curtain goes up and you are stunned by a magnificent stage set, you don't think of asking the designer how he did it.

Adam and Sándor immediately became good friends. They romped together on the settee and in between the fragile ornaments of china and glass. It is the mark of a truly great actor when he can convince you not only that he is Hamlet or Cyrano or Richard III, but a hungry lion about to devour a little boy.

With such noisy antics in the background, Kató spoke about readjusting to life in Budapest after being abroad for so long.

'When I look back, my life has been so full of ironies. When we left in 1956, I had an image of the American world of theatre and films, Broadway, Hollywood, Greta Garbo and the rest of the big stars. But none of it really existed any more. Those stars were already old and Hollywood had changed, and my illusions were empty, based on a lost era.

'So I went to America only to become disillusioned. But I learned to accept it. I adapted to the life we discovered there. And eventually I got used to it — the supermarkets, the television commercials, the Chevrolets and the unfamiliar customs. I never really felt at home in America, but I was content.

'Then came the decision to come home. And the same thing happened to me again, in reverse. The way I remembered Budapest and the kind of life we had here, the people in the streets — all these had changed. We returned to a different Hungary. I'm still out of my element. I've little in common with those who've been living here all along. I have no family any more. I live through Sándor, for his success and fulfilment.

'And as I get older, my children and grandchildren become more and more the centre of my life. And then what does it matter if an old woman realizes that most of her life has been spent in the wrong place at the wrong time, caught between two worlds which don't exist any more?'

Sándor, in the middle of his performance as a yapping bulldog under the dining table, heard the word 'children' and called out, 'Kató, have you told them about the boys yet? Don't forget the boys!'

We heard that both of their sons, now in their late thirties, are living successfully in the U.S.. One is an artist in Hawaii. He was commissioned to do a huge wall mural for the headquarters of a major trade union there. Sándor and Kató attended the unveiling. They were not surprised when they saw that it was done mainly in red-white-green, the colours of the Hungarian flag. These colours are featured in all of his work. The mural showed workers united by their hard but noble work. The sort of scene which would go down superbly in any socialist country. But in America they still believe it.

The other son is a Californian businessman. Many years ago he met a Hungarian girl while on a trip to Budapest. He fell in love, got permission to take her back with him to America and married her. Then she left him. Now he's trying to find a new wife. Occasionally he travels to Hungary hoping to meet another nice young girl. It hasn't occurred to him to look anywhere else.

Five

Early on the following Sunday morning the gates to our driveway swung open and a square black Moskvich drove through. Dódi's cousin Miklós had arrived to take me to their country bungalow at Zebegény, in the hills above the Danube Bend. With him were his good-natured, plump wife, Gizi, and their ten-year-old son, also Miklós but known as Little Miki.

Little Miki looked very American. His tubbiness was accentuated by his crew-cut hair. He had the awkwardness and baby-pink face of someone not quite into adolescence, so it was strange to find him wearing a wristwatch that would have done justice to the leader of an Apollo space mission.

Adam and I sat in the back of the Moskvich with Little Miki. Mári and Dódi followed us in their car with my mother. It was a fine, warm day. We crossed the Danube and drove through the outskirts of Budapest, past drab factories and a well-known shipyard along the river. It didn't strike me as odd that this land-locked country should be building ships. After all, Hungary was ruled for many years by Admiral Horthy, who hadn't a navy to his name. Hungarians aren't bothered by such minor details.

I had given Miki a set of model cars from London. Throughout the hour-long journey to Zebegény he spoke to me about them.

'I've never seen a car like this in Hungary,' he said, studying a Triumph TR7. 'Are there a lot of cars in England that we don't have here?'

'Do you want to see a really great car?' Miklós called to me from the front seat. 'Have a look at that.' He jerked his head towards the scene of a car accident straight ahead. We were slowing down abruptly. A car stood in between the two lanes of the highway, beside some policemen who were waving the traffic on. As we neared and then came alongside it, I saw that it was a white Trabant estate car, smashed up in what must have been a head-on collision. But what astounded me and gave rise to a sardonic laugh from Miklós and long whistle from Little Miki was the fact that the car's roof had completely detached itself. It lay on the roadside next to the Trabant, flapping in the wind like the flimsy side panel of a bathtub.

'What a car,' sighed Miklós. 'Have an accident in one of those and the good Lord Himself wouldn't know which prayer to say for you.'

Before long we reached that stretch of countryside north of Budapest where the Danube starts to curl towards the Czech border. To our left was the river and on the right the lush hillside rose steeply.

'Look up there,' Gizi said, pointing up the hill. 'See all the new *vikend* houses?' (If there is Franglais, there is also 'Hunglish'. Many English words have muscled into the Hungarian language. This expression, to describe the small bungalows built as private weekend retreats, is commonly used. Like that other Hunglish word, *szendvics,* sandwich, the Hungarian accent is phonetically built in, just in case some peevish individual might decide to say it properly.)

'A few years ago,' said Miklós, 'there was barely a house or two in these hills. And now look at it. Soon they're going to start building on the other side of the road, too, by the river. That will be really awful.' He clicked his teeth disapprovingly.

'People here must have a lot of money,' I said, 'if so many second homes are cropping up everywhere.'

'There are people who have piles of money. Of course, it's best not to ask how they got it.'

'What about your place?' I asked.

Miklós smiled. 'The bungalow is at least 150 years old. We inherited it from Gizi's parents. Her father rebuilt most of it with his own hands and her mother now lives there most of the time. So it's not just a *vikend* house.'

'And if we want to keep it, ' said Gizi sternly, 'we've got to do some more work on it, with *our* own hands. The plaster is peeling, the outside walls are crumbling. We'll be busy in the spring.'

Miklós nodded in reluctant agreement. 'I know. I don't suppose we'll be able to find any decent builders who are reliable and won't charge us a fortune. That's the problem in this country.'

What Englishman could be homesick in a country like that?

'What about that gypsy who did some work for us a few years ago?' Gizi asked.

'Yes, the gypsies are our last hope,' said Miklós.

'Zroom, zroom, ZROOM!' said Miki, driving a Ferrari up his father's neck.

Then we arrived at our destination.

A black mongrel bounded down the long flight of stone steps to the gate, barking furiously.

'*Szervusz*, Jancsi,' said Miklós. 'That's enough, Jancsi.' He called out to his mother-in-law to open the gate, which was locked, but the old woman couldn't hear him. So he put down his three bags bulging with food and drink for our lunch, and climbed onto it. Jancsi jumped up to greet him and nearly knocked him back down on top of us.

A few minutes later we followed Miklós up the steps, which were overhung with trees bearing big ripe peaches. The dwelling itself is primitive, but it is set in the Garden of Eden. All around it are fruit trees, and they were in full bloom. Almost from the front door a vineyard spread in a lush rectangle up the hillside.

On the terrace was a long wooden table with chairs. Here Miklós and Gizi began to unpack what they had brought, and Gizi's mother added her own items from a larder set into the hillside. Soon the table was covered with sausages, salami, goose liver paté, smoked ham, bread, grapes, apples, red wine, white wine, peppers, tomatoes and pickled cucumbers. And this was just the pre-lunch snack.

We ate a little and drank a little. Then Miklós, Dódi and I strolled into the village. For a while we walked beside the railway line and Miklós told us that during the summer hordes of day-trippers come up to Zebegény by train. They take a walk in the hills, or swim in the river, have lunch in a village *csárda,* then do the rounds of the wine cellars where they drink until they are tipsy enough to face the boring train journey back to town.

'The more intelligent ones might also visit our museum,' he added, with a slightly boastful air.

Dódi lit his pipe and puffed on it thoughtfully. He studied me for a moment. 'Do you think our relative from London is intelligent enough?' he asked Miklós.

The museum was once the home of a celebrated national artist, István Szőnyi. It has been preserved as a memorial to him, with most of the rooms unchanged, and his works line the walls of the corridors and staircase. Upstairs his studio is untouched since his death, with his half finished painting still on the easel.

He wasn't originally from Zebegény, but had loved the area of the Danube Bend and it was what he liked most to paint. He had owned a large stretch of the hillside behind his house, and when he died in 1960 he left the house and land to the state. For several years it has been used as a residential summer school for artists.

I suddenly remembered that I know someone who used to teach there. Laci has the appearance of a typical artist. Lanky and bearded. By his mid-thirties he was one of the most successful young artists in the country. He had one exhibition after another and was often invited to show his work in the West. As an eminent Hungarian artist he was warmly received everywhere by colleagues and patrons.

He became friendly with many influential Westerners living in Hungary. This indirectly led to his decision to seek asylum in London, for he was approached several times by government officials, hoping to extract information from him about his friends. His refusal to comply, he said, had an adverse effect on his career. During a brief trip to London he convinced his wife, Magda, that they should not return home. They were granted asylum.

But the friends and contacts who had been so gracious while he was a bona fide artist from Hungary made themselves scarce now that he was an exile needing help. For a few years he and Magda struggled along in a flat above an office in south London. Magda, an ex-pupil of Laci's from the Zebegény summer school, produced several exquisite drawings and etchings. Once in a while she sold one, but she couldn't bear to part with most of them. Laci painted great apocalyptic canvases and tried to sell them everywhere, but he couldn't make enough money.

They left London and went to Vienna. There Laci could at least do reasonably well painting portraits for the rich. But that gave him little satisfaction. They continued for a few more years, without fame or a great deal of money or happiness. It seemed as though they'd had to give up too much in leaving Hungary behind. And Magda began to be homesick for her mother and her friends. She was still only in her early thirties.

One day Laci learned that they had been granted amnesty by the Hungarian government. Once so fervently in favour of exile, he now considered going back home. He made one or two tentative visits. And so began his gradual re-entry into Hungarian society. He had forgiven the state and the state had forgiven him. Like a capricious child who had run away and been horrified at the cruel reality of the outside world, he returned, sulking but thankful that at least his parents still wanted him. Magda, however, who hadn't wanted to emigrate in the first place, refused to go back. She stayed in Vienna and has since become a highly successful artist.

We left the museum and wandered up the quiet, unpaved road leading to the summer school dormitory. It was now closed. There was no one else around. I could see why Szőnyi liked to paint there, and why the school was so popular with aspiring artists. It was a romantic place. I stood beneath the tall, old trees. Was it here that Laci and Magda fell in love?

When we got back the lunch was nearly ready.

'Just smell that!' said Miklós. 'You've never tasted fish like this before.' He led me into the kitchen.

'What is it?' I asked, sniffing at a school of white fish being grilled to a golden colour.

'*Hekk*. Imported from Russia. *Delicious.*' He could hardly contain himself. 'So clean, so pure. They have so many of them in their rivers, they don't know what to do with them. So they sell them to us.'

We sat down at the table and feasted. Miklós kept pouring the wine, which was all homemade. The fish was good. Then we went on to the ham, bacon and sausage which was also made by Miklós and Gizi.

'Have another slice of ham,' urged Miklós . 'It's all from the pig we slaughtered last winter. What a beautiful fat pig she was.'

Gizi's mother then passed around a pile of *pogácsa,* little savoury cakes which she'd baked that morning.

I ate until I felt as if I was nine months pregnant and about to go into labour. Everything was fresh and pungent and demanded to be eaten.

Then a strange thing happened. There was a plateful of tomatoes which Miklós had picked from his allotment in Budapest. Idly I took one, cut it up and started to eat it. I had seen that they looked particularly nice — large, firm and very dark. But I wasn't prepared for the taste. I had never eaten such a tomato. It tasted more like a tomato than you would have thought possible. Like an unashamed addict, I ate one after another until they were all gone.

This gastronomic experience made me stop and reflect for a moment on the Hungarians and their food. It is well known that of all the Soviet bloc countries, Hungary is in the most fortunate position. Its economy is relatively healthy and its people are not too badly off materially. In fact there is quite a lot of 'keeping up with the Kovácses' going on.

But the real reason why there is not the sort of discontent and rebellion in Hungary as in most of the other satellites is that there is plenty to eat. When your stomach is full, you don't feel like waving banners and shouting slogans. You just want to lie down for a while.

There is always meat and fish and good bread, fresh fruit and vegetables, a variety of spices to titillate the palate and more than enough wine to wash everything down. Hungarians love to eat well and they love being hospitable. Much of Hungary's produce is sent out to poorer nations in the bloc, as well as to the U.S.S.R. But there are so many private individuals with their rich little gardens and allotments, devotedly nurturing their crops, that there is never a shortage.

Nobody wants to contemplate the horrors of another 1956. While Hungary is well fed, it will be well behaved. Can it be entirely coincidental that the Hungarian word for tomato, *paradicsom,* also means paradise?

After lunch Miklós took us into his wine cellar and showed us the three casks which contain enough wine for 300 bottles. Each autumn they produce enough wine to last for a year, and that includes selling some of it to their Zebegény neighbours.

Then we climbed up the path that runs alongside the vineyard. The vines were covered with nylon netting to keep the crows from devouring the grapes.

'A few years ago I had to sit for hours at the top of the hill and take pot shots at those damned birds, if I wanted to save my grapes,' Miklós explained. 'Then I heard about an inflatable falcon, a sort of balloon, which is supposed to hover above your crops and scare the life out of the crows. It was made somewhere in the West. I saw a picture of it in a magazine. Anyway, I tried for months to get hold of one. I wrote to a dozen places. No one had ever heard of the thing. So I just forgot about the damn falcon. Probably just another one of our illusions about the great big wonderful West.'

From the top of the vineyard we could see far into the distance. I followed the curve of the Danube until it disappeared into the hills of Czechoslovakia. It was all a misty green, like an Impressionist painting. I sat down on the rough, untended grass. There were a few plum trees up there, and Miklós picked a bagful. I ate about six. Adam ate ten. They were excellent, but I still preferred the peaches I had earlier. Those peaches weren't yellow inside but white, and very sweet and juicy. How do you swallow a tinned peach after eating something like that?

At about six o'clock it started to get dark and we packed up our things, cleared the table, put everything away. We were all given wine and fruit to take home. Miki put his cars gingerly back into their box. Jancsi said good-bye as enthusiastically as he'd said hello.

On the way home Miklós spoke about the chandelier business in Pest which he and Gizi own. They make as well as sell chandeliers.

'There's an awful lot involved,' he said. 'We try to cut our overheads by doing everything ourselves. That's the only way we can make a profit. We even manufacture our own nuts and bolts.'

He went on to discuss materials, profit margins and turnover. But while he was talking I had to smile to myself. Miklós hasn't the heart of a true businessman. He's a country squire. When he's on his little 'estate' at Zebegény, making wine and smoking ham, picking plums and peaches, surveying the countryside from the top of his vineyard, entertaining his guests, then he's really alive and in his element. Then life is rich and good and simple. And I have the feeling that whenever he's anywhere else, he's only passing the time.

Now and then, since I had arrived in Budapest, I had caught a glimpse of the elderly couple who live next door to my mother's house, Imre and Mária. They moved in some time during the war, and were a part of that brief early childhood which I spent on Budakeszi Avenue.

Imre is now eighty. His life story reads like the plot of a John le Carré novel — suspense and intrigue, danger and drama played out in the shadow of great world events. Over the years I had heard his name mentioned by various Hungarian emigrés, sometimes by my father or his friends. And so by chance I picked up snippets about his career, his Francophile tendencies, his near-execution during the war. But it wasn't until I paid an informal social visit one mid-morning, Adam in tow, that I was able to piece these things together.

Rather than cut across the vaguely defined border of our two gardens, we went out onto the pavement and rang the bell by their gate. The two mongrels lept to their feet and bounded over to us, barking loudly. In a moment a diminutive elderly man wearing a brightly coloured cap came to open the gate for us.

He knew who we were and greeted us quietly but warmly. He

pulled the dogs away. 'Come inside, I'll get Mária. She's just upstairs doing a bit of tidying up.' He led the way through the front door.

I had been to visit them during my Hungarian holiday a decade earlier, but for some reason had forgotten both what they looked like and what the inside of their house was like. So when I entered their sitting-room/library I was pleasantly surprised once again. I sat down on a satin window seat before the satin-draped bow window and studied the room. From the floor to the lofty ceiling was nothing but books, big leather-bound volumes in deep shades of red and brown and green. Not one mahogany shelf was adulterated by a paperback or cheap edition.

I knew that he had been a publisher, and the room was nothing if not the sanctum of a man of the world of books. But it was also obviously the home of people with discerning taste in the fine arts. There weren't many *objets d'art* in the room, but what there were were beyond reproach, such as the two Sèvres porcelain figures on a marble-topped table by the door. No wonder the dogs were always kept outside.

Imre came back and sat down next to Adam and me. He grinned shyly. 'Like my cap?' he asked. 'My son sent it to me from Guatemala.'

Mária walked into the room, looking slim and fit despite her seventy-odd years. She had on a pair of trousers and a loose shirt with rolled-up sleeves. Her hair was hidden underneath a scarf. Like Imre, she seemed pleased to see us in a calm, casual, quiet way. Not the usual Hungarian greeting. It came as a nice change, because I was growing a little tired of all that hugging and kissing and having my hands squeezed as if they were bottles of washing-up liquid.

I admired the library. Imre said that he and Mária had been building up the collection for many years, obtaining books one by one, with much difficulty, from abroad. 'Most of the volumes are French,' he said. 'We both prefer to read in French. Reminds us of our time in Paris.'

'When were you there?' I asked, watching uneasily as Adam climbed onto Imre's knees in order to remove his Guatemalan cap.

'Oh,' he waved a hand carelessly, 'when I was a student. Very long ago. I went there to learn about publishing and printing. It was the most exciting place in the world to be. I met a lot of writers, poets. Including our own Attila József. There were so many exciting enterprises going on at the time. So many talented people were writing or publishing books or just sitting in cafés being witty and brilliant.' He stared at the Persian carpet in the middle of the room, half smiling. 'But I came back to Budapest. I wanted to carry out an enterprise of my own.'

'What did you do?' I asked.

'I founded a publishing firm, under my own name. It seemed to me that there was a need in the thirties for a certain type of anti-Nazi, anti-fascist book. Here was a cause, I thought, which I could strongly support. And I hoped that I could influence people. I felt I was riding high on the tide of history and that the tide was coming in overwhelmingly fast. Those were good days for me.'

Mária came in with iced tea, pastries and *pogácsa*. 'Right now Imre is reliving all those old times,' Mária explained. 'He's been asked to write his autobiography. So we have to dredge up our old memories, some of which I'd personally prefer to forget. But for Imre it's a good thing. It keeps him busy and gives him a goal to work towards. What can be better for a man of his age?' She put four small plates of Herend porcelain on the table in front of us. I didn't say anything, but giving a Herend plate to a child who is used to melamine is really pushing your luck.

'What happened after you published these anti-Nazi books?' I asked. 'Did you get into difficulties because of your political views?'

'For a while the climate here was not so bad. My books were even well received. It was not yet impossible to hold opinions which were left wing, or as I prefer to call it, socialist.' He sipped his tea. 'But then the relationship with Germany became stifling. The climate changed and my books became unacceptable.' He paused. 'Being Jewish didn't help much, either.'

Mária removed her headscarf and smoothed back her hair. 'And then came the espionage business,' she said coolly.

'Espionage?'

Imre cleared his throat. 'Yes, that was in 1941. I was in prison for seven months, accused of being a secret agent for British intelligence. I was told I would be shot. I was tortured, too. I still have a few scars on my back where the prison guards put out their cigarettes.' He said the words as casually as a pensioner ordering an extra pint from the milkman.

Seeing my questioning stare, Imre said, 'It was all a fabrication. Not that that would have saved me. I was lucky to be eventually set free.'

'But why did they think you were a spy?'

'I had established a reputation as being fervently anti-German. Hungarians living abroad were also aware of this, including a man named Páloczi-Horváth, a left-winger of aristocratic origin. He was in London working for British intelligence, with special responsibility for recruiting agents in Hungary. He wrote to me, hoping to enlist my services. The letter was brought to me by a secret courier, an attractive young woman. Unfortunately this woman was having an affair with another British spy, whom she told about her errand. He turned out to be a double agent. The police waited until she fixed a rendezvous with me and gave me the letter. Then they stepped in. We were caught and thrown into gaol.'

'What happened to the woman?' I asked, completely absorbed in the exploits of this octogenarian.

'She was lucky; she survived.'

'And all these events will be recounted in your book?'

'Indeed. The authorities have been most helpful to me in my researches, by allowing me to go through top-secret wartime files and documents pertaining to my own case. So there will be material in my book which has never before been made public. I will be able to give facts, substantiated by evidence.'

'Will your autobiography extend to the present?' I asked.

He and Mária looked at each other then he turned to me and shook his head. 'It ends in 1944 with the Soviet liberation.' He finished the rest of his tea and sat back against the window. Framed by sunshine and the pink satin drapes, he seemed like a kind old angel in a surrealistic heaven. 'Life has improved here a great deal,' he said, 'but there are still some things we can't do.'

The 'some things', I presumed, included writing an honest appraisal of the nationalizations of 1950, which resulted in the liquidation of all private businesses and the branding of entrepreneurs as 'class enemies'. In that year Imre's firm was taken away. He considers himself lucky to have then been given employment by one of the state publishing houses.

Outside the window, buses and lorries were thundering by. There were fewer and fewer pastries on the Herend porcelain. Imre's cap had been tossed into every corner of the room and was now perched, once again, on his head. Adam was lying on the floor looking at an American comic book left behind the previous year by Imre and Mária's grandson.

Imre told me about their son and daughter. 'András left when he was only seventeen. He went to America. That was in 1948.

Since then he has written to us every single week, except for the two years when he fought in the Korean War. He wrote then, too, but all of his letters were confiscated before they could reach us. He's in California now, working in computers. He married an American, they have a twenty-year-old son. András visits us occasionally, but he doesn't like Hungary very much. He says he hasn't anything in common with the people.'

'Well, that's not surprising, is it?' Mária said with a faint smile which was not really a smile, but rather the pre-empting of something like a frown. 'After all, he's hardly spent any of his life here.'

'And Kati?' I asked.

'She left in 1956 after being refused a place at university. She was determined to study French literature, and eventually to get her Ph.D. She, too, chose America. For several years she's been a professor of French literature at a university in North Carolina. But this year —' Mária shrugged, 'she had to leave her job. There weren't enough students wanting to study her subject. Times are difficult for academics.'

Imre also shrugged and let out a brief helpless laugh. 'Times are always difficult for somebody or other. Once in a while they become difficult for everyone at once and we've a real mess. Wars, revolutions. . .' He took off his cap and twirled it in his hand. 'If only we could steer away from those.'

Mária continued. 'Kati also married an American, another professor at the same university. And she's stayed close to us. She comes back each year, usually with her teenage boy. Her husband is very American. He doesn't come here often.'

Our conversation was interrupted by noisy growling and barking from the garden. Imre stood up. 'The dogs are fighting again, I'd better go and see to them.'

'These dogs,' sighed Mária. 'They're more demanding than our children ever were.' I heard Imre outside, acting as mediator in the canine controversy. The growling had stopped. Now there was only yelping and scuffling. 'You know, we've had many dogs of all sorts, and loved most of them. But my fondest memories are still of Doki. Do you remember him?'

It would be impossible for me to forget the unique and legendary dachshund called Doktor, Doki for short. He started out as my parents' pet, and for a few years was content and quite ordinary. Then my brother was born. He was kept in a crib in one of the upstairs bedrooms. Doki had jumped onto it once or twice and sniffed the baby with curiosity and suspicion. After that the bedroom door was always kept firmly shut and Doki was not allowed in.

But nobody reckoned on the hound's exceptional sensitivity. The banishment was too much for him. He became restless, resentful and nervous. A real case for the psychiatrist's couch. One day my mother was sitting in the garden with my brother. Doki was slouching nearby. My mother went inside for a minute and emerged with something for my brother to eat. 'Look at the nice treat I've got for you!' she called. Doki thought it was for him, being as greedy as he was sensitive. He jumped up and tried to snatch the food from my mother's hand. She scolded him severely. And that did it.

Doki left my parents' house for good. He moved in next door, with Imre and Mária. When any of my family went near the place, Doki raised the alarm, barking and snapping as if at a total stranger. Then he ran off and hid.

He never came back to us. A year or two after we left Budapest we heard through relatives that Doki had been killed by a car. A dog is supposed to be man's most constant and devoted friend. He's supposed to forgive you all those sins that your parents, your children and your marital partners would never let you live down. He's supposed to accept your authority unquestioningly. But dogs are really just like people. Terribly touchy.

My frequent visits to the theatre while I was in Budapest taught me about the difference between the function of the theatre there and, for example, in London. It might be compared to the way two people, one with a full stomach and one with a ravenous hunger, might react to the delicious aromas drifting out of a restaurant kitchen. The hungry person can't resist, he's drawn to it, knowing that the smell suggests the possibility of food. But he who has been eating good food all his life takes it for granted, and probably won't notice the aroma. As he isn't looking for a place to eat, he might not even see the restaurant.

Hungarians may have enough meat and vegetables, but they often seem to hunger for the nourishment of unrestrained laughter. The opportunity to joke in public at the expense of authority is highly valued in an undemocratic society. And in Hungary it can be done in only one place, the auditorium of a theatre. It is true that this 'freedom' is really only an illusion. It is granted by the government, which is shrewd enough to realize that contained rebellion in a theatre can help prevent the other type, which takes to the streets. Better a cocktail in the bar during the interval, than a Molotov cocktail outside. The government knows this, and the people know that the government knows. Everyone is in the picture. But a good political review which puts the knife into every aspect of bureaucratic stupidity and hypocrisy is nonetheless funny. And the country has a long tradition of what the Hungarians call 'political cabaret'. When it has been allowed to operate freely, it has had phenomenal success and influence. During the periods when it was 'guided' by political dogma, it usually managed to retain its integrity and the public's respect by outwitting its watchdogs. On the battlefield of humour, there are a million ways to strike a blow.

London's theatre is mainly a tourist attraction, the majority of Londoners rarely see plays. But in Hungary the theatre cannot attract foreign tourists, because they don't speak Hungarian. Foreigners will go to see an opera, ballet or perhaps one of those folksy operettas they perform on the outdoor stage at Margaret Island. But a play, and even more so a political cabaret, is something only a native can appreciate. And the natives do. Budapest has about twenty theatres, all thriving, and that is a lot for a city of two million inhabitants.

But, often, speaking the language is insufficient for understanding the subtle implications of a play or review sketch. You have to live in a country to recognize its ironies and idiocies. Escorted by Mári and Dódi, who are as *au fait* as anyone with daily life in Hungary, I was able to get an insider's appreciation.

The review at the Vidám Szinpad was entitled *It Stays in the Family*. The family in question is the Soviet bloc, and, as with most families, some of its members don't get along very well. Every once in a while there's a big family reunion. And there are smaller get-togethers going on all the time. But the 'biggest brother' only comes 'when he's called', for instance when he went to visit Afghanistan.

There were nineteen sketches in the review, written by various authors of national repute. They were sharp and witty and delivered devastating body blows to officialdom as well as to the corrupt cadre-on-the-street. It was clear that Hungarians know very well at what and at whom to laugh, but also harbour a deep angst regarding their nation's precarious position in the world.

98

The trouble, quite simply, is that it is answerable to the East, but relies heavily on the West.

Kádár, the Premier, alone remained unscathed by the ruthless humour. I could picture him hovering somewhere above the stage with a benevolent and patronizing smile on his face, not because he knew he would be untouched, but because he really had much to be proud of. For no other country in the 'family' can boast of such a free, unfettered theatre.

That all that is said can be said, is largely due to Kádár, and the Hungarians are grateful for this. Of the countries of Eastern and Central Europe, Hungary is the closest, both geographically and in spirit, to the West. What Kádár has been able to do is convince the 'biggest brother' that Hungary would never tolerate being part of an Eastern alliance without this crucial outlet, this licensed form of relief and criticism. If the steam can be let out sensibly through a legitimate opening, the kettle won't ever blow its top.

So Kádár is a popular man. No one is deluded into thinking he is a great statesman or politician. He leapt to power in 1956 when, during the turmoil of the revolution, he first tricked then stabbed in the back Imre Nagy, the democratic revolutionary Premier. Those are bad credentials. Rather, if he is liked and respected in Hungary, it is by default. For he could have been like the leaders of the other countries in the bloc, and made life a lot more miserable than it is.

Another production of the season was a new play by István Csurka, a playwright noted for his scathing condemnation of Hungary's socialist system. It concerned a team of sociologists which visits the lady porter of a block of flats in a poor district of Budapest. Their purpose is to research into the backgrounds and concomitant problems of people in this stratum of society. This sort of thing is common practice in Hungary.

But the tables are turned and the sociologists, instead, are in for a merciless grilling by the porter's alcoholic, disillusioned ex-son-in-law. He enters the play in a state of drunken dishevelment and starts everyone else drinking, too. Eventually the entire cast is in the same state as he, making it easy for him to 'undress' them emotionally to see what is behind their façades.

What he discovers in the other characters is a bitterness and cynicism to equal his own. For no one seems quite certain about his place in modern Hungarian society. Underlying everything is an existence without hope or joy. The play ends with the cast facing the audience and singing in unison the patriotic song which has come to symbolize Hungary's War of Independence of 1848:

> Lajos Kossuth sent a message:
> He's lost his regiment.
> If he sends this message again,
> We all must go to fight.
> Long live Magyar freedom,
> Long live the Homeland.

That song was last heard publicly in Hungary in 1956.

I left the theatre with Mári and Dódi in a slightly dazed state. The rest of the audience seemed to have been affected in the same way. The people were silent and their faces were thoughtful, even a little anxious.

As I stepped out into the cool darkness of the evening I heard a man behind me say, 'I wonder what the outcome of this will be. Do you think they'll close down the play? It does go a bit far.'

There was a pause, then his friend said, 'I wouldn't worry too much. The authorities have already approved it, otherwise it wouldn't have been staged in the first place.' Then he lowered his voice. 'I'll tell you something, though. One evening even the authorities might get a real shock. What if an audience has the nerve to stand up and sing with the actors at the end of the play? That *would* be something. And I just hope I'm not around if it happens.'

But the theatre in Hungary is nothing if not broad-minded; there are also plays depicting the miseries of capitalism and the Western way of life. Besides *The Signalman's Apprentice* in which Sándor so expertly portrayed the cheating, lazy, cruel station-master who is meant to embody all of rotten, maggot-ridden Britain, there was a production of Arnold Wesker's *The Kitchen*. It was staged by the National Theatre Company. In the play, the kitchen staff of a big, swanky restaurant owned by a ruthless Capitalist Pig becomes a microcosm of the outside world. All the good and evil, the conflicts, hopes and illusions which man is prone to are played out among the frying pans and stew-pots. But I couldn't really concentrate on the symbols and significances of the plot because I was so impressed with the acting. It was excellent.

The style and technique of the actors as well as the direction and staging, reminded me of countless high quality productions I have seen at the Aldwych and National Theatre in London. In the leading role of Peter was a tall, blond, young actor who has achieved national fame not only because of his skill and talent, but due to his erratic, volatile behaviour. It seems the Hungarians also like their showbiz personalities to be eccentric. On stage he gives the impression of frightening combustibility. This must have occurred to him as well, because once, during one of his performances, he threatened to burn the theatre down. That sort of thing does wonders for the box office. So everyone loves him. (Except for the leading lady he once threatened to strangle. She only likes him.) How can you not love an actor who is enormously attractive without being handsome and has a riveting stage presence, who has gestures like lightning and a voice which may not quite be like thunder but can at least be heard up in the gods?

In a socialist country like Hungary there is none of this business called 'resting', which is a euphemism for 'starving'. Every actor has work all the time in the theatre, in films, radio or television. There are very few actors who don't belong to a repertory company. And that means a regular salary and secure future. How many members of Equity can say they have that? The notion of the 'freelance actor' all on his own without the paternalism of a company to support him is a relatively new one in Hungary. Very few exist.

Neither do they believe in the 'star system' in a socialist country. Everyone receives the same salary. Of course, this does not mean that there aren't any stars. If someone considers himself a star, there's very little that will dissuade him. And he will suffer for the privilege of being one. One of the most famous of all Hungarian actors, let's say of the calibre of a Richard Burton or Peter O'Toole, is always getting plum parts in films and plays, although he earns a fraction of the income of a mediocre newcomer. While the star gets the same fee for a plum that the newcomer gets for a dud, the celebrity refuses to take on the sort of work which he instinctively knows a star worth his salt wouldn't touch with a ten-foot pole. The newcomer accepts any offer as a challenge, hence, he earns more money. And yet, the world is the same wherever you go. People prefer a big shot of modest means to no big shot at all.

I briefly mentioned the ballet earlier. It's true that, on the whole, anyone can go to a ballet in any country and comprehend it. Princes and dying swans transcend the bounds of language. But in Hungary, the foreigner might find himself baffled even in this wordless domain. My only encounter with an American during my

101

trip took place at a performance of a new work called *The Cedar* at the Hungarian State Opera House. A distant relative of mine is a prima ballerina with the company and she was dancing that night.

The ballet is based on the scenes depicted in seven expressionist paintings by Kosztka Tivadar Csontváry, an early twentieth-century artist. He is considered to have been a mad genius whose work conveys a fragile, disturbing world. But his paintings are absorbing even without his complex symbolism. The chief characters in the ballet are the artist himself and two women who appear in the paintings. The one dressed in white represents his muse, his guiding spirit. The one in black is the demon of death and devastation. The women struggle to win the soul of the artist. That was the inner conflict which eventually drove Csontváry mad.

During the interval a tall bearded man sat down in the seat next to me.

'I wonder if you speak English?' he growled amicably in my direction.

He couldn't believe his luck when I told him I was brought up in New York.

'Could you please explain what this damn thing is about?'

I did my best, not leaving out the fact that my cousin Lilla was dancing the role of the woman in black.

'Say, is that your cousin?' he asked, suitably impressed. He stroked his beard. 'Boy, she's got a cute little butt there.'

Just then the lights dimmed and the curtain went up. But the American kept on talking. 'Gosh, I'm glad I ran into you. A person can get real lost in this place if he doesn't speak Hungarian. Do you know any good restaurants?'

I whispered the names of one or two places where the food is good.

'I'll tell you something,' he continued, 'I've just come from Bucharest where I've been undergoing a cure for my rheumatism. I'm staying here for three days, then I'm off to Poland and Bulgaria. My rheumatism is a lot better but I got a feeling I'm gonna go back to Seattle with the biggest goddamn set of ulcers you ever saw.'

At the end of the performance the audience, as always in Hungary, broke into the so-called 'iron applause', slow clapping in unison. This originates from the Soviet Union. The American turned to me. He was shaking his head and his beard was fairly bristling with disapproval.

'This stuff really bugs me. I always try to mess it up by clapping out of time.'

'Isn't it difficult for just one person to do that on his own?' I asked. 'Let's mess it up together.'

'Look, honey,' he said, 'I've got some pretty big hands here. Have a listen.' He began to clap in between the main clapping and he succeeded in making such a din that after a minute or two the rest of the audience was thrown off its metronomic beat. The iron applause splintered up and everyone rose to leave. The American bellowed with laughter. 'Not bad, huh?'

I said he had done admirably, slapped him on the back, and informed my mother that we had a guest for supper.

The artist Anna Éber couldn't be further removed from the surrealistic fears and agonies of Csontváry. She visited us one morning to inspect the portrait of my mother which she had painted decades earlier and which had been slightly damaged by rain when the roof had leaked. She was wearing a cheap nylon raincoat and her grey hair was pinned to the top of her head. She was small and quiet and elderly, like everyone's idea of a perfect granny.

'You might not like what I'm going to say, Vali,' she told my mother, 'but I should leave this picture as it is. I was never completely satisfied with the colours. I think the rain improved them.'

'Yes, but the nose! All that water pouring down the painting has taken my nose with it. It looks so *long*. Can't you do something about that?'

Anna thought for a moment. 'I think I may be able to touch it up. You know I always admired your lovely nose. Have the portrait brought to my studio.'

Later, Anna and I left the house together. I was going into town and agreed to accompany her back home first so that she could show me some of her work.

In the middle of the garden she stopped and looked around. She looked at the uneven path, now strewn with over-ripe plums from the tree above it. She glanced up at the pines and at the heavy golden cones which hung from them. 'I haven't been here for years,' she said. 'But I have always liked this garden. It is an artist's dream. Every leaf and every stone seems to be harbouring its own little tale.'

We waited for a bus. She looked frail, standing patiently by the roadside. But she isn't frail at all. Her hands are strong and capable, and her thick fingers, now somewhat distorted by arthritis, seem to belong to a farmer's wife, not an artist. Her face is creased and pale. But it doesn't require a lot of imagination to see that she was once an exceptional beauty.

Her studio/flat is on a wide, busy avenue in the middle of Pest. The building is a typical one, old and dreary, with the usual sort of entrance amid dustbins. The lift, however, was a total surprise. I had already been in some really cramped, creaky, ancient ones in Budapest, but the lift in Anna's building made the rest seem capable of rocketing to the top of the Empire State Building. It can only be operated by a key. Anna unlocked it, opened its decrepit double doors and we stepped in. By some miracle, we were feebly dragged up to the fifth floor.

'Well, this is it,' Anna sighed, once we were inside the flat. 'I've been here for forty-five years. It used to be bigger but after the communists took over, as you know, a private individual was only allowed a certain amount of space, so a couple of rooms were walled off to make another flat.'

We squeezed past a large wardrobe and entered her studio. There were paintings everywhere, on the walls, stacked closely together in corners, piled onto tables. And where there weren't paintings there were plants — of all types and sizes, seeming somehow to thrive on the thin light coming through the blackened net curtains which hung across the windows. There were also piles of magazines, books and papers, which must have been untouched for so long that they had aged into each other, like the stones of a Roman wall.

A few very large pieces of furniture stood here and there, maintaining an uncomfortable dignity among this array. But what could have been a den of dust and gloom was an enchanting place. For warmth and life radiated from the paintings on the walls. She had taken her obvious love for whatever she painted — whether a person or a place — and transformed it into shape and colour. And as I began to see the world through her eyes, I was amazed by all the natural beauty she had found.

She had spent her life surrounded by art and artists. Her father and late husband were both well-known artists, and her brother still is. The Éber family comes from Baja, a small town in southern Hungary, on the banks of the Danube.

Anna cleared some paraphernalia from a chair and motioned for me to sit down. After a while she brought some espresso and mineral water on a tray. The table in front of me was stacked with books and sketching pads. Anna balanced the tray on top of this mountain and poured the coffee.

Then, for no reason at all, she asked whether I'd been to Florence. I told her I hadn't. She peered at me through her glasses like a disapproving schoolmistress. 'But you must go, and go soon. Florence is for young, hopeful people.' She took a jar of paintbrushes and a cloth from the chair opposite me, and sat down. 'I went there in 1928, just after I finished my training. It is the most beautiful city in the world.' I suppose I didn't look too impressed, because she smiled at me and shrugged. 'I didn't believe it either, until I went there.'

'Have you ever wanted to return?'

'No. I never felt I had to. I can still remember it perfectly, although it was over half a century ago. I only want to go back to one foreign city before I die — Paris.'

'Why Paris?'

'I was there with my husband shortly before he died. It was the last time I heard him laugh. It was the last time he was happy. Then we came home, he fell ill and had a great deal of pain. He couldn't laugh again. If I go back to Paris, it'll almost be like having him with me just one more time. We were very close.' She pointed to a portrait of him when he was young; she had painted it soon after they were married. He was attractive and thin, with delicate features and long, slender hands. He looked very serious.

'Are you working on anything now?' I asked, searching the studio for an easel with some half finished canvas.

She shook her head slowly. 'It's a terrible thing to say,' she confessed, 'but I've simply lost the desire to do any more work. People ask me, family and friends, why I'm not painting now. I say it's my age, or my heart, I tell them I'm tired, feeling a bit under the weather. But none of that is true. I just don't want to paint anymore. And that makes me sad because there is still so much I could capture.'

I wondered whether her loss of inspiration had something to do with her husband's death. Perhaps, without her realizing it, he had been her inspiration. For a moment I thought she might cry. Her eyes were so gentle and vulnerable.

But then she lifted her head. 'You're young,' she told me. 'Do you realize what that means? That you mustn't think of anything sad. Live brightly, be happy, laugh. And go to Florence.'

I decided not to use the lift again on the way down. Anna and I said a warm farewell, and I started to walk down the stairs. The wrought-iron handrail was covered with several years' dust, and Anna warned me not to touch it. The whole staircase was fusty and dirty. But it must have been lovely once. It was wide and of a fine design, the stairs were of marble.

'If I get back my desire to work again, I'll do a portrait of you!' Anna called down after me.

'Oh, please, I'm not an actress, you needn't do that.' I forgot about the handrail and grabbed hold of it as I craned my neck to look up at her.

'That doesn't matter. I'm only interested in *character*. I may yet paint again. We should always keep hoping.'

At the bottom of the stairs I nearly collided with an old man. He was bent, and wearing worn and dirty clothes. An exact personification of the building itself. He stared at me, as startled as if I were a ghost.

I found him frightening too, so I shuffled past and hurried out to the street.

Six

I have a friend in England called George Szirtes, a poet. We're sitting in my small study in Highgate, which overlooks the wide, crowded valley that is London. In fair weather I am often distracted by the hills of south London on the horizon. But today George and I are not admiring the view. We are comparing notes as two refugees of the Hungarian Revolution.

George left Budapest with his family on the 2 December 1956, three days after his eighth birthday. His brother Andrew was five. George's first volume of poetry won the Geoffrey Faber Memorial Prize for 1980. Andrew is now a violinist for the Birmingham Symphony Orchestra. The long journey which began on that night in December, when the Szirtes family walked across the Austrian border in a party of twenty refugees led by a guide, and which has resulted in such a successful absorption into English life, has not been without its jolts and disturbances. But neither does George seem particularly surprised by its outcome. As he says, Hungarians often start out with the dice loaded against them and yet manage to win.

I can remember very little of my pre-revolution years, because there were so few of them. But as George was double my age when we left, he has a little store of disjointed memories. He was that much more independent at eight, and besides, he was at school.

'I can remember little which is whole and coherent,' he says as we sip our lemon tea. 'Only fragments, little broken bits, the touch of someone's hand, a face at a window, the sound of a voice. I can't pretend to know more than I do.'

'Does that mean that, as a poet, you can't really draw upon those memories?' I ask.

'It's true that very few of my poems deal directly with immigration or the state of being a refugee. But I still feel it is a rich vein which can be tapped, even if indirectly. They are referred to as "authenticating experiences" by the existentialists.'

Yet George has written at least one poem which makes effective use of his 'broken bits', 'Budapest 1951'. These are its last three stanzas:

> What were the names? What address?
> Whose were the cars that sped
> Late and fast along the street?
> Whose were the visits and the feet?
> The startling jaw whose touch lacked gentleness;
> The hands, the lips? And are they dead?

> But this is too peculiar to time and place;
> That these images persist does not bring grace
> Nor the right to dwell,
> Because we cannot see them as they were,
> Not really young; not at all like us:
> Figures seen descending from a bus
> Or heard indistinctly through a door —

> Staccato days, quick imprints in the snow
> In the park where my father and I would go,
> And he would exert all his strength to pull
> Our wooden sledge across the frosted grass,
> And the wind blew away his trilby hat
> In one big gust; and he charged like a bull
> Over the path to get it back.

George says he would never want to push 'Hungarian-ness' away from himself, only to embrace Englishness, which is different. But what does this Hungarian-ness consist of?

'Oh, several things,' says George swinging one leg on top of another. He is dressed casually, in corduroy trousers, woolly pullover and jacket. His dark hair is untidy, as a poet's hair should be. He looks as though he has just had an earnest tussle with an iambic pentameter.

'For a start, I enjoy rich and resonant imagery. That's a Hungarian quality, I believe.' He smiles. 'This is held in check by my developed English sensibility. But I have also been told that my work has a certain "edginess", that the borders of nightmare are never far away. There are two poets who have made a big impression on me — Anthony Hecht and Joseph Brodsky — in whom I can recognize the same kind of edginess. The pleasant images very nearly tipping over into nightmare. . .'

'But why should you have nightmares?' I ask.

'I'm not sure,' he says, turning towards the window. For a while he seems mesmerized by the red light blinking on and off at the top of the Post Office Tower. 'But there is one possible explanation,' he continues, looking at me again. 'I have a nervous fear and mistrust of crowds. I intensely dislike being in large masses of people. My father told me that during the revolution I saw a lot of violence in the streets, that I even witnessed a man being torn apart by a bloodthirsty crowd. My father says I woke up screaming every night for weeks afterwards. I can't remember anything about this myself.'

'Maybe it's a case of wilful amnesia,' I say.

'Maybe. Who knows about these things?' He leans forward and his face suddenly brightens. He has obviously flung his nightmares to the wind for the time being. 'I'm certain of one thing, though. If you want to know about my Hungarian-ness, just play a bit of Magyar music for me. It always moves me deeply. Of course I like Liszt, Bartók, Kodály. But for some reason I even respond profoundly to the most schmaltzy gypsy clap-trap.' He sighs. 'That must mean something. Even though my father once took me by the shoulders, shook his head and said I wasn't really Hungarian.'

'Does he think you are completely assimilated into the English way of life?'

'Yes. And of course he's right. I am. Funnily enough I think it was easy for me to blend into English society. I was born with certain characteristics generally considered to be rather English. I'm shy, easily embarrassed, a bit awkward, and I have a distrust of rhetoric.'

I nod my head fervently. 'Yes, the English are brought up to have a certain code of behaviour which strikes Hungarians as strange. Here you aren't supposed to ask people about themselves. It's thought of as prying. You are supposed to be content to feed on any meagre morsels of information as may be thrown your way. While a true Hungarian will confront a total stranger with any question, he'll be nosey about anything he damn well pleases. After all, he's only being friendly and *showing interest*. Not to show interest is terribly rude in a Hungarian's eyes. That's being stiff and cold and, well, rather English.'

'Neither do the English like it when you blab on about yourself,' George adds. 'Here you must learn to be circumspect, modest.'

I am defensive. 'Let's get things straight, old chap,' I say. 'The

Hungarians aren't the only ones who blab on a bit. Look at the Italians and the Greeks and the Poles and the Americans. It's what's known as being gregarious.'

'And what about all of this confusing business of kissing people hello and good-bye? You know how the Hungarians go in for rapturous greetings. Some years ago I used to be stared at here as if I were some sort of freak whenever I tried merely to shake hands.'

I explain that there are some people I am on single cheek-kissing terms with, some on double cheek-kissing terms, some people I shake hands with and others I wouldn't touch with boxing gloves on. I've never actually seen anyone kiss a lady's hand, except my father. And the effect of that on English people can be remarkable, as though the Austro-Hungarian Empire had risen from the dust before their very eyes.

We sit and look at each other for a while, across the massive desk which fills most of my study. We're like two people on either side of a window, each seeing the other as well as his own reflection.

'Tell me, George,' I say, with typical Hungarian inquisitiveness, 'how do you see yourself, I mean, what are you, really?'

'Simple,' he answers. 'I'm an English poet. You see, it's just impossible to be Hungarian and write English poetry. With the English language, you must say English things. I know I'll never be absolutely English, but I feel patriotic towards this country, I feel a part of it. And I would like to be thought of as belonging to the English tradition of poetry. I certainly don't want to read like a poet in translation.'

'Ah, yes, it's all quite straightforward for you,' I sigh. 'You only emigrated once. You know where you came from and you've been here ever since. But my life is divided into three parts — Hungary, America and England. I feel like one of those ridiculous little microscopic organisms that goes on reproducing itself all over the place.'

'That sounds like fun.'

'Oh, sure. But which tradition am I supposed to belong to?'

'None. You've got to be a kind of union of all three.'

'Unions are for the T.U.C. I'm a person. I've got to be one thing or the other. Haven't I?'

'Not necessarily. You know, I almost envy you in a way.'

'Why on earth should you envy me?'

'Because you can take the best things from those three parts of your life and put them together, and end up with something better than what the rest of us have. Or at least something more interesting, more varied. Be positive.'

I decide to be positive.

'*Még beszélsz jól Magyarul?*' I ask, testing his Hungarian.

His face reddens slightly and he grins. '*Hát. . .igen, egy kicsit.*'

We laugh. 'When you speak English,' I say, 'you have a very faint accent. Nothing much, but enough to rouse a bit of curiosity, to spread a little mystery. But when you speak Hungarian,' I shrug my shoulders and smile, 'you've got a big accent, chum.'

'So I'm told. Hungarians find it amusing. But it's not really my fault. My parents never encouraged me to speak Hungarian at home. They settled in this country determined to make a go of it, and that meant total submersion. We all spoke English at home. This has evolved into the present strange language we use, mixing up English and Hungarian in a real mess. But it seems natural.'

'Yes, we do it too, in my family. Although my parents' policy was the reverse. They didn't want my brother and I to forget Hungarian so they generally spoke it to us, and always with each other. And there were always so many other Hungarians around. . .'

'Same with me,' George nods. 'I know the emigré scene. Not intimately, but well enough. I wrote a poem about it, 'Reunion'. It's about my parents and their friends, people who came here twenty-five years ago with nothing and are today comfortable and happy and well adjusted. Even a little overweight.'

1

A dark road. They drift across the field
like wastepaper down a city street. The wind
seems to carry them over trenches concealed
among ruts and folds with a disciplined
and paradoxical tenderness. Their hands
prevent them from flying apart, mother, child,
father with suitcases, while the moon stands
perfectly still, a dead post. The clouds are piled
haphazardly, haphazard too the motion
of the group, into Egypt, anywhere
out of the heart's range. There's no time for caring
too much about anything. They drift on.
The wind has blown them far off course, on air
that clings to faces, hands, the clothes they're wearing.

2

They have landed on their feet. Tonight they sit
around a suburban table, telling jokes.
Their stomachs have grown sadly delicate
but at each punchline the narrator pokes
his neighbour in the ribs and everyone laughs.
The hybrid language serves and makes the point.
One hands round some recent photographs
of cousins back home. The hostess carves the joint.
My God! I remember them. He served with me
in forty-eight and they got married when
He was, how you say, demobbed. We sometimes write.

They're doing well then?
                              Isn't everybody?
Well, let's drink to that, ladies and gentlemen.
To wealth, old age, and a sound appetite.

'Hungarians are often thought of as being introverted and melancholy. But I haven't met any like that over here. The Hungarians I know are all convivial and doing well, ' says George.

I ask about his father and mother.

'My father is Jewish,' he begins to explain. 'He spent most of the war in a Russian labour camp. Afterwards, he worked in the building industry, in a private company which was later nationalized. It was a plumbing and heating company and he eventually became its manager. My mother was from Transylvania, a press photographer. She always had a weak heart, so no one could understand how she survived Ravensbrück when all the rest of her family perished. When we left Hungary she packed a suitcase full of her photographs and dragged it with her across the border. She died in 1975.'

'Did they intend from the start to settle in London?'

'The plan was to go to Australia. My father has a cousin there. But they wouldn't let my family in because my mother didn't pass the physical examination. So when we left the Tidworth Refugee Camp in Wiltshire, we lived for a short time on the south coast. Then we came to London. We lived at various addresses in the poorer northern suburbs.

'I learnt to speak English at a primary school in Algernon Road, Hendon. I picked it up quickly, I was an academic child. Unlike

Andrew. He had difficulty adapting to the new life. He was never really happy until he began to concentrate on music. He left school at fifteen to study the violin at the Trinity College of Music, under the tutorship of a Hungarian, funnily enough, Professor Katona. Meanwhile I did science A-levels to please my parents, who wanted me to become a doctor.

'My father got a job with a plumbing and heating firm, visiting sites, and eventually he became its contracts manager. Slowly my family climbed up the conventional social ladder. We bought our first terraced house, our first car, our first semi-detached. At last we advanced to a mock-Tudor place in Wembley.

'It was at about this time that I noticed a profound change come over my parents. Before the revolution, they had been strict socialists and atheists. I remember we had a framed portrait of Stalin on the wall in our flat. During the period of de-Stalinization in the early 1950s we had some visitors one day who glared disapprovingly at this portrait. "Don't you realize," they told my parents, "he was never all that he was cracked up to be?" My mother became angry and upset. She took the picture from the wall and held it up proudly in both hands. "What do you mean?" she cried. "Of course he was! I don't understand. First you tell us one thing, then another. Are you all crazy?" Then came 1956 and we left. And for several years my parents maintained their rather left-wing views here in England. But they began to drift towards agnosticism and a kind of mild bourgeois conservatism. One day I woke up to find that they'd become honest-to-God Tories. I think it was Harold Wilson that did it, actually.

'While this was going on, I, too, was discovering myself, both as a poet and as an artist. Art came first. I studied at the Harrow School of Art for one year. There I met Clarissa, whom I later married. Then I went on to the Leeds Polytechnic Faculty of Art. I did a lot of painting there, all vaguely Chagallian. After the first year I took part in a group exhibition in Bradford. The review in the *Bradford Telegraph and Argos* called our work "childish daubs". But we were undeterred. I was taught by Jeff Nuttall at Leeds. Martin Bell, my poetry tutor, also guided and encouraged me. We later became good friends. At the end of my second year I was granted a travelling scholarship, and Clarissa and I went to France and Italy. I graduated with a First and was awarded the Art History Prize. These things surprised my parents, who still viewed my paintings with scepticism.

'I was writing a lot of poetry throughout this time. And Martin

Bell guided my reading — Pope, Tennyson, Shakespeare, T.S. Eliot, Baudelaire, Rilke. From 1976 my work started to appear more regularly in print, especially in *Encounter* and *The Listener*. Martin recommended my work to Peter Porter and Edward Lucie-Smith. It was through Porter's support that my poems were included in Faber's *Poetry Introduction* anthology in 1978. That, in turn, led to my own first volume. And the prize. My second collection will be out at the end of the year.'

'A remarkable success story. Now tell me about the life you lead in Hitchin.' To my mind, Hitchin and Artistic Creation are not exactly inseparable. 'Doesn't the artistic spirit flourish best in Paris garrets and London bedsits?'

'I've been there since 1973, teaching art and art history at a comprehensive school for girls. A poet can live anywhere. Keats said they were all chameleons, adapting to their surroundings, soaking it all up. And my children, although born and growing up in a rural market town in England, are well aware of their connection to Hungary. For a start, they've got a funny foreign name to contend with. That takes a bit of explaining. But they're interested in my origins. And they even speak a few words of Hungarian, although their accent is even worse than mine.'

'Are your pupils aware that you are from Hungary?'

'Yes. But to them it's just another queer little country far away that they've never seen, and probably never will. My children will see it, though. We are going there next year. It will be their first trip abroad.'

'How often have you been back since 1956?'

'Just once, in 1968. My parents took my brother and me for a holiday in Budapest. My mother and father were disappointed in what they found. I suppose everything had changed. But I loved it. And I was perpetually amazed by the fact that everyone was speaking Hungarian.'

This sounds familiar. 'How long did you stay there?'

'Not for very long. The Czech invasion intervened. We cut short our trip because we all felt rather uncomfortable.' George looks thoughtfully at a stain on my carpet. 'I suppose the natives were a damn sight more uncomfortable than we were. But even then I had the feeling that Hungarians are born survivors. They scrape by. And that's a quality I admire. I won't talk about the régime there, mainly because I'm thoroughly apolitical and such matters don't hold much fascination for me. I couldn't ever imagine myself siding with any political party or advocating any political dogma.'

114

I tell George that perhaps that is why he is drawn to poetry and art, which are finest when practised by those who reject the strait-jackets that others so readily put on.

'Do you know what inspires me more than anything to write poetry?' he asks. 'The sheer pleasure of being witness to the uniqueness of things, small and ordinary things. Louis MacNeice called it to "feel the drunkenness of things being various". Suddenly a mundane sight will catch my eye in a different sort of way, for example a row of supermarket carriages sparkling in the sunlight, and I will have the basis for a poem. And I like to catch a moment and suspend it in time. The more perishable something is, the more wonderful it is, and vice versa.'

'So your view of life is essentially an upbeat one. You find pleasure in what you see, rather than pain.' I refrain from looking at him in case he is annoyed by my impromptu efforts at critical analysis.

'Just so. And I'm not an *intellectual* poet, either. I want to present not concepts, but thrills. And there are a lot of thrills to be had in life. There are poets like Philip Larkin and Alan Brownjohn, whom I find very entertaining, but who seem to spend most of their time denying these thrills.'

'What about Hungarian poetry?'

'I have read Sándor Petőfi and Endre Ady since I was a child. There weren't very many books in our home, but those were always available. They knew what it was like to be thrilled by the sensation of "things being various".'

'I agree with you poets. Sometimes I think the minutiae are the only things you can really hold onto. The trouble with life is, we're all so damned busy, we haven't always got time to read the small print. If you know what I mean.'

George nods.

We have long since finished our tea. Beyond the window London flickers sublimely for as far as we can see, but the red lights on the Post Office Tower still steal the show. We sit back and consider in silence the way in which the past and present have fused for both of us, dissolving distance as well as time. Memories have become objects to be passed around. By now my small study is bursting with them.

It has seemed so easy to us, but this may be deceptive. Behind our words are many years of metamorphosis. By a painful, circuitous route I have arrived in Highgate. George's journey from Hungary to Hitchin has been more direct. But we are still travellers

115

in time, even if we have stopped moving around the map. He says that the 'borders of nightmare' are never far away. I think that might be a good thing. You needn't be afraid of being near those borders, only of stepping across to the wrong side.

Seven

The Budapest gypsies were still selling their flowers by the entrance to the underground terminus in Moscow Square. I brushed past them and entered the terminus building. You can travel anywhere for one forint on the underground. There are no tickets. You simply put the forint coin into a slot in a machine which looks like a pair of metal gateposts. There is no 'gate', actually, and the impression is that forint or no forint, you can just saunter through the posts and down the escalator to the trains. But just try going through without putting the coin into the slot. A metal bar slams into your stomach with lightning speed. And it doesn't matter whether you were intending to beat the system or were merely in a state of absent-mindedness, you're likely to die of internal injuries before you can explain.

But being down in the bowels of the station is a soothing experience. Underground stations in Budapest are light, spacious, clean places. The decor is modern; each station has a different colour scheme. There are marble walls and pillars. Not a speck of graffiti anywhere. And no advertisements. Of course, there is precious little to advertise but the state, anyway, and the entire underground system is itself an advertisement for the state.

It is based on the Moscow system, and the fast, efficient blue and green trains are imported from the Soviet Union. In most stations there is a digital clock on the wall recording the time since the last train's departure. They arrive every three or four minutes. If someone steps too near to the edge of the platform he is scolded over the loudspeaker by an irate schoolmarm-type voice. There are no chocolate-bar dispensers and smoking is forbidden. In other words, it's the flip side of the London tube: that grim underworld where shady characters wait around interminably for stale-smelling trains, flicking Milky Way wrappers and fag-ends onto the line.

But maybe precisely because of these things, the London tube is more edifying than the Budapest underground. Anything can happen on the tube. You can meet a flasher or have your bottom pinched or start a relationship with a married man. In Budapest the best you can hope for is a quick glance down the tunnel without getting caught.

Nevertheless, I will always think fondly and warmly of the underground in Budapest. And for one very good reason: it is intimately associated with my birth. Let me explain.

I was born in the summer of 1952, when my father was working as screenplay writer for the Hungarian state film studio. Rákosi had just declared that Hungary was a nation of iron and steel, and to prove that this was really so, several great projects were initiated under the Five Year Plan. One of them was the construction of a new underground system. There was already a small shallow line, built in 1900, but that served only a tiny section of the city. Budapest required a comprehensive network.

At that time, film production came under the supervision of the Motion Picture Department of the Ministry of People's Education. The Ministry was headed by József Révai, a rigid Stalinist, and all film scripts had ultimately to be approved by him. His orders were clear — the eight or so films to be produced yearly had to concern themselves with at least one of the following: the life of the workers in a place created or improved under the Five Year Plan; the life of the peasantry, with particular emphasis on the expansion of collectives; the progress and conflicts of intellectuals loyal to the people (preferably the technical intelligentsia); the People's Army; the struggles of an outstanding Hungarian during the Party's underground period; or some aspect of history, showing how contemporary struggles and goals arose directly from Hungary's past. A lot of fun themes.

The task of writing a script about the building of the underground was given to my father. His colleagues considered the job to be hopeless. How could the film end with a triumphant display of socialist achievement when not one section of the underground had been completed? In addition, there were the problems of making the complicated techniques of construction interesting to an audience and overcoming the monotonous setting of an underground maze.

But my father was enthusiastic about the theme. The excavations had captured his imagination. He was given a permit to roam underground at will, and spent the following six months finding out about the intricacies of tunnelling, drilling, caisson lowering and deep construction. He spent most of his evenings drinking cheap wine in a nearby bar with the workers, and got to know them well — peasant boys, former criminals, former aristocrats.

My mother was pregnant with me at this time. One morning, as my father was leaving the house on his way to the excavation site, my mother went into labour. A taxi was called and she was taken to hospital. Several hours later, as my father was crawling along one of the poorly lit, stifling tunnels, someone called out to him the news that he had a daughter. I think that the two of us must have had spent those hours having a similar sort of experience.

My father was pleased with his script, *Under the City*. There were a variety of interesting, authentic characters and a dramatic climax in which the tunnels were flooded. He described the effects on people of long hours underground, how they became deeply involved with each other, and at the end, how their common suffering forged them into a solid unit.

The script had to be approved by the following people: the head of the drama section; the studio art director; the drama committee composed of the studios' directors; the head of the Motion Picture Department of the Ministry of People's Education; an art committee created by the Ministry; an operations committee made up of deputies of the Ministry; the directors of the underground construction and the Party organization for the project; the Deputy Minister of People's Education, György Non; and finally, Révai himself.

The script failed to win approval at its first reading. Kovács, the head of the drama section, didn't consider the conflict authentic. The flood, he declared, couldn't simply be an accident. It had to be an act of sabotage perpetrated by an enemy of the people. Kovács and my father argued excitedly. Their voices were heard all over the studio. My father tried to be firm but the pressure was too great. He made the required revision.

The studio art director, Mrs Kemény, said the script was interesting, but 'there aren't any right-wing Social Democrats in it, and in the present circumstances we cannot make a film about workers without showing the danger of right-wing Social Democrats'. My father bowed to her orders.

The next version went to the drama committee, which decided that the Party Secretary had to be given a larger role in the film. A fourth version was written. That went to the head of the Motion Picture Department of the Ministry of People's Education. He demanded more action by the Party organization — 'A Party Secretary, after all, cannot carry out the work alone.' My father hammered out a fifth version.

The art committee objected that the script ignored the fact that the walls of the underground stations were to have frescoes. The importance of the project to artists would have to be stressed. The sixth version went to the operations committee, which complained that the story failed to emphasize that the Budapest underground was based on the Moscow underground. Soviet leadership could not be ignored. A seventh version was written.

The construction managers and Party organization wanted certain technical processes to be described more clearly, and modern methods to be shown. This meant an eighth version. György Non read it and expressed distaste for the whole thing. 'Too many grim underground scenes. Put in a few cheerful scenes on the surface. Perhaps the construction workers could take trips to the lovely hills surrounding Budapest. They could go by train up János Hill.'

The ninth version was read by Révai. He said the story was just too confusing. It tried to do too much. Social Democrats, saboteurs, frescoes, excursions into the hills — all these were superfluous and ruined an otherwise good plot. It would have to be rewritten completely.

The tenth version should have been closest to the spirit of the first. But by that time my father was worn out and demoralized. The speeches, characters and scenes no longer had any meaning for him. The last version was by far the worst. A young film director, Herskó, began shooting, and by the autumn of 1953 the film was complete.

On the day of the première the government suddenly announced that work on the Budapest underground was to be terminated. But the film was shown, and it was a success. One of the central characters, a sceptical engineer, says, 'I don't believe we can ever do it. It's too big a task, the product of a feverish mind. We don't have the strength it takes.' When the audience heard this it roared with laughter and applauded wildly. My father was never forgiven for those words.

In the years that followed, Stalin died and, in Hungary, the Rákosi dictatorship was shaken to its foundations. Imre Nagy proclaimed a new course of democratization. But his plans and programme were short-lived. Before long, Rákosi repealed all the concessions he had been forced to make. Yet, as my father later wrote, 'Despite this, the general atmosphere did improve. The truths proclaimed by Nagy survived — hid in office corners, in the winding corridors of public buildings, in the cracks of walls. No ideological spring cleaning could root them out. Truth, like a faithful dog, cannot be banished; once it has found a home and affection, truth clings to its owner, despite occasional kicks.'

But for my father and others like him, it was already too late. When the floodgates of the country were opened in November, 1956, they grabbed the chance to leave these invidious practices behind.

The Hungarian cinema has undergone many changes over the past thirty years. Some Hungarian films and film directors now have an international cult following. They appear at film festivals in Cannes, Venice, London, San Sebastian. They win prizes and admiration for their gritty, realistic depiction of life in a 'People's Democracy'. The films are obviously honest, say the critics, because they don't deny the problems and failures of the system.

But I wonder whether there isn't a residue from the Révai days. Nothing too obvious, which would show up on the big screen as an open-and-shut case of censorship or oppression. Just a lingering apprehension in the breasts of the film-makers themselves, as to whether honesty is wholly the wisest policy.

Shortly before my return to Hungary I was at my parents' flat in Munich. One evening we had an unexpected guest for dinner, a Hungarian film director, an old friend of my father's from his days at the studio. In the early 1950s Károly had been a young assistant, a green boy who simply muddled through those dangerous years as best as he could. But now he is among the top three or four directors in the country. And he had been given the most sought-after award: the freedom to work with foreign production companies abroad. So he was in Munich directing a German film, and we spent an enjoyable evening together, hearing the latest news about Hungarian film stars, new films and television plays, writers and directors.

'Phone me when you arrive in Budapest,' he told me, 'I'll be flitting back and forth between here and there over the next couple of months. And I'll arrange for you to meet anyone you like, or to see as many films as you want at the studios. Call me — here's my number, if I'm not there just leave a message.'

I thanked him warmly, but he shook his head and said it was only natural for him to help, after all, my father was one of his dearest friends. I asked whether it wouldn't be unpleasant for him to be seen in Budapest with me, as some of my father's writing has made him *persona non grata* in Hungary since the revolution. He almost looked offended.

'I make no secret of my friendship with your father,' he replied.

I was cheered by this remark. Well, things really have come up a bit in the Homeland since the days of the Ministry of People's Education and ten-version scripts, I thought to myself.

I arrived in Budapest. I rang Károly. He wasn't there, so I left a message. And I did that twice a week for four weeks until it was time to go home. Perhaps he was detained indefinitely in Munich and couldn't flit back and forth as planned. Perhaps.

Then there is Zsuzsi, the overweight screenplay writer. She is my father's cousin. She is also highly successful. Her films are always being shown abroad. And when she or one of her associates visits the West, my father is usually contacted.

I rang Zsuzsi's number, too, while I was in Budapest. Several times. But they were shooting her latest film at the time, and she could hardly get away from the studio. They were shooting at midnight and in the early hours of the morning and all during the day and when they weren't shooting they were sleeping. I left a few messages with her laconic husband who is a famous photographer and equally famous Communist Party member and who always sounded as if he had just been woken up from an annoying dream about Western imperialism. I never did see Zsuzsi. I didn't meet her husband or her colleagues.

I did manage to get a look at the studios, however, if only from the outside. The old, original studio is still there. It's an art deco building with a large sign — *Mafilm Studio* — above the main entrance. But more buildings have been added since then. The complex is surrounded by a white iron fence topped with barbed wire.

It is in Pest, in an area which is surprisingly peaceful and residential. The streets surrounding the complex are lined with tall trees. One of them bears a familiar name; it is called József Révai Street. He was, obviously, a man *sans pareil*.

But to go back to my starting point. The underground. I sat on a smooth plastic seat and sped along through a tunnel which perhaps my father once crawled in on his belly. There are three lines, called simply 1, 2 and 3. The first two were completed in the early to mid-1970s. Line 3 is only two years old.

Each time we pulled into a station I half expected, just for a split second, to see a feast of ads for tights and temps and new horror movies. But each time we stopped at what seemed to be an elegant theatre foyer. At last I arrived at my destination: Vörösmarty Square; the hub of the downtown area, and a short walk from Ervin's murky dungeon which I was going to visit.

Váci Street is the most famous shopping street in Budapest. There is even an old song about it, which I can dimly recall my mother singing, extolling its sophistication and the beautiful women to be seen strolling along its pavements. I peered into some of the shop windows. There is an Intertourist shop, which was crammed with passport-clutching customers waiting impatiently for their bottles of Johnny Walker and cartons of Marlboro. There are a couple of flashy stores selling traditional Hungarian items of a folksy nature, handmade tablecloths and shepherd's jackets and the like. They were empty except for a small group of wealthy American widows looking for something 'typical' to buy with their late husbands' money.

There are bookshops and children's clothing shops and dress shops, all quite ordinary. And there are shoe shops. I had been warned not to buy shoes in Budapest. Shoes are a sore point, it seems. The foreign imports are exorbitant, so no one can afford them. But recently even the domestic products have risen in price enormously. An average pair of shoes can cost an average monthly salary. And the worst of it is, the shoes are useless, made with inferior materials and inferior methods. They usually come with a little instruction leaflet. 'Let's not wear these shoes in wet weather,' it advises, 'because the soles are likely to peel off. Neither should we put them on when it is very hot, for the uppers may shrink, making the shoes difficult to remove. . .'

Instructions for the use of clothing are also written in this strangely patronising way. I bought a cotton pullover from an inexpensive department store. Attached to it was a tag filled with such phrases as 'Let's not put this into the washing machine!' and 'Let's not spin dry this item!'

I turned into a narrow side street and found the steps leading down to Ervin's basement workshop. I pushed open the heavy iron door. It was dingy inside. The only light was at the other end of the small room, and Ervin was sitting underneath it, examining something through one of those monocular magnifying lenses.

Ervin heard the door's rusty groan and looked up. His expression was strained, but in an instant a broad smile brightened his face and he jumped to his feet, letting the lens drop into his palm.

'I knew you would come to see me,' he declared.

A minute later I was seated opposite him and he was studying me closely and asking me about the many years which had passed since we last met. I, in turn, studied the dungeon while we spoke. I imagine a medieval alchemist's den would not have been dissimilar. Ervin once had a jewellery business, a small shop up on the street in the same building. But it was confiscated in 1950 and since 1952 he has been down below, forbidden to handle silver and gold, something only state-owned establishments are allowed to do. As a *maszek* (self-employed businessman), Ervin can deal only in what he calls 'bijou' items. So he repairs jewellery and other little objects which people bring to him.

In the dimness I could make out unfamiliar dusty objects and jagged heaps. There were rows of bottles, empty and blackened with age. It was a place in which everything seemed to have been discarded. Protruding into the centre and almost totally obstructing the doorway was a winding iron staircase. But even in the half-light I could see that it led nowhere. There was only a blank wall at the top.

Ervin sat in his white work-coat, his hands folded on his lap. He was all attention, and had the appearance of an amiable family doctor discussing a minor ailment. It occurred to me that in fact he was a sort of doctor. His delicate patients lay scattered about him, waiting to be examined through his magnifying eye-piece and mended.

I couldn't imagine, however, anyone spending day after day, nearly thirty years, amid these stale subterranean mounds.

I think he read the thought on my face. 'When I was first banished to this cellar,' he said, as if letting me into a big secret, 'they told me that within a few years I'd either be blind or rheumatic, or both. But here I am, nearly seventy, and I've never felt better. Many jewellers up there —' he jerked his thumb upwards, 'on the surface, have ruined their eyes through work. But not me. And look at these walls. They seem dank, don't they?' He laughed. 'But they're dry as a bone. In fact I'm nice and cosy here in the winter. It's like hibernating.' He reached across a petrified mass of metal scraps to turn on another light. This lit up the space between us and I could see him more clearly. His grey hair was combed straight back, away from a face which was lined, but in a peculiar way appeared to be young. Perhaps it was because of the almost childlike curiosity in his eyes.

'What is life like in England?' he asked leaning back and cradling a knee.

'It's good. There are problems, of course, people are always complaining about the economy and politics, the trade unions, unemployment, race relations — just about everything, I suppose. But I still like it there. When I moved to London I was green as a gooseberry. I feel I grew up there. I think London has that effect on people.'

'Yes, you have grown up.' He smiled. 'And as for all of those complaints and problems you mentioned, just consider them the inevitabilities of life. I don't bemoan our troubles here. There are too many of them. But when I am in danger of becoming depressed over something, I remember a conversation I once had with your father.

'It was in December 1944. We were prisoners together in a Soviet P.O.W. camp near Sambor, in the Ukraine. There were several hundred of us lying on the bare wooden floor of a large hall. Your father and I found ourselves next to each other. We talked and became good friends. One morning we woke up to find that the young fellow on the other side of me had died of typhus in the night. I was thrown into complete despair. Our outlook seemed very bleak.

'Your father put an arm around my shoulder. "Listen, Ervin," he said. "Let's not go overboard about this. You've got to keep one thing in mind: no one plays the starring role in his own life; we're all just extras." Those words have come back to me many times over the years. Once you realize you're an extra, you're grateful for what you have, not unhappy about what you haven't got.'

He paused for a moment, I looked at him inquiringly and he went on.

'One midnight we were all rounded up for a roll-call. We were marched down a dark hallway, or a tunnel of some sort, and then divided up. I was sent to the infirmary because of a shotgun wound inflicted on me by a Soviet officer. Some of the prisoners were sent to other camps. Still others, your father among them, volunteered to join the Red Army for its assault on the Germans holding Budapest. So by a quirk of fate, he arrived home on the day the war ended for Hungary, 4 April 1945.

'I was only released from the camp many months later. I returned to Budapest not knowing what I would find. I learned that my mother had been killed. I hadn't dared to hope that my wife, Magda, would still be alive. When I found that she was, I was filled with the most inexpressible joy. That was my greatest piece of luck.' He rapped twice on the wooden table in front of us and a cloud of dust rose gracefully into the air.

He continued. 'My marriage to Magduska has been a story of happiness and success. I'm an extra who is grateful for what he has. And as for what I haven't got, well, when you've been through the horrors and tragic experiences of the war, these other little disappointments don't seem so bad, do they?' He nodded towards the iron staircase. 'Thirty years ago I was kicked down those stairs and condemned to this "cell". But I haven't been hungry or thirsty or cold or chained to the wall. So why shouldn't I be content?'

He asked about my father. And I wanted to know whether they had kept up their friendship after the war.

'Certainly. He came to see me from time to time. We would speak about our days at Sambor. Later, in the fifties, we often discussed the political situation. The whole country was like a volcano and we wondered when it would erupt. The last time I saw him was in early October 1956. He was sitting in the same chair you are in right now, facing me in the same way. He had recently returned from the International Youth Congress held in Vienna, which had been the first foreign event Hungarian journalists had been allowed to attend since the war. He was proud of the new tweed jacket he was wearing and showed me the label on the inside pocket, bearing the name of a Viennese shop. Then the revolution broke out. We never met again.'

One of Ervin's customers creaked open the door and peered into the room, blinking at us.

'Come on in, Ilona!' he called. 'I'm just having a chat with the daughter of an old friend of mine. She's visiting from London.'

A middle-aged woman walked in. She nodded politely to me and kissed Ervin on both cheeks. She was a neat, quiet person, and she began to speak earnestly to the jeweller about a chain necklace which she was carefully removing from her handbag.

'It's not very valuable,' she said apologetically, 'but it's very precious to me. My husband gave it to me when we were young.'

Ervin nodded in an understanding way. He was the family doctor again.

Ilona's eyes began to fill with tears and she took out a small white handkerchief, although she didn't use it. 'He died less than a year ago,' she whispered. 'He was only fifty. Don't you think that's too young to die?' She looked at me. 'Why did it have to happen?'

Ervin took one of her hands and held it in his. 'Dear Ilona,' he said, 'anything can happen to any of us. You must realize, we don't play starring roles in our own lives. We're only the extras. If we remember that, we don't let ourselves get too bitter about our misfortunes.'

The woman held the necklace tightly in her fist. I don't think she quite heard his words. But Ervin and I looked at each other with a kind of conspiracy. He winked. Ilona loosened her grip on her treasure and gave it to Ervin.

'Please mend it for me. It just needs a new clasp, I think. I'll come back for it next week.' She smiled at us both, turned and left.

Ervin looked thoughtful. 'I haven't communicated with your father in any way for twenty-five years. But I still think of him as my spiritual brother.'

A couple more customers came to leave beloved 'patients' in the hands of their trusted doctor. One woman brought an unusual serving spoon to be mended. The handle was made of metal but the bowl was wooden. The two halves had become loose and wobbly. 'I cherish this funny old spoon,' said its owner. 'It's the last of the set, and they just don't make this sort of thing any more. It's from the olden days.'

After she had left I asked whether many Hungarians were feeling so nostalgic.

'Every new wave in the West washes over us here, too, sooner or later. Trends in music, clothing. It's the same with this longing for bygone days. Everyone wants to see the films we made in the thirties and hear the old pre-war songs. They are re-issuing 78 rpm records made by singers no one has even thought about for decades until now.'

'Do they think of my mother?'

'Of course.'

'But I don't mean the older people. I mean my generation.'

'Yes, I'm telling you the entire country is immersed in nostalgia. The other day I heard someone on the street humming, "In a small café by the side of the Danube, there's such atmosphere and charm. . ." you know, one of your mother's hits at the Hangli. The next time someone comes in I'm going to introduce you as Vali Rácz's daughter. See what happens.'

Ten minutes later he carried out his threat in the presence of two gentlemen aged about forty who had come to have a watch strap repaired. Their reaction was as Ervin had predicted. I was nearly gobbled up by their enthusiasm. Suddenly I was a V.I.P. And a V.I.P. from the West, at that. I felt like a visiting princess or Hollywood film star. The men left reluctantly, but only after lengthy hand clasps, head nods, smiles and avowals of lifelong devotion.

I was elated. I had grown up in places where my parents' names were unpronounceable. And suddenly, they are not only pronounceable but celebrated. And their celebrity has rubbed off on me.

I began to see nepotism in a new light.

Soon after this, I, too, took my reluctant leave of this time-encrusted cell and its occupant. I had another call to make. We said our fond farewells, but when I had clanged his great rusty door shut, I hesitated. I had a feeling I wouldn't see him again and my impulse was to go back into the dust and dimness and say something else to him, I don't know quite what, but something.

I didn't go back. I would have looked foolish, standing gaping in his doorway. So I started slowly up the stairs and as it grew brighter and noisier and the street came into view, Ervin receded into the background of my mind. I was back in the world of shoppers and taxi drivers and little street corner kiosks selling corn-on-the-cob to peckish pedestrians. What will I ever really know of Sambor and boys dying of typhus? While I was sitting opposite Ervin in the chair my father had sat in so long ago, he said he hoped my generation would always remember what happened during the war — the camps, the torture, the deaths. But it's impossible to remember something you never knew in the first place. In Europe, in the West, my generation has not been required to produce martyrs, heroes and survivors. All we have to remember or to forget are other people's nightmares.

I stood before the block on Bajza Street where my father's Uncle Sanyi and Aunt Manci live. They have a one-room flat at the top, on the fifth floor. For as long as I can recall they have been old and ill.

I was worried because I knew that I was about to disappoint them. They were expecting me to bring Adam along. I had wanted to, but at the last minute my mother had persuaded me that it wasn't really a good place for him. 'After all,' she had said, 'their flat is practically a sick room.' So I left him behind. But now I regretted it. He would have been a bright interlude in two uneventful and unfortunate lives. Sanyi and Manci have no children, and their only two relations in Budapest (Zsuzsi the film script writer and her brother András) refuse to have anything to do with them.

I looked up at their window and the narrow balcony in front of it. When my father was a young man, he and my grandfather had lived in the adjoining block, on the second floor. There are a few such blocks in a row, in various shades of grey and with little balconies. My father moved from there when he married, my grandfather died there.

From behind one of the windows an aged face peered down at me. It was perfectly still. Only the eyes seemed to have life. I couldn't tell whether it was a man's or a woman's face, but it studied me with what I felt was mild hostility. I moved towards my relatives' doorway still eyeing this motionless visage and nearly stumbled over an ancient, discarded icebox.

It was dark and quiet inside, as though no one lived there at all. The sort of building in which any number of eerie, ailing geriatrics could be languishing. A block of flats ought to be pervaded by the sound of children and the smell of chicken soup.

When Manci opened the door her gaze was at about knee level. Her lips were parted in anticipation. She lifted her eyes up to me.

'But where is he?' she asked plaintively.

I started to make some excuse, but by that time Sanyi was also standing at the door. He was smiling and holding out two thin, trembling hands and seemed unsteady on his feet.

'Let's go in,' urged Manci, 'Sanyi is getting a bit over-excited. Let's sit down. Oh, how miraculous that the three of us should be together again like this!' She forgot about Adam for the time being.

Manci and I sat down on either side of a little table and Sanyi lowered himself with some effort into the only armchair in the room. He watched me wordlessly. From time to time his mouth quivered into a faint smile. He didn't move, except to lift a hand every now and then to his chin, in order to pat at a small plaster. When Manci saw him doing this she scolded him.

'Just leave that plaster alone. It's fine.'

'I just thought,' he began weakly, 'that perhaps it was coming off.' He threw a nervous glance at me.

'Well, it isn't,' answered Manci crossly.

'Is the blood coming through?'

Manci sighed and frowned at him. 'No.'

Sanyi seemed relieved. He relaxed back into his chair. 'Then everything is in order,' he said.

'He has a tiny cut on his chin from shaving this morning,' Manci explained. 'It's nothing, really. I don't know what he's so worried about.'

He squirmed slightly. 'Ask her about Peter,' he told Manci in a low, hoarse voice.

'My father is doing well, thank you. Busy, you know. . .' I looked out the window at the concrete building across the street which was the same shade of grey as Sanyi's complexion.

'Is he happy?' Manci asked.

I wished Adam were there. Then he would be the centre of attention. He would laugh and sing and play the clown, and I wouldn't be asked questions which I don't know how to answer.

Soon Manci retired to the kitchen for a few minutes to make us some coffee. Sanyi and I looked at each other in silence.

Then he said, 'This is a special treat for me, coffee. I'm not really allowed to drink it.' His gaze fell to his thick, black lace-up shoes. They were done up very tightly, as though to give his ailing feet all the support they could. He shook his head. 'I'm not well,' he said quietly.

People who live in England are simply not prepared to deal with the ill and the aged, let alone the phenomenon known as death. Such things interfere with social decorum. And that, above all, must be maintained. Thus cancer, tuberculosis, scarlet fever and all other diseases known to mankind fall into the single category of 'How are you?'/'Not so bad, thanks' and can be dispensed with painlessly. The only ailment the English can be seen to suffer from is stiffness of the upper lip. It's chronic and contagious.

But elsewhere illness is given full rein, especially among the old. It is a badge of courage to be displayed proudly, like the Victoria Cross. Sadly, that is very often what it is.

'Why aren't you well, Sanyi?' I asked.

Weakly, he shrugged and gestured with a pale hand. 'I have many problems,' he said. 'Sometimes my legs just give way underneath me. My circulation is very poor.' He looked around the room. 'And we're stuck up here, day after day. No one ever comes to see us. If the lift breaks down, and it often does, we're like prisoners, unable even to go down to the shops to buy some food. If you want to know the real trouble — it's that we're both pensioners. And the government has hardly any money for pensions.'

Manci came in with the coffee and a plate of chocolate biscuits.

'He's right,' she said. 'Sanyi is eighty-two, he's been retired for twenty-two years. I've been retired for seventeen years. We're of no use to anybody and the government knows that.'

She told me about her heart problem. Every once in a while it stops beating for a couple of seconds. Each time it happens she is terrified, convinced that it won't start again, that the end has come. 'And one day it will stop beating for good,' she said matter-of-factly, 'and then I don't know what will become of him.' She nodded towards Sanyi.

He shook his head emphatically and took a sip from a cup which he had lifted carefully from its saucer. But instead of putting it to his lips he rubbed it against his chin, and suddenly I saw a look of horror come into his eyes.

'The plaster,' he mumbled helplessly. 'It's come off now. . .'

'No it hasn't,' Manci reprimanded him. 'Why can't you be more careful? Leave it alone.'

It was too late. Sanyi was already fiddling with it. The slight knock against the cup had caused the cut to start bleeding again. Sanyi held the plaster in one hand and desperately dabbed his chin with the other. He got a drop of blood on his finger and tears came to his eyes.

'Now look what you've done!' Manci was angry and viewed him with disdain. She went to the bathroom for some first-aid things. I looked at him, unable to speak.

When she came back she was calmer and spoke to me as though Sanyi wasn't there. 'See what he's like? He's like this all the time. More trouble and aggravation than a baby.' Gently she cleaned his chin and held a tissue over it until the bleeding had stopped.

'Yes, I'm like a baby,' Sanyi said in a muffled voice.

'Don't speak or you'll start it bleeding again!' She put a new, bigger piece of plaster over it, and pressed it down firmly. 'There. You're fine now. So don't say a word.' Her efficiency seemed to reassure Sanyi. Manci rapidly put everything back into a box and offered me another chocolate biscuit.

'Would you believe,' Manci said in a tone which was suddenly softer, 'that this man fought in two world wars? In the first one he was shot in the thigh with a dumdum bullet while fighting near Udine, in Italy. He was in hospital for six months with half his body in plaster. Afterwards, he walked on crutches for two years. But when the second war came, he was still strong and fit enough to fight again. So much of his life has been spent fighting, trying to stay alive, watching other men die. And now he's a baby, crying because of a drop of blood on his chin.' She fell silent. Presently she got up and walked over to her husband. She kissed his head. He looked up at her and I saw that his cheeks were damp.

I felt a strong urge to get up and leave. Although it angered me, I could see why Zsuzsi and András kept well away from this roomful of misery. How can you witness all of this and ever be light-hearted again? I wanted to go away and forget their troubles. I suppose I feared that now that I knew about them, I would be partly responsible for their existence. I'm like most other people — full of such despicable instincts.

Manci sat down again and the conversation turned towards the days when my father lived next door. I barely knew my paternal grandfather, with whom he shared the flat. All I can remember about him is a phone call from Hungary to our home in the Bronx one day in 1960. My father spoke for a minute or two, then put the receiver down and went into another room, closing the door behind him. My mother told me my grandfather had just died. I can't remember what I did. I probably went down to the playground.

'Where is he buried?' I asked. 'In the same cemetery as my mother's parents?'

'Oh no,' Manci answered. 'He's in the other one, near the airport. It used to be a humble cemetery for the common people whose relations couldn't afford a plot in the exclusive cemetery in the Buda hills, which was for the 'somebodies', the well placed in our society. But after the war, the well placed became the badly placed and the common folk became the élite. And so the cemetery in Buda is now humble and neglected, and the one by the airport is kept very tidy because the ruling class always has to keep up appearances.'

When I finally rose to leave, Sanyi rose, too. He still wasn't speaking for fear of loosening the plaster on his chin, but he held my shoulders shakily and kissed me good-bye. I told them I would come back on another day with Adam. Manci said that would be wonderful and Sanyi nodded eagerly.

I tried to call the lift, but it was stuck somewhere on another floor. Perhaps someone hadn't closed its door properly. I hurried down the dirty staircase.

The taxi drivers in Budapest bear a close resemblance to the bus drivers. Often, they inspire less confidence sitting behind the wheel of a taxi than the driver of a No. 12 bus in Oxford Street would if he took over the controls of a jumbo jet. But they have boundless confidence in themselves, and maybe that's what counts.

The taxi I hailed that evening to take me out to dinner was driven by a young man with longish hair. He screeched to a halt beside me, his front fender rubbing against my kneecaps. He wore jeans and a leather jacket and when I slipped nervously into the back seat he squeaked around to face me and asked, 'Where to?'

I gave him the address.

'You're not Hungarian, are you?' He watched me through his rear-view mirror.

'Yes I am.' I'm not one of those people who likes to indulge in intense, all-revealing dialogue during ten-minute taxi rides.

But he was persistent. 'Odd accent you have.'

'Mmm.'

He asked me which route he ought to take and, as I hadn't the faintest idea, he clicked his tongue and announced, 'So you *are* a foreigner.'

I acquiesced. 'I left Budapest in '56. I live in London now.'

Our eyes met again in the mirror. 'Nice,' he said.

'Ever been to the West?'

'No. I will one day, though. But I've only recently finished serving in the army, and according to the regulations, I have to wait four years for a visa to the West.'

'And then where would you like to go?'

'I don't know. Anywhere.' He stopped at a red light, leaned back and stretched his arms. 'The truth is, I don't speak any other languages.' He shrugged. 'Of course, that may not be so disastrous. If I take evening classes and get a diploma from the technical college, I may be able to use my training abroad.'

'So you've already decided to leave Hungary?'

He nodded. 'The system here just isn't made for me.' he said.

'It might not be so easy to get a job in another country, you know. There's a lot of unemployment around, governments are tightening up the laws on immigration. . .' I stopped short. It was evident, even from the back of his head, what he was thinking. I turned to look out of the window at the early evening traffic. 'I wish you the best of luck.'

He began to speak in more detail about his plans, but his words were lost as we rumbled along over the cobbled streets. At last we arrived. He swung around in his seat and waited patiently as I counted out his fare. He wasn't exactly smiling, but the expression on his face was companionable, as though we were members of the same club. As I opened the door to get out he spoke again.

'You did the right thing.'

'Pardon me?'

'In 1956. When you got the hell out of this prison.'

'Is this a prison?' I felt like an idiot, asking so many questions.

'Haven't you noticed? The whole country has got bars round it.'

Then he put his hands on the steering wheel. I got out and shut the door at the same instant that he made a U-turn with a lot of noise and drove off into the dark.

I was left on an empty street in the outskirts of the city, where the lights were just beginning to come on in some of the buildings. Music poured out of a window somewhere above me. As I walked up the pathway to the building where Géza's brother Pista and his wife Judith lived, it grew louder. It sounded like one of those punk groups often to be seen on television, whose songs always sound exactly the same, namely terrible. (In purely visual terms, however, the performers are really quite versatile. They can combine the facial distortions of constipation with the stance of someone suffering from acute diarrhoea.)

I began to climb the stairs and the closer I got to Pista and Judith's place, the more obvious it became that that was where the music was coming from. It came as a surprise that they actually heard my knock. Pista opened the door and the full force of the bass hit me squarely on the jaw.

'Come in! We've been waiting for you!' He held a glass of red wine in one hand and a cigarette in the other.

I entered an audio-visual paradise. Along one wall was a massive music centre flanked by two great speakers. Underneath it were battalions of cassettes and records, in neat single file. Opposite this were two televisions, one of which was on but with the sound turned off, showing a football match between Hungary and East Germany.

Otherwise the room was modest. There was a low, modern settee and a couple of chairs. Hanging on the wall above the settee were several posters, some had pictures of rock groups and others showed women without much clothing on.

'Not bad, are they?' asked Pista, obviously pleased with the collection. 'My friends are all envious. I tell them, "Go and buy some for yourselves. They're from a little shop in Leicester Square." '

He started to tell me about his one month's tour of Europe the previous summer. But the bass pounded on relentlessly and the treble taunted my eardrums, so I didn't catch much of what he was saying.

'Can you lower the volume?' I pleaded.

He was glancing at the football match. 'No, we haven't scored any goals yet,' he answered.

I pointed to the music centre.

'Oh, the music!' said Pista. 'Yes it is good, isn't it? It's a band called Q-Tips. I brought this album back from London.'

I put my hands over my ears.

'You don't like it?' he asked. 'Why didn't you say so? I'll put something else on.' He turned the record player off and with the utmost care, like a surgeon performing a heart transplant, he prepared to put another LP onto the turntable.

'Please don't bother. Let's have an intermission. You can tell me all about your trip.'

Judith came in from the kitchen where she'd been getting dinner ready. Pista poured us all wine.

'It was sensational,' Judith said. 'We just got into the Skoda and drove off. We went to Vienna, Munich, Paris, London, Brussels, Frankfurt and then back here again. By the time we got home the car was groaning with goodies. The latest records and cassettes, Benson & Hedges cigarettes, copies of *Playboy* and *Club International*. . .what a haul.'

'Often we slept in the car,' Pista explained, 'to save money so that we could do things.'

'Like what?' I asked.

'Oh, see the sights. Go up the Eiffel Tower and into the sex cinemas of Soho. Things you can't do over here.'

'In London,' Judith said, 'we stayed at my half-brother's house in Friern Barnet.'

'Yes,' Pista added, 'on Hollywood Avenue.'

'Hollyfield,' she corrected. 'I practised my English with his two teenage sons. Unfortunately they both speak with a lisp, so it didn't help me much.'

'Judith is a linguist. She speaks fluent English and German,' said Pista, with one eye on the television.

'My parents wouldn't let me study English at school. They said it was German or nothing. So reluctantly I learnt German, but I was still very keen on English. I decided to go to evening classes. I think it's the most beautiful language in the world. Now I have a good job as a secretary with special responsibility for writing and translating official letters in English. And once in a while they even send me for a week to the firm's office in London. The very first time I ever went there I felt at home immediately. I can't explain it, there was just some sort of affinity. I sat at a desk in the tiny old office in Holborn and looked out the window at the secretaries and office boys going into the sandwich bars for lunch, and I thought — I could always be happy here.'

'Oh, DAMN!' cried Pista, jumping to his feet. 'The East Germans have won the match!' He slumped back down into his chair and buried his face in his hands. 'Well,' he moaned, 'we might as well eat.'

In the kitchen a table was laid with cold meats, peppers, tomatoes, bread. 'Can you please tell Grandma we're eating?' said Judith, and her husband disappeared into an inner sanctum to fetch the old lady.

'I didn't realize you had a grandmother living with you,' I said.

Judith explained. 'For a long time we had two grandmothers living with us. But Pista's died last year, so now we just share the flat with mine.' She sighed. 'It's not really such a bad arrangement. She's eighty-two now, and can be rather trying at times. But we get along all right.'

Pista returned, followed by a frail, white-haired woman who seemed indifferent about eating dinner. I was introduced to her and we sat down at the table. But Pista jumped up again after a moment.

'Let's play some more music. Do you like Blondie?'

Somehow, Blondie didn't strike me as the ideal music to eat salami by. But we ate and drank happily enough, and even Grandma seemed content with the choice. Pista opened another bottle of *tokaji* and soon it didn't matter much which record was on. There was a rich chocolate layer cake for dessert. After that we could barely move. But we managed to transport ourselves back to our seats underneath the naked women and rock groups.

After Blondie came Fleetwood Mac, and then some music which Pista told me is described as 'heavy metal'. An apt term, for it sounded like a score of brimming saucepans being dropped to the floor at once. Grandma sat all the while in a corner, her hands folded in her lap, watching us patiently.

The coffee table in front of us was covered with record sleeves and magazines, empty bottles and glasses, and ashtrays filled with the butts of Benson & Hedges cigarettes. Our conversation was beginning to fade, losing out to the stiff competition from electric guitars and rasping high notes. Then, to everyone's astonishment,

136

in a momentary lull between songs, the old woman uttered her only sentence of the evening.

'What,' she inquired, 'Does Q-Tips mean?'

We giggled. 'Your grandmother is really amazing,' I said. 'I mean the way she sits around and listens to all this music, never complaining.'

'But she can't hear any of it,' said Judith. 'She's been with us for six years and stone deaf for the last five. How could we get on otherwise?'

Pista and Judith drove me home. It was only eleven o'clock but the city seemed asleep. The river lay dark and invisible below us as we crossed it.

'When will you come to London again?' I asked.

Pista snorted. 'Good question. We've blown every forint we had. It'll be quite a while before we can afford another jaunt to the West.'

'Will you do me a favour?' Judith asked.

'Of course.'

'I've embroidered a cushion cover for my brother's wife. Could you take it back with you? Maybe you could drop it in the next time you're passing through Friern Barnet. . .

Budakeszi Avenue was in its usual week-night blackness. It was still in my mother's house and at first, when I opened the door, I thought everyone had gone to bed. Then I noticed that Juszti's door was slightly ajar and that her transistor radio was on ever so softly. Little Mári had told me that Juszi suffers from insomnia and often listens until late at night to the broadcasts from Austria. I whispered her name and looked into the room.

'Hello,' she said, as she moved like a shadow across the dark room to where I stood.

'Are you all right?'

'I've just been putting my feet up. I've done a lot of cooking today, preserving plums and peaches. My ankles are swollen.' She switched on a lamp, illuminating a bedroom which was crammed with mementoes. Every surface was obscured by a myriad of little objects and the whole room revealed a devotion to the past which was sad and touching.

'May I sit down for a moment?' I asked. I had glanced into her room before, but never been inside. It made my head spin.

'Who did this?' I asked, pointing to a large painting of Jesus, kneeling by a large rock and praying, his long fingers interlocked in a weird way.

137

'Your grandfather.'

I studied it more closely and found in a corner his name and the year 1907. Juszti pointed out other pictures which he had done, as well as the pheasant on top of her wardrobe, which he had stuffed himself.

'He could do many things,' she said, standing reverently in the middle of her little private museum.

I peered through the glass doors of a cabinet at scores of curiosities — animals made of porcelain, carved wooden figures, souvenirs whose origins I couldn't begin to guess at. Then my eye was caught by a small framed engraving on the wall. It was of a castle, and, judging by the attire of the ladies in the foreground, it must have been during the last century. I asked about it.

'That's the castle at Karlsburg. We called it Oroszvár in Hungarian, because of course at that time it was in Hungary, near the Austrian border. Now it's part of Czechoslovakia. That's where I worked when I was a young girl.'

'You worked at that castle?'

She nodded, and sat down on the edge of her bed. 'My father was a gardener there, and my mother worked in the kitchen and did general housekeeping chores. It was a lovely estate, with beautiful grounds where I used to wander when I was a child. I had a happy childhood.'

'Your family lived on the estate?'

'No, in the village of Karlsburg. Not many servants lived in the castle itself. When I was twelve I started to work there, picking fruit and vegetables from the orchards and fields of the estate.' She bent down to rub an ankle. 'I left Karlsburg when I was fourteen.'

'To come to Budapest?'

'No, I worked for several years elsewhere in the country. I didn't come here until 1938. I arrived here, at Budakeszi Avenue, to work for the *művésznő* in 1954. You were two years old and I was warned that you were a terrible eater. It was absolutely true. I never knew what to cook for you. Now your brother was different. He ate well. We had other problems with him, though. Sometimes he picked up a naughty word from your parents or their friends and teased your grandfather with it. Then he got chased with a stick all over the house and the garden. But your brother was very fast, he was never caught.'

I was interested in the portrait of a young army officer which hung beside her bed. Perhaps he had been an old fiancé. There had

138

to have been a romance some time, somewhere, I thought.

'That was my brother,' she said. 'He died a long time ago, along with the rest of my family. So I have no one, you see. The *művésznő* is the only one who still cares for me. That is why I'm still here in this house. This is where I belong. I just hope I can carry on doing what I have to, with these tired old feet of mine.'

The house was chilly and I shivered slightly. I left her sitting there, bending over her ankles. The Austrian radio station was playing a waltz by Strauss.

Eight

At last Mári and Dódi's 'free Saturday' arrived. The Zsiguli rolled through the gates of our drive and we were on our way to Gölle. It was a misty morning. The sun cast a pale light over the hills of Buda. Yellow leaves and wild chestnuts were falling from the trees above us. It was a morning to make you feel serene and content.

Soon we had left Budapest and were driving southward along a slender highway. There were hardly any other cars. What would await me at that tiny village, that alien spot on the map which was just a name to me, but still part of my heritage?

My grandfather had moved to Gölle from another village in the county of Somogy in 1910. He was then a young man, well educated. He was an exceptionally gifted singer, with a fine tenor voice. Almost immediately the village elected him as its 'cantor-teacher'. He taught at the village school and led the singing in church. Before long his talent became renowned throughout the *Dunántúl* region.

My mother was born soon afterwards. I still remember a photo I once saw of her aged four or five, with blonde pig-tails, wearing an old-fashioned, rustic frock, standing on a dusty road. It seemed strange to think of my mother having such beginnings, she who was later thought of by the Hungarian public as being their answer to Marlene Dietrich.

When my mother was still a small child, my grandfather was asked to go up to Budapest to audition at the opera house. The company required a tenor. He sang his arias so well that he was immediately offered the chance of a year's private tuition in bel canto in Italy, followed by a position as tenor with the company. His instinct was to grab the opportunity, to leave the dusty village for Italy and make his name as an opera singer. But my grandmother wept and pleaded with him. She didn't want to be left without him for a year, looking after their child alone. So he turned the offer down. He put away his dreams and returned to being a simple village schoolteacher. Later he became headmaster and moved into the headmaster's house opposite the school. But perhaps all was not abandoned. When my mother declared her ambition to be a professional singer, it was my grandfather who encouraged and pushed her. He overpowered the fears of my grandmother, who was against her daughter becoming anything other than a decent, ordinary and obedient wife. Someone like herself.

For many years my grandmother's sister also lived with them at the headmaster's house. In those days there were five main families in Gölle, who had been there since time immemorial. Their names were Bíro, Deres, Puska, Bodó and Esküdt. Any young woman marrying a young man in Gölle would most probably get landed with someone from that rather limited lot. My grandmother's sister married a young Esküdt. Apparently he was something of a tearaway. He was a former pupil of my grandfather's, always getting into mischief and being beaten for it. He never could be tamed.

They had a daughter — Big Mári. About 2,000 people now live in Gölle, and Mári is related to most of them, as these five families have been inter-marrying for a long time. This has always been one of my great reservations about the peasantry: a distinct lack of imagination in matters marital.

'Good Lord!' Mári cried as we entered Gölle's one and only street. 'It's been paved! I never thought I'd see anything but dust or mud on this street. Doesn't it look smart?'

'It just goes to show you — anything can happen in five years,' said Dódi. 'It seems even longer than that since we've been here.'

The two sides of the street are lined with rectangular houses of a single storey. But they don't face front, as most houses do. Rather, they are side-on, turning windowless backs on each other. Their front doors are in the middle of the rectangle, all facing busy little yards.

Dódi parked before one of these houses.

'Who lives here?' I asked.

'I am closest to two of my relations in Gölle,' Mári said. 'They are sisters, both in their fifties, called Boriska and Mariska. This is Boriska's house. She's not expecting us, nobody is. Let's see if she's in.'

We opened the front gate and were met by a huge white dog with great thick fur, who studied us like a benign polar bear, and a scattering of nervous hens. There was a vaguely familiar odour in the air, and a little further down the yard I spotted a pig-sty with a couple of inelegant snouts poking out. We were in the country, all right. Compared to country pigs, the ones in Regent's Park Zoo could pass for matinée idols.

A woman appeared at the door of the house. She wore a dark dress with a dark apron over it, she had a scarf around her head and shapeless black ankle socks and broken shoes on her feet. The shoes seemed to be composed purely of dust, and I found myself staring rudely at them.

'Boriska!' called Mári with her usual intensity of emotion.

'Mári! Dódi!'

'We've brought you someone. Can you guess who this is?' asked Dódi, nudging me forward.

The woman came up to me curiously and put her face close to mine. It was an extraordinary face. A lifetime of tough, endless drudgery was impressed upon it. She looked much older than she really was. But it was an open, honest face with which you could feel at ease. Her hands were also honest, hard-working, with square dirty fingernails. The sleeves of her dress were rolled up to the elbow. For some reason her bare arms seemed young. She had the tanned, smooth arms of a young woman just back from a seaside holiday.

She smiled but shook her head. She couldn't guess who I was. When Mári told her, she flung her arms around me and I felt the bristles on her chin as she kissed me on both cheeks.

'Let's go inside and have a drink,' she said.

We followed her up the steps and into the rectangle. Traditionally, the door leads directly into the kitchen in these peasant homes, because that is where the stove is, so it is the warmest room of the house. Then on one side of it is the 'parlour', for Sundays and guests, and on the other side are the bedrooms. We were led into the parlour, which was untidy and airless. Boriska put a bottle of wine and some glasses on the table. I suppose I must have been a completely unknown quantity to her, because she asked me hesitantly, 'You do drink wine. . .don't you?'

I nodded, but I wasn't paying much attention to her, because I had just noticed, to my grave consternation, that the table-top was made of melamine. And the settee and two matching armchairs were covered in the sort of imitation leather you would expect to find in the lounge of a cheap bed-and-breakfast hotel in Llandudno. There was a television in the room, and a plastic ashtray and chipped mugs like the ones we used to drink from during our

142

frequent tea breaks when I was staff writer on the weekly *Local Government Chronicle* in London.

All this was profoundly disturbing. For God's sake, what had become of the *genuine, rustic, peasant existence*? Only a few days before I had wandered around the National Museum in Budapest and been charmed by the old carved wooden chairs and tables and cabinets, all with delightful hand-painted scenes on them of animals, flowers and trees. Obviously the state had scoured the countryside for those items, leaving in return great wads of vouchers from Woolworth's and John's Bargain Basement.

Mári was taking photographs out of her handbag and handing them to Boriska. She was obviously going to be brought up to date on the doings of Little Mári, Little Pali and Big Pali. I said I was just stepping outside to inspect the chickens.

The front porch was bathed in bright sunlight. As I walked onto it, the polar bear stood up and wagged its tail at me. I sat down on the top step and nearly jumped up in alarm a moment later, when a one-eyed cat rubbed against my back. As I sat there in the warmth and tranquillity, I began to like Gölle. I would have preferred it with hand-painted, carved wooden furniture, but it wasn't so bad, anyway. And I thought about my mother being a little girl there, and my grandfather's singing pouring out from the church and resounding among the houses.

Soon the others came out, too. 'Shall we visit Mariska?' asked Boriska.

It only took about five minutes to walk to her house. It was somewhat bigger than Boriska's, and there were more animals in the yard. There was a barn with cows, more pigs and chickens and various vegetables growing in a disorganized, bohemian way.

Unlike Boriska, Mariska had a son and grandson. She is a widow. I don't think Boriska was ever married. But in other ways they are very alike. Mariska's hands were dirty from picking walnuts, so she didn't shake hands with me. But she seemed excited by my visit, as well as a bit embarrassed.

'Why didn't you let us know you were coming?' she asked. 'I would have put some decent clothes on and tidied the house and cooked you a proper lunch. Oh, I wish you'd written to me first!' She told us that her son and his wife were away on holiday, but that her seven-year-old grandson was around somewhere. 'Gyula!' she yelled. 'Gyula! Come out, you little scamp!'

A plump figure in strange, ragged clothes emerged from behind a grain storehouse and moved warily towards us. His face was very mucky, but more striking was its shape — like that of a perfectly cooked *palacsinta,* a Hungarian pancake. A woollen hat covered his head and was tied under his chin.

'Say hello, you rascal. And go clean your face,' ordered Mariska.

Gyula said nothing and went nowhere.

'Well, this is a marvellous surprise,' said Mariska, beaming at me and shaking her head as if with incredulity. 'Tell me about yourself. What do you do in London?'

'I'm a journalist.'

'Ah, yes. So now you're going to write a book about Hungary.' It wasn't a question, it was a conclusion.

Her statement completely dislodged my cosmopolitan smugness. In Budapest, not even the most urbane of my friends inquired as to whether I was intending to write about my experiences in Hungary. I never mentioned the possibility to anyone. Yet they all know that I'm a journalist. Then along comes a simple peasant woman with walnut-stained hands, who can take one look at you and size you up to the nearest millimetre. So another one of my illusions about the peasantry was firmly wrenched away from me. The 'simple peasant' isn't simple. And Mariska wasn't the only shrewd and alert inhabitant I met in Gölle.

Mariska's house is lighter and neater than Boriska's, but the decor is not vastly different. On our way into the sitting-room we passed through a sort of morning-room with a fold-out dining table in it. Sitting on a stool next to this table was an ancient woman whom I was told was the mother of Mariska's late husband. She wasn't a 'little old lady', but a large one. The palms of her hands were resting on a cane propped up in front of her. Her legs were spread out and a long, dark dress covered them completely, almost touching the floor. All in all, she was shaped like the Liberty Bell, and she looked at least as solid. I shook hands with her and said, 'Good day', but she merely made a sound like a suffocating bird. Then she surprised me with a big, toothless grin.

I noticed that Mariska also had a television. I pointed at it and started to mumble something. But Mariska interrupted.

'We all have one of those. Nothing new in that.'

'Do you watch it a lot?'

'When I have time. A little bit in the evenings. I always watch the news. And sometimes, for light entertainment, we'll watch *Charlie's Angels* or another one of those noisy series. It's nice to have a little noise once in a while. In Gölle we don't get many car chases and police shoot-outs.'

Gyula lay sprawled on the floor, putting together a puzzle. Mariska went out of the room to get a cold lunch ready — some of her own smoked ham and pickled cabbage salad, tomatoes, peppers and bread.

'Go and help your grandmother,' said Boriska.

Gyula waved a foot in the air but stayed put. 'No.'

'I'll give you a hiding!'

'No you won't.' The lips in the middle of the *palacsinta* were pressed together stubbornly.

Mariska called out from the other room, 'Talking about the news on television, have you heard about the latest terrorist bombing in West Germany?'

I said that I hadn't. So she told me all about it. I felt I had to make some excuse for my ignorance.

'I haven't had time to read the papers here. . .and I can't read Hungarian very fast. . .and I don't know how to work my mother's radio. . .'

'That's quite all right. We can't all know what's going on all the time, can we? Lunch is ready.'

The ham was cut into thick slices and bordered with rich, white fat. Mári and Dódi tackled it with great gusto, fat and all. I've always admired people who are able to eat that repulsive substance. I still pick out all the white bits before eating a slice of salami, which may be considered an eccentric digression from my Central European upbringing.

As we ate, Gyula hung like a gibbon from the back of his grandmother's chair. He eyed me with a mixture of fascination and suspicion. For a long time he stared at the Hampstead boutique version of cowboy boots I was wearing. They seemed to remind him of something.

He muttered under his breath.

'Are you saying something?' asked Mariska.

'I said *Gary Cooper,*' he answered. Then he dropped onto the floor and crawled under the table to my feet to inspect them more closely. I felt him prodding my big toe.

'Sometimes I just don't know *what* that boy is prattling on about,' Mariska sighed, pouring us more wine.

After lunch the sisters offered to walk with us down to the headmaster's house and school. I said good-bye to the old bell-woman and was on my way out when Mariska called me back for a moment.

'Would you like to see my other son?' she asked.

I didn't understand. 'You have two sons?'

'Look in here,' she said, leading me by the arm to the door of a room which we had not yet entered. She opened the door wide and stood back.

The curtains were half-drawn and it took me a moment to focus on the figure lying on the chaise longue, resting against a large cushion. And then I gaped awkwardly and dumbly into the eyes of a man with a closely-shaven head. He was lying still except for his hands which were twitching and fiddling on his lap. He groaned, but there was no expression on his face besides that of total incomprehension. Mariska closed the door again.

'He's twenty-eight,' she said, 'but mentally he's still a baby. Can you imagine how much work he is? He's become very heavy and it's difficult for me to clean him and change his clothes alone. I've had no help since my husband died.'

'Can't he live in an institution?' I asked.

She hesitated a moment. 'Yes, he could. But try to understand, I need the modest allowance I get from the state for looking after him. It'll be another couple of years before they pay me my husband's pension, because he died before retiring age. I must get money somehow.'

We started to walk down the street together and I looked through the gate of each house. Cats and dogs were sleeping in the sun, chickens were beating their feathers into the ground and raising dust, the smells of animals and dung, hay and ripe fruit mingled in the air around us. Saturday is a working day in Gölle. But it seemed as devoid of people and as peaceful as Cornhill on a Sunday.

But a few houses down we met an old woman, the only person on the street besides us. She was leaning with her back against a gate, holding her knees. She wore the usual peasant clothes — shapeless dark dress, apron, headscarf, black stockings. She didn't move, but her eyes, which were embedded in a maze of deep wrinkles, followed me as I passed by.

Behind me, Boriska stopped and asked, 'Mrs Szabó, who are you waiting for?'

'I'm not waiting,' I heard a hoarse voice answer, 'I just *am*.'

The headmaster's house is different from the others, it is L-shaped. We went around the side to the entrance and knocked on the door. Boriska and Mariska, who had left us at the gate, had told us that the current headmaster and his wife were youngish and

146

keen Party members.

We were greeted by a woman of about thirty-five who was obviously not of peasant origin. Mári explained who we were and why I was interested to see the place. She asked whether we could take a quick look around.

At first I thought the headmaster's wife would refuse. She looked as though she were in the middle of an exacting chore, like bottling black cherries. But she flashed a smile at us, revealing her two gold teeth, and asked us to step inside.

We went from room to room. Mári would look at a floor or the shape of a room and say, 'It was different in my childhood.' But as we stood in the front hallway she smiled with recognition, nodded and told me, 'This hasn't changed. Your grandfather's writing desk stood right in front of this big window. Here he had plenty of light by which to read and correct his pupils' papers.' She opened the door to the room at the end of the hallway. 'Your mother was born in here. The bed lay against the wall by the window and the great tiled stove was in this corner. Your grandfather kept this room very hot in the winter. He always liked the warmth. You're the same, aren't you?'

I couldn't muster a great deal of emotion during this sentimental tour. A house to me is only a geometrical shape, stone and wood and glass, spaces and corners which alone mean very little. My grandfather was no longer at his desk correcting papers, my grandmother wasn't obediently going about her chores and there was no longer a girl with blonde pig-tails in an old-fashioned frock. I could hope for no miraculous vision of times past. It was just another strange house with strangers in it.

What I did find moving wasn't to do with the house, but just outside it. In the garden was a tall pine tree, a soulmate of the pines at Budakeszi Avenue. Like the others, it was overhung with golden cones. I suddenly realized that one man had planted a great many trees. Neither did the religious connotations of this fact escape me. Joyce Kilmer, in her famous poem 'Trees', speaks of 'A tree that looks at God all day,/And lifts her leafy arms to pray.' I think that at that moment I began to understand the one-time headmaster from Gölle, who for so long was only a shadowy figure in a distant dream.

The garden has become overgrown with weeds since those old days. No one has the time to tend it any more. And opposite the house, what used to be the school building is now the village cinema. So Gölle has a cinema, a bus stop, a paved street and an

147

imposing office for the local farmers' co-operative. What else could a socialist village require?

We moved on to Lajos *bácsi*'s house. It was a hotbed of activity. Old women were hovering over steaming cauldrons like panto witches, little boys were stuffing themselves with bread and honey in the kitchen, Lajos's son was tinkering with the engine of his car, and there was Lajos himself — a big burly man who pressed my hands into his brown leathery palms.

I was expecting to be regaled with news about his stud bull or something of that sort but instead he brought us up to date on the Leader of the Opposition's latest speech in the House of Commons. He asked what my opinions were on Mrs Thatcher's economic policies. I looked into his craggy face and said I hadn't thought about them much lately.

In the kitchen we were given more wine and some pastries which his wife had just baked. Lajos had recently seen a television programme on the Middle East crisis and spoke with some authority on the subject. Without my knowledge, another little war had broken out somewhere in the region. I said nothing, but shrugged and nodded sagely.

'Disturbing, isn't it?' Lajos asked.

'Oh, quite.'

Fortunately, he began to speak about his childhood after that.

'Your mother and I went to school together,' he said. 'I remember the way your grandfather kept control of his class. The trouble-makers and louts behaved like angels with him. He had a cane on his desk and didn't mind using it. He drummed learning into our heads. Took no nonsense. We were all afraid of him. But he was the best headmaster Gölle ever had.'

He showed us his latest calf in the barn. It was dwarfed by three or four huge, glossy cows. Dódi admired them, took the pipe out of his mouth and whispered to me, 'There's a fortune in this barn. Animals like these are worth tens of thousands of forints. Of course, Lajos devotes his life to them. He's never once taken a holiday.'

Outside the barn there were haystacks and piles of building materials and old troughs and other bits and pieces lying around. It was like a small Moscow Square, with places being dug up and other places being covered up. I wondered what a typical Swiss farmer would make of this wild Hungarian spectacle. I felt a surge of affection for everything that I saw. Except perhaps the dunghill.

Opposite Lajos's farm lived another family related to Mári in a complicated way. It consisted of an elderly couple, their son and his wife, and a small grandson who liked to eat sugar cubes. Jancsi, the son, showed his elaborate new milking machine to Dódi while his wife made us espresso so strong that I had to chew it before it rode like rattlesnake venom down into my guts.

My mother had given me various little presents to take to these relations, and for this particular young woman she had set aside the latest issue of a very chic German fashion magazine. As I looked at her, in her drab, shapeless dress covered by a stained apron, her hair in a tangle with an odour about her of hard work and fatigue, I wondered what on earth she could want with it. Later, Mári told me that she was most competent with a sewing machine. She would study the latest styles and designs, send off for materials, and make her own haute couture clothes. At Gölle's special social occasions she always wore the most fashionable gear. She seemed to me the very embodiment of hope.

Her husband spoke to us about agricultural matters, but so thick was his regional accent, I could barely understand a word. His face was fascinating to watch. His mouth was formed by two perpetually good-natured curves. He was missing a tooth or two and there was one of silver which, when he laughed, caught the sunlight through the window. He was short but powerful. His rough hands were stained with work and cigarettes, but they were tender as they stroked his child's head. He too, like everyone else, looked about fifteen years older than he was.

We sat in their living-room, on cheap modern furniture. The only ornaments were the empty miniature liquor bottles with their colourful labels which filled a shelf on the wall. Outside, a horse-drawn cart passed slowly by, and then a sports car. There was a brief silence when we just sat watching each other. We were all Hungarians. But I wondered what my place was in this human collection. We were like ocean currents, sometimes swirling around each other in pursuit of our own very different directions. Yet even by swirling it's possible to reach and touch someone, to come nearer than you were before.

It was dusk when we left Gölle. The menfolk had finished their work in the fields and meadows and were driving home in their cars. They were thinking, no doubt, of their suppers and that evening's programmes on telly.

149

Two rows of straight-backed chairs were laid out in the cavernous hall of the Museum of Fine Arts, Budapest. All around were paintings and frescoed arches. At one end, tuning up their instruments, was the Tinódi Chamber Orchestra, of which Little Klári was the sole female member.

We waved to each other as I took a seat. The twenty-five musicians were wearing black suits and frilly white shirts. It is not an ordinary orchestra. The Tinódi, which is subsidized by the Ministry of the Interior, specialises in renaissance and baroque music. The Ministry has spent a vast fortune equipping the players with reproduction renaissance instruments such as the viola da gamba, krummhorn, cornetto and dulcian, all imported from West Germany. Klári plays the baroque oboe. Dulcet tones were floating up to the neo-Grecian columns and all around the Roman statuettes.

When all the seats were taken, the concert kicked off with the French dances by Praetorius. Then they proceeded to play some works by Giovanni Gabrieli, Johannes Pezel and Scandeli. Soon my ears began to buzz with all the sonatas, intradas and cantatas, the concertos and chanzonas. Klári's inflated pink cheeks blew forth a series of perfect trills. Curious faces appeared from behind pillars. At any moment I expected a band of minstrels to appear in the gallery and shower their songs upon us.

It was a cold Sunday morning and after the concert Klári and I went back to her flat where Laci was waiting with a bottle of his redcurrant wine to warm us up. From the kitchen came the comforting fragrance of newly baked *pogácsa*, those indescribable little savoury cakes which can, through a single sniff, encapsulate a Hungarian upbringing.

Fleur, the poodle, was sitting majestically by the window.

'She's a very pretty girl today,' said Big Klári, stroking the dog's fat rump. 'She's had another visit from her beauty therapist. Her hair and nails have been nicely trimmed. She had a lovely bath and her ears were cleaned.'

'Does the beauty therapist call often?' I asked.

'Once a fortnight.' Klári caressed a supine belly. 'Just to keep the little girl in good shape.'

Little Klári had invited a few of her musician friends over for drinks before lunch, and just as we were all admiring Fleur's feminine grace, the doorbell rang.

A short, stocky man with a ginger moustache came into the room. Zoltán, I was to learn, was a bachelor, a bon vivant and cello player, and probably in that order.

He gripped my hand firmly and shook it once and immediately began to tell me that I reminded him of a girl he once knew when he was studying music in Moscow.

'She was a violinist, a charming girl. She lived in a little room that was so cold in winter she used to go to bed in her grandmother's beaverskin coat. This is only what I heard, of course. Never witnessed it myself. Unfortunately.'

Soon the others arrived. There was Karcsi, a thin, bespectacled piano teacher with long bony fingers, and Julia, a plain, sour-faced flautist who looked as though she had given up men for the sake of Art and just realized it had been a terrible mistake. Last to arrive was Csaba, who deftly took a *pogácsa* from a plate on the table before collapsing in a subdued mound on the floor beside his fiancée.

At first the young people exchanged bits of news and gossip about friends and work. They mentioned forthcoming concerts and discussed the cancellation of the Tinódi orchestra's foreign tour caused by the Ministry withdrawing its grant.

But I wanted to hear about other things. How do they see their lives, their futures in Hungary, a country which is at times infuriating, at times uplifting, and nothing if not unique?

The musicians' demeanours changed when they heard my questions.

'You have to realize,' Zoltán began with a tug of his moustache, 'that while our lives are not very easy here, we never expected them to be, so few of us are really embittered. There are certain serious problems which must be solved, but — '

'But until then,' Karcsi cut in, 'we will be content with simply trying to get by, to live as fruitfully, as comfortably, as our circumstances will allow.'

Julia shook her head. 'We all know that isn't good enough,' she declared. 'Why should we be content with the present situation in this country? After all, we do have the power to make it better.' She folded her hands on her lap and looked at her long, dowdy skirt.

'Not alone we don't,' said Zoltán. He turned to me with a smile. He leaned forward in the manner of a kindly, informal university tutor. 'Shall I tell you what our real problem is here?' He put his hands stiffly to either side of his head. 'We're like horses wearing blinkers. Our vision is severely impinged. We see only our own routes — our ambitions, dreams, desires. But we can't see

151

ourselves in a wider context, from a national or even international perspective. We're always asking, "Where am I going and how fast am I getting there?" not "What's happening to Hungary and how can I help change its direction?" '

'What we need is a new leader. Kádár has been all right, but we're all getting bored with him,' said Julia.

'No,' Zoltán said emphatically. 'That isn't the answer. That's just an excuse. Our situation will grow better only when the perspective of the ordinary citizen widens at last so that the entire picture becomes clear. When we stop thinking and acting selfishly. And a change like that can come only from within ourselves, not from political leadership.'

I asked in what way Hungarians were being selfish.

'We have three main goals,' said Zoltán, and he counted them out for me on his fingers. 'A little flat somewhere, a car and a *vikend* house in the country. To have these three things is equivalent to success and contentment. It doesn't matter how we acquire them, either, whether honestly or dishonestly.'

Karcsi's words rushed at me. 'But don't think that we are like this because of some terrible shortcoming in the nature of the Hungarian race. Our history and our circumstances have forced us into this attitude. We're human, that's all.'

'The trouble is,' Julia said, 'that in the meanwhile we're just a nation hobbling along, with one arm leaning against Russia and the other stretched out for aid from the West.'

Zoltán nodded. 'And it's every man for himself. Neither the present nor the future are too secure, so we toss these deeper issues to the wind and enjoy ourselves. Eat well, drink well, watch television, spend the weekends in your little country places. . .'

'And why should we work our heads off?' asked Karcsi. 'What for? The more you work the more money you earn — for the state. The state owns everything, us included. We can't do a thing about it. So why not make merry?'

'How pathetic.' Julia was shaking her head. 'After a thousand years of struggle the Hungarian people, who have always been forced into acts of heroism, have finally succumbed to apathy.'

I said I didn't agree. Perhaps the nation is only keeping a low profile, biding its time, slowly and cautiously building up its confidence. Even apathy is a type of action. And for those old enough to recall the war, Stalin, Rákosi and 1956, the terror and the anguish, apathy might be considered a luxury.

'Oh, it's true that we are a lot better off than many other

countries,' said Zoltán. 'And most of our problems seem to exist just about everywhere else, as well. Maybe that is why we dare to ask for more and more material things for ourselves.'

Csaba straightened himself and spoke out. 'I hate to interrupt this discussion,' he said. 'But no one has yet mentioned one particular aspect of our lives here. If you want to know the difficulties of the young in Hungary,' he said, turning to me, 'consider the way in which the young and the old are so totally interdependent that they can never hope to be free from each other, to have privacy. We might as well be bound to each other with ropes.' He threw a quick glance towards the kitchen door, beyond which my cousin's parents had tactfully banished themselves. Little Klári looked somewhat shocked by his speech.

I wanted to know what this interdependence consisted of.

'It begins with enforced physical nearness,' Csaba explained. 'I think that's the worst of it. Isn't it true that, in the West, when a young person reaches the age of eighteen or twenty, he leaves his parents' home and starts an independent life?'

'Most of them seem to prefer a bedsit or sharing a flat with friends to living at home.'

'Well, we would prefer it, too. We would also like to come and go as we please, make our own decisions and be responsible for our own lives. But there simply isn't a choice in the matter. It's difficult for married people with families to find a flat, but for young singles it's just impossible. There aren't any flats to be had. So we stay at home. When we marry, most of us still have to live with one or the other's parents, sometimes for years and years, even after the babies are born.

'Perhaps if we are lucky the parents will have some money put away, enough to help us find a home of our own. Because we wouldn't be able to afford it otherwise. But then we are indebted. And the debt has to be paid. When the parents become old-age pensioners, we feel obliged to support them. By then, you see, they are the ones who are finding it hard to exist on their pensions. They're worried about having enough money for food, for the rent. So they probably come to live with us.'

My cousin seemed acutely embarrassed by these words. Her cheeks were flushed. I remembered that a few days earlier I had asked her when they were going to set the wedding date. When they knew they had somewhere to live, she replied. Csaba had rejected the idea of moving in with Laci and Big Klári, who had kindly offered them their own bedroom. No one could understand it, she told me. So she and Csaba were simply carrying on with their dateless engagement, waiting for some miracle to happen.

Zoltán jumped up and clapped his hands together. 'Come on! Let's switch on Laci *bácsi*'s splendid record player and listen to some Mozart. I haven't heard the old man for ages.'

We drank some more wine, ate more *pogácsa* and listened to the Sonata in B flat Major. Laci put his head around the door and smiled benignly at us.

'Having a nice time? Ah, how I wish I was young again.'

The massive grey building throbbed with the beat of rock 'n' roll. Students by the thousands were unleashing tapping feet and snapping fingers. The Budapest Technical University was holding a dance and that evening the drums and electric guitar were the main items on the syllabus.

This was a treat for me from Pali, a student at the university. It wasn't easy to get the tickets; these dances were very popular. So I was determined to enjoy myself, despite the fact that I was about seven or eight years older than everyone else. In fact, after the music started, I forgot all about this age gap. It's incredible how rock music can not only immediately wipe out the barriers between countries, but also reduce everyone to the same juvenile (but invigorating) common denominator.

The hall in which the band, the Old Boys, was playing was so packed that it was literally impossible to take a step in any direction. Neither was it easy to see what was happening onstage, there were so many swaying, shaking and bobbing heads. But the atmosphere was so intense, and there was such a deep underlying sense of yearning, that it would have been difficult to remain unmoved by it.

The Old Boys sang the old hits from the 1950s, wringing the best out of Elvis, Chubby Checker, Roy Orbison and Bill Haley. Not only did they sing in English, but with totally untainted accents. They even ad libbed in English: 'Hi there, all you great kids' and 'Hey, how's your Hungarian?' quipped the lead singer into his microphone. The audience howled with glee, whistled and stamped its feet. The whole evening was pounding, thundering into my skull and I suddenly realized that I felt no differently from any of them. They were *my* young people, and a part of that illusive heritage which I had journeyed here to find and capture. I had found them easily enough, but I knew that there was little I could take away with me. When the music was over and the crowds had dispersed, I would once more be that ocean current which keeps flowing and swirling around, drawn on by the sun and the wind.

The Old Boys wore pink and blue Teddy Boy jackets and dark sunglasses. Neon signs flashed behind them — *7-up, Cadillac, Hot Dogs* and *One Way Street.* Catch-words, exotic Anglo-Saxon sounds. The hall was packed with moving bodies, Coca-Cola bottles and smoke. And the yearning was total. It was for Western words, music, clothes, idols, manners. It was youth, with all its eccesses and limitations. Youth, which is its own ecstasy and its own damnation.

There is nothing quite like being young and *en masse,* free-spirited and yet in a way a prisoner of that same spirit. This is the only time in life when you can live with such intense concentration, purely for the moment. It's the only time when you might suddenly be blinded by the realization that what counts in life is the struggle, that the struggle *is* life. It's not getting the girl in the end that's important, but knowing that somewhere, somehow, there's a girl to be got.

When finally, after half a dozen encores of 'Rock Around the Clock', 'Blue Moon' and similar golden oldies the band was allowed to leave, everyone poured into a lofty lecture theatre for a different kind of show. They played a clip from a Bruce Lee film. It was scratchy and the sound quality was poor, but the hero's high kicks, chops and screeches produced great merriment nonetheless.

After the Kung Fu another band, hard rock this time, took the stage. Pali and I couldn't find seats in the packed hall so we stood up front to one side of the platform. When the music began we were almost blasted off our feet by the sheer force of the volume. A particularly crazed individual sat at the electric organ, a combination of Andy Warhol and the Phantom of the Opera. He was thin and his fingers crept like spiders over the keyboard. He stared intermittently at the audience and spent the rest of the time flinging his lank hair out of his eyes. Then they played a hard rock version of a Hungarian Rhapsody by Liszt. And I realized that they were actually excellent musicians. All they needed was a damned good melody.

By eleven o'clock the dance was over. Pali and I walked through the fast emptying building, the stale air. In all corners there were discarded paper cups and paper plates with half-eaten sausages, napkins and empty packets of Bulgarian cigarettes, producing a pervading sense of satiated indulgence.

There was something depressing about the faces and the voices in that drab building. The students were of all types. Some sported the collegiate look, wearing blazers and ties, while others were unkempt and shabby. All had their Western counterparts. On face value, they could have been students at a polytechnic anywhere — in Paris or London or Los Angeles.

But as we stepped out into the black, drizzling night, it suddenly dawned on me just what the difference was, and why I had felt a vague sense of depression. In the West, the music of the young is a reflection of their lifestyle and values. In Hungary, it is a reflection of their unattainable dreams.

Nine

We are in the kitchen of Paul Neuburg's house in Hampstead, London. It is small and at the end of a narrow corridor. The rest of the house seems as though it might be a little cold and draughty, but the kitchen is cosy and friendly and filled with the smell of his wife's cooking.

Paul is hungrily watching his plate being piled high with noodles and meat and then topped with a thick, tomatoey sauce. A tabby cat jumps onto my lap, I suspect in order to get a better view of the food.

Paul is in his early forties and has been a professional journalist since 1967. He is my fellow ex-refugee from 1956. But unlike me and my friend George Szirtes, he wasn't a small child carried across the border in his parents' arms. He was a young man of eighteen and he came out of Hungary alone, leaving his family and friends behind.

At first he is more interested in his dinner than in raking up old memories of the revolution, and who can blame him? He puts a great forkful of noodles into his mouth and chews it thoughtfully.

'I was living with my mother in Pest when the 1956 revolution broke out,' he says. 'I was in my last year of high school. I can remember vividly my sense of astonishment at finding myself "in the middle of history", as it were. On 23 October I attended the mass demonstration and moved on with a lot of other people to the radio station where a group of student revolutionaries wanted to make a broadcast. That's where the first shootings took place. I was too young to understand what on earth was happening. All I knew was that these events were unprecedented. And I kept thinking to myself, one day all this will be in the history books.'

Paul's trim American wife, herself a television journalist, pours me a glass of wine. 'You escaped unhurt?' I ask.

He nods. 'I made my way home in a sort of stupor and told my mother what I'd seen. I woke up the next morning to find tanks

157

and men running down the street with guns outside my window. Within a month I had made up my mind to leave. I had only vague plans. I remembered the pictures of England in the school book from which I had studied English. And I thought it might be a good place to try. At least until the situation settled down in Hungary. My intention was to see something of the world, find out what the West had to offer, soak up as much as I could, and then return home and make use of my experiences there.'

'What did your parents say to that?'

'My mother has always been a selfless person, thinking of others first. She agreed that it would be best for me to leave, even though we wouldn't meet again for a long time.' He leans back briefly to allow his wife to give him a second helping.

For a while Paul eats in silence. The cat jumps off my lap and scrambles onto the boiler. 'Some time in November I met a schoolmate on the street who told me, to my amazement, that the borders were open. Guides were leading groups of refugees into Austria. It was impossible to tell for how long this would be the case, so I decided to make my move. The revolution came after a few years of political thaw during which a lot of the barbed wire had been taken down from the border and the land mines had been removed. It was still a risky business, though. There were no organized border patrols yet but there were guards watching. The refugees always had to escape at night, and when the guards' flares went up, we all hurled ourselves onto the ground and prayed or cursed.'

Paul says he spent eight weeks in refugee camps in Austria. The English quota had temporarily been filled, so he had to wait, but he was told to reapply in early January. By the end of January he was in England.

'I came in under the wings of the British Council for Aid to Refugees. There was a fabulous woman there who was in charge of us, an enormous, silver-haired lady called Miss Perrin. Over the next couple of years she steered me through my "A"-levels at the Westminster College of Commerce. The British looked after their refugees very well, a lot better than the French looked after theirs, for example. The British took on only as many as they knew they could cope with comfortably, the French let in a lot more and then forgot about them.

'In 1959 I went to Cambridge to study English. I came down to London three years later with my degree and got a job as a trainee with an advertising agency. I didn't like it, so I began teaching at a secondary modern in Clapham. By then I had realized that my emigration was not temporary. I could no longer go back to live in Hungary.'

'Why not?'

'Because during those five or six years I had grown to manhood here. Going back to Hungary would have meant reverting to the ideals of childhood, in a way. The years between eighteen and twenty-two are all-decisive. By twenty-two my mind was formed, and it had been formed by England. In 1964 I published an article in *The Listener* precisely on this subject — what goes on inside someone who emigrates to a strange, unknown place. At that time I put the refugee's success or failure down to the age at which he emigrated:

The over-forties have had it. Some of them may not even learn the language beyond what is inevitable and may die without ever properly speaking to an Englishman. The over-thirties, if they are especially gifted or indispensable in their old professions, may hope to integrate and have friends of choice and not of necessity, but more often than not their jobs hardly correspond to their young ambitions, and their wives, unless from home, are nothing even like a second best. It is we who have come here in our late teens and early twenties who stand the best chance. Adopting a new language, we were young enough to assume a new personality.

'Since then I have met several people, young and old, who do not fit into these generalizations. So if you ask me now which factors determine the outcome of a refugee's life, all I can say is, I don't know. But I do know that you have to be able to undergo a painful, lengthy process of rebirth if you want to emigrate without getting stuck in a state of isolation for the rest of your life.'

Paul has finished his dinner. His wife Nora clears away the plates, then she asks whether we would like some of the poppy-seed cake Paul's mother sent from Hungary. I nod eagerly. I begin to feel as though I am sitting in a Hungarian kitchen. I haven't had this seasonal sweet for a long time. Every Hungarian's mother makes poppyseed cake. Nora may be American but you can tell she knows all about these things.

We discuss the events which followed the publication of Paul's article in *The Listener*. A talent scout from Secker & Warburg read it and liked it so much it led to a commission for a novel on the same theme and an advance of £150. That was a hefty sum in the early sixties. So during the summer vacation (he was still a teacher)

159

he went to Greece on the money and wrote most of the novel there. *The Long Birth* was published three years later. The hero is based not only on himself but on other young refugees on the revolution.

In his article Paul had already described those things in England which had made the strongest impressions on him when he arrived and which had infuriated him the most:

The 'jolly good' and the 'fine show', the tolerance and cosy dirt, the slums, the bottles of milk standing at the doors for days untouched, pale little girls of five in the streets with nails varnished red and buttons falling off, ye olde whatsit. . .I was used to hard speaking, to intolerance, to dirt which was either cleared up or left there but never cosy, to milk queued for, fought for, or pinched, to sunburnt children kept tidy whatever the cost, the brashest new whatsit or none at all. . .

He was eighteen and felt 'a mixture of free exhilaration and desperate uncertainty'. He wrote, 'I could not have reacted in any other way. Because adolescence and totalitarianism have a lot in common even if they are not looking at the world from the same side of the fence. There is an idealism about them, true or feigned no matter, an arid kind of vision, a way of mapping life in black and white, and a ruthless desire to sweep opposition out of the way.'

As I look at him reaching for another slice of his mother's poppyseed cake, he does not appear to be idealistic or ruthless. He is just tired from overwork . His face is lined and pale but he doesn't look particularly old. He is in that mysterious phase which is suspended between youth and middle age, when elements from both seem to compete for the upper hand. Just under the surface the young man is still lurking, the newly arrived immigrant excited by his discovery that in England 'You could say what you liked and people did, to no apparent use; papers whipped public opinion any way they cared to, from left, right, and centre, and with a ferocity which would have created a revolution within a week in any other place you could think of.'

During the late sixties and seventies Paul established his reputation as an Eastern European expert, writing for the *Guardian, The Sunday Times* and *Daily Telegraph Magazine.* Since 1966 he has travelled back to Hungary eight times, as well as visiting the other Soviet bloc countries. From these trips a book was born — *The Hero's Children,* which gave a comprehensive picture of the postwar generation in Hungary, Romania, Czechoslovakia, Poland and Bulgaria.

'Whenever I go back to Hungary,' he says, 'I try not to let on to people I speak to, in the street, in shops and so forth, that I'm a Hungarian visiting from abroad. They treat you differently if they know that. So I pretend I still live there and hope I don't come unstuck.'

'But isn't your Hungarian dated?' I ask. 'I know my parents and other 1956ers still use words and expressions from before the revolution which would be immediately obvious to those who have been living in Hungary for the last twenty-five years.'

'I've kept in touch,' says Paul. 'I have a circle of old school-friends with whom I've never lost contact. I see them whenever I'm there and still speak the same language. So I never really feel like an outsider when I'm in Hungary.'

'And you obviously don't feel like an outsider here,' I add. 'You're at home in both places. Unlike me, who feels a bit of a bloody foreigner everywhere.'

Paul is shaking his head. 'That's not quite so. I do consider myself a foreigner living here, but that doesn't matter. There is a well-respected place for us in this society. Despite their reputation, the English aren't more xenophobic than anyone else. My God, look at the French.

'But in any case, I don't think of myself in terms of nationality. Even though others do. For instance if I stay up all night working in my office, when my colleagues come in the next morning they say, "I don't know how you Hungarians do it." It makes things easier for people if they categorize you, it enables them to make judgements.

'There is one thing which I have always felt distances me from the native English. My lack of an English childhood. When I was in my early twenties, all around me my peers were going to the weddings of friends they'd grown up with, been at school with. And the children's literature which is second nature to the English, all of that rich background is unknown or, at best, third nature to me. And such things are important.'

When he was thirty-seven Paul entered a new medium — television. 'That's quite late to start something totally different,' he says. 'Television people asked me why I didn't think of going to them fifteen years earlier. But it was accidental, just a matter of chance. That's the way most things have happened to me throughout my life. I was throwing out some newspapers when an advertisement caught my eye. London Weekend was looking for a reporter to work on *The London Programme*. I had nothing better to do that day, so I just went along. . .'

Paul had grown a little tired of his role as commentator on Eastern European affairs. The ad offered an opportunity for change. All of a sudden he realized that he had been living for twenty years in one of the most exciting, newsworthy places in the world and yet never written about it. So he escaped from his pigeon-hole.

He is now one of the five producers of *Weekend World* and the programmes which he originates deal with every sort of topical subject. His work has at last widened to include the affairs of the entire world, but perhaps his imagination will continue to be fired most effectively by the dramas of Eastern Europe. His most acclaimed work since entering television has been the five-part series, *Stalin — The Red Tsar*, which he co-wrote. As I said in my introduction, you can't get blasted into the air by a revolution and not remain somewhat scorched.

His views on the state of immigration and the state of mind of the immigrant were written nearly two decades ago, but they are just as apt today, when there are more refugees than ever to whom they might apply:

Your complete freedom from roots, from burdens, as well as from absolutism, is also a freedom to all. There is nothing to rely on there, except a vague terrifying knowledge that no one but yourself can pull you up. . .It is also then that the new life flows in on you and with luck recreates itself and that you go through in a short time the unconscious assimilation for which the natives had had all the leisure of childhood. . .It is as near as we shall ever come to the outmoded mystic notions of death and rebirth. . .

What becomes of us — what does one become? English? No. Hungarian? No. A composite which is stronger and weaker than the environment. But perhaps that is part of what maturity means. I could not say for certain because uncertainty itself is part of it. A child with a freshness of vision and an adult in not dismissing with contempt the child in itself. A being with some standards which are the flexible ones of tolerance and thus hardly standards at all, but which would yet be worth fighting for. Like a man's right to be what he is and not what he does, or to defend the basis of his life even if others think he should live another, nearer the ideal. A suspect for all kinds of fertile vices and fruitful indecisions, with memories mused over till they are painless and plans which if unrealized are ploughed back to make the ground for new ones. An unruly character with some respect for the freedom of order and a heretic who gives the god his due for the price of ignoring him. Altogether, someone belonging here.

Ten

One afternoon Little Mári, Pali and I took the two children for a ride on the Pioneer Train which runs to the top of Freedom Hill. It is operated and manned mostly by pubescent 'Pioneers', the Hungarian equivalent of boy scouts and girl guides.

We rode through pleasant woods, the sun streaking thinly through the trees. On board were a party of German tourists, a few parents with small children and a couple of elderly people out for some fresh air. Soon after we left the quiet little station a boy of about thirteen, looking frightfully efficient in his blue uniform and conductor's cap, came around punching tickets. His complexion was like a half-ripe peach. He wore a red neckerchief which Adam (with his scant regard for authority) tried to grab. The downy-cheeked cadre frowned with disapproval.

We sat in an open carriage, enjoying the pine-scented fragrance of the hillside. Pali pointed to a fenced-in complex of buildings.

'Look there. That's a Pioneer summer camp. Those who acquire special distinctions and awards are allowed to go there for a two-week holiday.'

I hate to be disparaging, but the only thing more absurd than one of those self-important uniformed teenyboppers is a uniformed teenybopper with a chestful of medals.

A short walk from the terminus at the top is an adventure playground, where Adam and Little Pali spent an hour clambering over and under and through all kinds of bizarre constructions. Then we took a long slow stroll. We passed a group of picnickers and that made us feel peckish so we had coffee and cakes at a nearby café. For a while we walked along a path beside the Pioneer railway line. A bright, neat train passed us by. Adam and Little Pali waved to the passengers. I caught a glimpse of another blue uniform, another red neckerchief. Then the upright young conductor gave us a short, swift salute. For an instant I was reminded of an old Shirley Temple film I'd once seen. I think she did something like that. But at least she had dimples.

When the sun fell below the trees and it began to grow cool on the hill, we returned to the terminus and took the next train down to Budakeszi Avenue. As we neared the house we could smell the *krumpli paprikás* that Juszti had made for dinner. I hoped there was plenty of cucumber salad to go with it. These are the joys of being Hungarian.

'It's nice on that hill,' I told my mother as we sipped drinks together on the terrace.

'What did you see?' she asked.

'Oh, a lot of lovely trees, the summer camp, the playground at the top.'

'Playground?'

'Yes, near the terminus. Just down the road from a big hotel, the Red Star, I think it's called.'

My mother finished her Campari and put the glass down on a small table. 'Well,' she said, an odd look coming over her face, 'there was no playground there during my "holiday" on that hill. But I do remember the Red Star, certainly. The hotel I stayed at wasn't far away.' Her voice was strange. I looked at her.

'What do you mean, when was that?'

'November 1944. I was staying at the Hotel Majestic.'

'With whom?'

'About forty other detainees. You might say we were all the "guests" of Peter Hain, the head of the Gestapo in Hungary. He had taken over the hotel for his headquarters. One Sunday in November two plainclothesmen came to the door. I was just on my way out to the theatre where I was expected to give an evening performance. I was worried about being late. They took me to the Majestic. And I did miss the performance, by three weeks.'

Vaguely I remembered that my mother had had some trouble during the Nazi occupation. I knew several Jews had hidden in her house. An elderly couple still wrote to her from Tel Aviv, and another woman from Cologne. But now I was there, in the house where it had all happened. I wanted to know where they had hidden, where they had slept, what had happened to them, how they had escaped.

'Shall we go on a tour, then?' my mother suggested. I helped her to her feet. Her knee was still painful. She took hold of her crutches and led the way.

We went into her bedroom. There was a built-in wardrobe along one wall and she opened its heavy oak door. She slid a row of dresses to one side and patted the wall behind.

'That's a false wall,' she said. 'Behind it is a fairly large triangular space, the cavity above the staircase. But no one can see that. When the men called at the house that day, the cook kept them waiting for a while at the gate, pretending to search for her key. It gave us time to get everyone behind this wall and cover up the traces. There were six people in there, most of them weren't even able to stand up properly, because of the slanted wall. The men searched everywhere. They came into the bedroom, opened the wardrobe, scattered my clothes. But they found nothing.'

'Who were the six people?'

'There were the Mandels — Jenő and Szerén — who were already quite old by then, and Szerén's sister Olga. And Margit Herzog and her twelve-year-old daughter, Marietta. The Herzogs had been a wealthy industrial family with a large mansion on Andrássy Avenue. Margit's husband had already been caught and killed, his body thrown into the Danube. And then there was my cook's son. He wasn't Jewish, just an army deserter. One day he was home on leave, visiting his mother, the next day he had deserted. They beseeched me to let him stay. What could I do? He joined the others in the wardrobe. We all knew that the penalty for harbouring a deserter was the same as for harbouring a Jew. But he had nowhere else to go.'

'Why did they suspect you in the first place?'

'Before they threw the body of Margit's husband into the river, they searched his pockets. They found a piece of paper on which was scrawled simply "*Vali - művésznő*". I believe a friend had passed it on to him to let him know where his family was. But I only learnt about all this later, while I was being held up on the hill. Of course in those days it had another name: Schwáb Hill.

'So I was taken to Mr Hain. We slept in a cold, crowded room. There were women, old people, children, mostly Jewish, mostly awaiting deportation. I remember one police guard was kind to me. He was wearing a pair of thick, fur-lined gloves. He took them off and gave them to me to put under my head as a pillow. When the Soviets took over, this same guard came to me asking for help. He was being interrogated, and hoped that I would say a few words on his behalf. I told the communists all that I knew — that he had been kind and humane.' Silently she closed the wardrobe door.

'Why did Peter Hain finally let you go?' I asked.

'First of all they couldn't prove anything. They hadn't found anyone here during their search. And that same night, after I was

166

taken away, the people who had been hiding here slipped out into the darkness and fog to find some other refuge. They left carefully, one by one. They didn't know it, but the occupation was to end within a month.

'I was lucky, too, because certain friends in the resistance movement acted on my behalf. One of them was very close to me, he was a well-known writer, a Jew. Shortly before my detention he was escorting me home one evening, when he suddenly stopped and asked me to wait outside a house while he went inside. He was only there for a moment. When we reached home I asked him who lived there. "It's a safe-house," he replied. "I had to speak to the man who runs it, an extraordinary person, a Swede. Perhaps you've heard of him. His name is Raoul Wallenberg." My friend didn't survive the war. Not long after he helped me to get released from the Majestic he was killed by the Hungarian fascists, the Arrow Cross. I heard that he was first tortured. They did a lot of that. I know, because there was not one day or night during my three weeks on Schwáb Hill that I didn't hear the screams, the cries.' She shuddered. 'Come on, let's go down to the cellar.'

My mother leant heavily on my arm as we went downstairs. There was a light switch by the cellar door. But even when the dark steps had been illuminated, it didn't seem an inviting place. It smelled of dry rot and old, discarded things. It was a large cellar, composed of three separate chambers. We entered the first one. The atmosphere crawled up my spine.

'I've taken you here because this is where Jenő and Szerén slept. On a camp bed in that corner there.'

'It couldn't have been very pleasant or warm here in November,' I said.

My mother looked at me briefly. 'You say some damned obvious things, my girl.' She stood with one hand against the wall for support, studying with intensity the place where the bed had once stood.

'Did the plainclothesmen come down here, too?' I asked.

'Of course. And when they saw the bed they asked who had been sleeping in it. One of the men felt the sheets to see if they were warm. "Someone's been lying here recently. Who was it?" he demanded. I told them my cousin from the country had been staying with me and only left that afternoon.'

We went upstairs just as Juszti was laying the table for dinner. For once, the room actually seemed cheerful. The odours from the kitchen were tantalizing, lights were burning everywhere and Pali had lit a fire in the big Transylvanian tiled stove, which filled the room with warmth.

My mother sat down at the piano and began to play an old song from some battered sheet music. I asked what had happened to her after Peter Hain let her go. She answered without looking up from the keys.

'Oh, my problems had only just begun. I soon found myself in even worse trouble. The Gestapo had been horrific, but no different from those seeking revenge after their defeat.'

'You mean the Soviets?'

'And the Hungarians, those who were out to get blood at all costs.'

She told me how, during the *ostrom*, the seige of Budapest, the Red Army had finally forced the German troops into the centre of the city towards their ultimate stronghold, the Castle. By 24 December the Budakeszi Avenue area was under Soviet control, although there was still some crossfire going on. On that evening, Christmas Eve, Soviet troops entered my mother's house. They used it as a resting place before the final attack on the Germans. When they learnt that my mother was a singer they asked her to sing and play the piano for them. The soldiers assembled in the sitting-room, they sat in the chairs and lay on the floor. Serenely they listened as she sang to them, 'Silent night, holy night'. They heard shooting in the distance. Then a stray bullet shattered the window beside the piano, it whizzed past my mother's head and wounded one of the soldiers on the floor.

The Russian soldiers had a reputation for raping women and ransacking homes during their conquest of the city. But a Red Army colonel decided to make his billet in my mother's house. He was an honest, respectable man. 'It was because of his presence here, I'm sure, that the soldiers always behaved impeccably with me,' she said. 'He had an unquestionable authority. I also swiftly realized another fortunate thing for me — the Russians are very fond of singers and actors.'

Further up the avenue the house of a friend of my mother's, a baroness, was raided by the advancing Russians. They vandalized the house and terrorized the woman and her family, shouting at them and calling them dirty capitalists. They were forced to flee. The baroness asked my mother for help. Through the colonel's influence and protection, the aristocratic family was allowed to move into my mother's house. She gave them her bedroom.

Another time she was in the garden watching captive German

soldiers being marched up the avenue by the Russian victors. One German officer could barely walk. His feet were swollen and his boots were falling apart. He was ordered to move faster. Instead, he fell to the ground. A mounted Russian trampled on top of him. My mother could stand it no longer. She ran to the iron gate and cried out for him to stop. She had learnt a few words of Russian by then. One of the soldiers from the house hurried out to the gate and pulled her back in. 'Do you want to get yourself shot?' he yelled.

But the greatest danger came later, when a group of newly empowered Hungarian communists came to my mother's door, announcing that she was to be taken away and shot as a Nazi collaborator. They claimed that she hadn't really been detained on Schwáb Hill by Hain, but had been working for him as an informer. She protested, she struggled. Just as she was being dragged from the house, the colonel, whose name was Valyushka, arrived back in his jeep. He demanded to know what was going on.

He wouldn't allow them to take my mother anywhere. 'She's coming with me,' he said. He put her into the jeep and drove her to the Red Army headquarters. There she was given a hearing and allowed to send for witnesses. It soon became clear that the charge was a fabrication. She and Valyushka drove home together.

Months afterwards, those who had tried to have her shot came to the house. My mother met them by the gate.

'We've come to apologize,' they said.

'I cannot accept your apology,' my mother replied. 'And don't ever come near this house again.'

Sometime in the mid-1960s Valyushka returned to Budapest, on holiday with his wife and teenage son. He wanted to show them where he had stayed during the winter of 1944/45 when the Red Army had crushed the Germans holding Budapest. He wanted them to meet the singer he had told them about. He rang the bell at the gate. Juszti came out and spoke to him.

'I'm afraid the *művésznő* doesn't live here any more. The family left Hungary in 1956, just after the uprising. When your army came for the second time.'

That was another winter to remember.

Géza's wife Gizi and I were rattling into town in her little off-white Trabant. We felt every crack, every lump in the road. We were like

169

the last two cigars in a plastic cigar box. We were out to have a 'women's day', just the two of us, and discuss all the things that women like to talk about when their husbands aren't there, like other men and in-laws and breast-feeding.

It was Gizi's idea that we should go to the famous Lukács Turkish baths at the foot of Gellért Hill. 'I haven't had my pores opened in ages,' she said. Budapest has many thermal springs, centred around the hill. The Turks, as everyone knows, have always taken advantage of such warm, natural mineral waters. The Lukács and other similar baths stand above the ruins of the original baths built during the Turkish occupation.

We bought our tickets, deposited our clothes inside a dressing cubicle and walked through the door into a great, labyrinthine orgy of heat. I have to admit, however, that the members were anything but orgiastic. There was no one under the age of about seventy (all women, of course) and I had never seen so many forms of decrepitude. There were a dozen pairs of bowed legs bending under the strain of roll upon roll of sagging, surplus flesh. As far as the eye could see (not too far because of the steam) there were bosoms which had long since given up trying to be anything like horizontal. There were pale, wrinkled, ancient bottoms. But like so many nymphs in the Fountain of Youth, the women were floating, paddling, swirling about in several thermal baths of various temperatures.

Gizi and I stood surveying the scene in the short white robes we had been given. Gizi's eyeglasses were getting steamed up, so she took them off to wipe them. 'Let's cool off in here for a bit,' she said and we went into a massage room. There we found fatty rumps and limbs being rolled and kneaded with some sudsy lotion by two sturdy women in white shorts and bras.

One masseuse with muscular forearms of Olympic proportions eyed us inquisitively, so we retreated back into the steam. Gizi sat down daintily by the side of a square, tiled bath and dipped her toes into the water. She kicked a foot playfully, narrowly missing an aged, bulging midriff. She was glared at with the sort of suspicion which a fur-coated housewife from Scarsdale could expect to arouse in Harlem.

We moved further down the labyrinth, encountering more tiled baths containing unsightly nymphs. Somehow neither Gizi nor I fancied the idea of bobbing up and down amongst them. We passed a row of showers, though, and finally took off our robes to sample a thermal trickle. Then we looked through a steamy window into the Turkish bath itself. There was plenty of room on the wooden benches. The outline of a solitary figure could be seen, hunched at one end, like a haystack in a hot fog. We went inside and took a deep breath. Our lungs groaned open, our eyes began to swell in their sockets.

I sat down. I don't know how long I sat in that Turkish bath. Surrounded by steam, time as well as vision is obscured until you lose your hold on reality. The next thing I knew Gizi was tapping at the window from the outside, trying to get my attention. She was pressing her face against the glass and watching me with horror. By then I was feeling like someone's lunch which had been left too long in a pressure cooker. This reminded me that it was just about lunchtime and that we ought to find a nice restaurant. I stood up and staggered out the door.

'You look like an overdone stuffed tomato,' said Gizi.

'Please,' I told her, 'I'm hungry enough as it is.'

On the way out, there is a 'recovery room' with rows of beds where you can lie down and wrap yourself in sheets like a mummy. There is also a hairdresser's salon for restoring limp locks. We wrung ourselves out, dressed and reapplied our make-up. And for what? Outside it had started to rain. We made a dash for the Trabant.

Gizi knew of a good restaurant along the embankment in Pest. By the time we got there it was pouring. We skipped over a few puddles and ran up the steps. From the outside it seemed an old-fashioned, elegant place, but I was glad to find that it wasn't. It had a friendly, careless ambience. The kitchen was noisier than a bowling alley and nobody cared if you sat down in a wet raincoat.

We shared a table with two glamorous Polish girls. They were drenched in jewels and French perfume. They were making their way gracefully through some rather exotic dishes. One of them wore her hair in two braids as though she were a country girl, but you could tell it was merely caprice. She had the well-used, nebulous look of someone bred on the limited oxygen of a big city. When she finished eating she turned and asked me for a cigarette. We studied each other for a moment. Perhaps she thought I was an atypical Hungarian. I had to admit she seemed an unlikely sort of Pole. So far the ones I had seen in Budapest were unjewelled and unperfumed, they were wearing cheap clothes and standing at street corners selling meagre possessions to passers-by. The first time I saw these Poles I asked Dódi about them.

'They come to Budapest for short periods,' he told me, 'bringing things from home which they sell here in order to buy food. They stock up and take the food back with them. Our country has always liked the Poles. We understand them. We influence each other.' He lit his pipe and took a thoughtful puff. 'Unlike the Czechs and the Romanians. Ghastly bunch.'

So I gave the braided girl a cigarette and I offered her a light and our curiosity mingled in the smoke between us. Something like geniality swept across her features. Then we were distracted by a clatter and a shout from the kitchen.

After lunch Gizi and I stood on the steps of the restaurant.

'Where would you like to go now?' she asked. I looked at the wet street, the grey outlines of the buildings along the riverfront and the sky dense with cold, autumnal clouds. 'It's a bad day to be outside. How about going to Corvin, our lovely big department store?'

I shook my head. 'I haven't much money with me.'

'It doesn't cost anything to browse!'

'No. But I'm not in the mood for it.' I looked across to Buda. The hills seemed unreal through the rain, like billows of pale green vapour which had somehow frozen and now stood clinging to the air. I felt as though I could stretch out and put a hand through them. All of a sudden I knew where I wanted to go. 'Have you heard of the Hotel Majestic?'

Gizi hesitated. 'Yes, I think so. I've heard the name.'

'It's on Freedom Hill. It was used as Gestapo headquarters during the war. It must be a well-known landmark, don't you think?'

She nodded doubtfully.

I told her about my mother's incarceration there together with many other political prisoners. 'It was all highly intriguing. Can't we go and take a look?'

She went back into the restaurant to ask someone for directions. When she returned she said, 'Nobody in there has heard of the Majestic. Are you sure that's what it's called?'

'The name may have been changed, I suppose, since 1944. Come on, let's get in the car and drive up there. We can ask for information along the way.' I took her by the arm and she agreed, rather reluctantly, to this idea. She started up the Trabant's little washing-machine engine, turned on the two baby wind-screen wipers and launched off in the direction of Buda. My spine shivered, partly from anticipation, partly from the chilly drizzle.

There was a lot of traffic. We waited for a long time to cross the bridge. The city was exploding with charabancs and street cars, dodge'em-car taxis and *corps diplomatique* Arabs in black limousines. Everything spun in front of me. And all around us, winding their way down with the rain, were curled brown leaves.

It soon became obvious that Gizi didn't know the streets of Buda very well. I had a map in front of me which I perused, twisted this way and that, and strained my eyes to read. Sometimes we would admire the villas on the more exclusive roads and so miss an important turning. Then I would have to hold the map upside down so that we could retrace our steps. We mistakenly drove down one or two dirt tracks leading to mysterious mansions. And the light grew steadily dimmer.

I had imagined that we would reach the Majestic at about tea-time and perhaps have a leisurely cup or two there before going home. But I became more and more doubtful as to whether we'd find the hotel at all. We knew we had to head for the Red Star Hotel and the terminal station of the Pioneer Railway, but we were having trouble enough locating those. Let alone some edifice from the past which might no longer even exist. Our navigation left a lot to be desired.

We stopped a few pedestrians but no one had heard of the hotel. Gizi went into a tobacconist's. At last we splashed and bumped along by the railway. The tracks ran through a heavily wooded area with narrow, steep roads and very few houses. The trees began to appear as shadows and silhouettes, for dusk was near. In the daylight these trees and hills had been refreshing, but now there was something sinister about them. The higher up we went the darker it became and the blacker the branches overhead.

At the top we found the Red Star. Gizi went inside. I waited in the car. The wind eddied across the bonnet, it forced its way in through the cracks and I felt the damp cold creeping down my back. She took a long time. At last she reappeared.

'No luck,' she said, and I could see that she was getting fed up. 'I think they must all be too young in there. Post-war people, you know. The only older person is new to Budapest and barely knows what side of the Danube he's on.' She sighed.

'What next?' I was hoping she hadn't already given up.

'Someone said we should ask at the trade-union rest-house and cinema down the road. It's worth a try.'

We parked outside its gates. Inside there was a young girl at the reception desk. A middle-aged couple had just come down from one of the bedrooms. They greeted the receptionist lengthily, nodded to Gizi and me and babbled something about dinner. When they left it was silent and empty in the foyer. The girl of course knew nothing about the Majestic. But she summoned an older woman, a cleaner or cook or something, whose eyes widened with recognition when we mentioned the name.

'You want to find the street that runs parallel with the railway tracks, it's on the other side of this building. Go around the corner and turn right.'

'What's the name of the street?' I asked, excited that we were finally getting somewhere.

'Couldn't say.'

'Is it still called the Majestic?'

'Oh no, it isn't a hotel anymore. Just a big block of flats. Most people don't know it was once a hotel. Just as well. If they knew what had gone on in that place, well, who'd want to live there?'

Our spirits lifted, we were on our way. We drove slowly so as not to miss anything. We peered through the dripping trees and found the street which the old woman must have meant, the one running alongside the tracks. Gizi wiped the inside of the windscreen which our exhausted breaths had by now completely steamed up.

The search was on in earnest. We were like Holmes and Watson on the trail of some den of evil. But we were to be disappointed again. The road contained no big block of flats. It was dark now. The atmosphere on Freedom Hill was menacing. The sudden turns in the road, the woods that half hid unlit houses, the winding lanes that petered out into nothing. We were lost.

We stopped in front of a house. There was a man of thirty-five or so in the driveway, getting something out of a car. He came to the gate smiling pleasantly.

'Looking for somebody?'

Gizi explained. I didn't have much hope. The man was far too young to know anything of Peter Hain or the Gestapo. But I was mistaken.

'Sure, sure,' he nodded. 'I know the place. It's on Melinda Road. Not far from here, but it's a bit complicated to find. You might not see the street sign, it's so dark.'

Gizi and I looked at each other. She was sceptical. I was sanguine. 'All right,' said the man, 'follow my car. I'll lead you there.'

'Oh, thank you,' I croaked, for by now my throat was sore from the intemperate wind.

He took a couple of sharp turns, we followed him uphill for a moment, then we dipped downwards. He braked at the junction of two narrow roads. He rolled down his window and indicated for us to take the one on the left. There was a sign on a tree. With some difficulty I could make out the name: Melinda Road. Then our guide swerved around and was gone.

We rolled cautiously down the hill and almost at once we saw it — a huge murky-coloured building with narrow windows and peeling plaster. A few steps led to a dimly lit entrance.

We left the car on the opposite side of the road and I stepped out into a bog of slimy leaves and dirt.

We just stood staring at the building. Now that we had found it, we didn't know quite how to approach it.

'Shall we go in?' I asked.

'I don't know what on earth you expect to find. Still, we might as well, as we've come this far.'

Inside the door, occupants' mail boxes lined the walls. The hallway at the end was dingy. From behind one door came the sound of a television, from behind another, the smell of cooking meat. We couldn't see anyone. We glanced at the list of names by the bells at the door, but there was no porter or caretaker.

'This place is creepy,' said Gizi, 'let's go. What I need is a cup of scalding espresso and another pair of shoes.'

'Yes, I suppose we can go. I'm ready.' It was difficult to hide the disappointment in my voice. What had I expected to discover? It was just another drab, old block. But I had been hoping for more. A little sign of the past and my mother's presence there, some indication of what had happened within those unenticing walls. I derided my own naivety. Had I expected to find, tossed carelessly into a corner, those fur-lined gloves the guard had given my mother for a pillow? I turned and followed Gizi out of the door.

At that moment a man walked by, wearing a heavy raincoat and carrying a briefcase. I hurried down the steps to stop him. He was strongly built and upright, but I judged that he must be at least sixty.

'Please excuse me...' I began, and for some reason I was out of breath.

He was startled. 'Yes?'

'This building here,' I waved a hand towards the block, 'do you know about it? Do you know if it was ever the Hotel Majestic where they imprisoned and tortured people during the Nazi occupation?' Only a dim light fell on his face, but I could see that he

175

was no stranger to this query, and that he was trying to figure out who I might be.

'This is it,' he replied. 'Of course it hasn't been a hotel for a long time. And it doesn't look particularly *majestic* now, does it? But it was once a very popular and elegant place. It used to be full of well-bred people during the summer months.'

'You knew it during the occupation?'

'I should say so. I've been living almost all my life just down the road. When Hain took over the hotel several of the residents were forced to move away under orders from the Gestapo. They wanted as few people as possible nearby, because it was obvious to anyone who wasn't deaf what was going on inside. There was terrible screaming.' He smiled at me and tilted his head inquisitively. 'Why are you so interested?'

I told him about my mother. 'I suppose you don't often think about those days as you pass by the old hotel,' I observed, as much to myself as to him.

'I wouldn't say that. And occasionally someone reminds me, just in case I should forget. For instance, a few weeks ago I was approached by the director of a Polish documentary film crew. They were shooting a film about the fate of Polish Jews in Hungary during the war. They filmed the building from all angles. And they had the right idea: they shot it at night. You see, at night the Majestic always became more terrifying. No one ever lingered around here, amidst the fear and death. But do excuse me, I'm getting very wet.'

We returned to the car. A few minutes later we were descending back towards the river. The distant lights and traffic noises were an immense relief.

'What an awful place,' said Gizi somewhat absent-mindedly. I believe she was concerned about her wet shoes, which, according to the instructions, were due to fall apart at any moment.

'I agree.' I turned around for a last look at the hill, the black mound which had, for me, come to embody everything which was evil and fearful. It was all so clear now why Hain had chosen that place as his domain. The endless dark woods not only screened his activities, but intimidated his victims. Here there could be no hope, they must have felt, only death.

I thought of Ervin's words: my generation must always keep in mind the tragedies of the war. I think that that night, for the first time, I sensed and understood what it must have been like for someone stupefied by fear on a wet, cold night, like that night in

November 1944 when my mother was taken to the Majestic. I think I sensed it. But maybe I am wrong. Maybe such things are beyond transmission.

I was called downstairs by Juszti. 'Someone has come to see you,' she said. I drew back the heavy curtains at the bottom of the staircase to find a tall, slim woman who appeared familiar. She greeted me warmly but casually. Juszti told me that she was Teréz, a neighbour and long-standing friend of my parents. Then I saw a Scottish terrier standing by her feet and remembered that she was the woman who had passed by the house one day and waved to Juszti in the garden while I watched from the terrace.

'I had to see you,' said Teréz. 'I wasn't sure when you were returning to London. I thought we might do something together one day.' There was a softness about her which I liked. Her voice was soft, her hair fell in soft waves around her face. And her eyes, although a light blue, didn't have that cold brittle quality which so often comes with blue eyes. She seemed a genial companion altogether and I said I would be happy to arrange to do something with her.

'Fine. Can you come to my house tomorrow, say at one? I'm just around the corner, past the headquarters of the State Security Border Guards.'

'I'll see you then.'

'Good. I'll think of an interesting agenda for us.'

The next day I strolled around the block and as I neared the border control compound I slowed my steps and then stood for a moment on the opposite side of the pavement to get a good look at it. Until 1948 it had been a home for Jesuits. Manning the barrier before the driveway were two green-uniformed guards. They were chatting amicably, rifles lying across their knees.

I thought of a tiny episode from 1956. During late October and the beginning of November, while the revolution was victorious, huge numbers of Soviet tanks and troops had been steadily streaming into the country. On Sunday, 4 November, they finally overran Budapest and crushed the revolution with one mighty military operation. After that there were tanks everywhere in the city. Some were stationed outside the border guards' headquarters.

In the middle of November my brother and I were playing outside and wandered beyond our garden fence. We crossed the gardens of one or two neighbours and emerged on the quiet road parallel to Budakeszi Avenue, where Teréz lives. We approached a tank and the Russian soldiers standing by it. I don't suppose we could speak to each other, but we must have hit it off rather well, for a short while later we ran home clutching a few Russian coins.

'Look! Look what the soldiers gave us!' we said excitedly.

They must have been nice young men. Yet earlier, they and others like them were responsible for the deaths of thousands, including small children like us. That is, if they weren't themselves killed, burnt alive in their tanks by a Molotov cocktail, the coins in their pockets the only remains.

The guards looked up and saw me. As I moved on, a shiny Lada drove up to the barrier. It carried a single passenger in the back seat, a man who bore the unmistakable marks of a V.I.P. fish in a small satellite pond. The guards saluted and let the car through. I hurried along to Teréz's house.

Her house is sparsely furnished. The single room downstairs has large windows with rusty grills, overlooking a simple garden. A staircase of dark wood leads to the two upstairs bedrooms. There is a wooden cross on one wall and a couple of religious pictures. No other ornaments or decorations. It struck me as a melancholy house. Not the sort of place where you can imagine a boisterous all-night party taking place.

'We're going on a guided coach tour around the city,' she told me. 'Afterwards we can take a look at some of the great Hungarian paintings at the National Gallery in the Castle.'

The tour departed from Engels Square. In our coach were several young Germans, a Japanese family and three Australian businessmen in immaculate pin-striped suits. The guide was a middle-aged Hungarian woman, a bit on the dowdy side. She was meant to tell us about Budapest in both English and German, but few words of either language were distinguishable. Her verbal concoctions were on a par with those of a slightly disorientated toddler. I felt most sympathy for the Japanese. They might as well have been riding along the streets of Ulan Bator. But I was all right. Teréz was my private guide.

We stopped at Heroes' Square, built to commemorate the Millennium in 1896. In the centre are the statues of Chief Árpád of the conquering Magyar tribe and his lieutenants. On a sweeping semi-circular colonnade behind stand the great kings, princes and regents of Hungarian history. King St Stephen, King Béla IV, János Hunyadi, King Matthias, Ferenc Rákóczi II, Kossuth. So many noble heads, fearless chins and broad brows. The sort of people you don't trifle with. The course of history depends not so much on battles and campaigns as on powerful faces.

And so we went on, past the famous Gundel Restaurant, the decaying zoo, the City Park, the Semmelweis Hospital. Then we crossed the river to Buda and climbed up to the Fishermen's Bastion, the Matthias Church and the Hilton Hotel where we had tea and cakes. From there it is a short walk to the Castle, so we strode off together down the cobbled street, leaving the others behind.

The gallery is vast; there are several entrances. It is spacious and modern and very clean. Rather like the underground. To see the paintings there is to learn the story of Hungary and the Magyar race. Wars, invasions, social upheavals, the poor, the aristocracy, the lush countryside with its peasant revolts, rape and pillage by the Turks, Sándor Petőfi writing poems in an army encampment, Hunyadi's last farewell, and always kings and sumptuous queens and patron saints.

Bursting from the pictures so forcefully that you could almost hear them were an array of emotions, all highly charged. Determination, pride, courage, anguish, panic, hope, misery. They added up to an overwhelming sense of *national intensity*. It's the sort of thing which leaps at you from most of Petőfi's work, for example 'I am a Magyar', written in 1847:

I am a Magyar. I look proudly over the sea of our past where my eyes encounter mountains that tower into the sky — these are your great deeds, my heroic nation. We have played on the stage of Europe, and ours was not the smallest role. Our sword frightened the world as lightning terrifies a child.

These sentences belong to an idiom which cannot really be translated into the English language, because English-speaking people are unaccustomed to expressing them. And so to us they are a little embarassing, they go a bit too far. But in 1848 Petőfi's emotive words ignited the Hungarian people, they lent fire to the War of Independence. And when he, a young poet of genius, died in battle, he became one of its greatest martyrs. In the final analysis, we remember words more than actions, the mood rather than the scenario.

The upper floors of the gallery command an exquisite view of Budapest. Teréz and I paused in front of a tall window. The colour of the city startled me. Perhaps it was due to the angle at which the sun was filtering through a bed of cloud. For while most cities seen from a distance appear grey or grey-blue or even grey-pink, Budapest was laid out before us like a giant, very old photograph which had been tinted ever so softly with sepia.

This delighted me and before I could stop myself I clapped my hands together and cried, 'How wonderful!' thus provoking a disapproving glance from the guard by the door.

'Yes,' Teréz whispered, 'each time I stand here I'm thrilled by this view. And I've been living here for forty years.'

'Where are you from originally?'

'Salzburg.'

'Do you mean you're not Hungarian?' I asked, somewhat bewildered. She had no trace of accent.

'I'm Austrian. I came here when I was twenty. I spoke nothing but German then. But soon I met my husband, a Hungarian, and it didn't take long for me to learn the language.'

'Well, you've certainly learnt it perfectly. I don't suppose anyone here can tell you're not really a native.'

She smiled appreciatively. 'My husband spoke beautifully and he was a patient teacher.'

'What was his profession?'

'He was a lawyer.'

'He died a long time ago?' (Several years' experience as a journalist has, I'm afraid, implanted within me an unconscious but compulsive tendency to interview people, to *get the facts*.)

'In 1961. There had been a great deal of difficulty ever since the revolution. He had been responsible for initiating a passive resistance movement after the suppression of the uprising. He drew together a group of people, many lawyers among them, whose aim was to reject the strictures of communist totalitarianism not by violent means, but simply by refusing to comply with them. By ignoring them, in fact, and withdrawing their co-operation.'

'How far did this movement get?'

Teréz shook her head and sat down on the leather window seat. 'They all lost their jobs and were blacklisted. My husband was finally imprisoned in 1958. He received amnesty in 1960, but of course they wouldn't allow him to practise as a lawyer anymore. He eventually found work as a porter in a warehouse, loading and unloading heavy boxes. Then he started as an apprentice lift repairman. But before he could finish his apprenticeship, he died.'

She paused, I watched her face attentively. She waited for a small group of tourists to drift past, then continued.

'Throughout all those terrible years he managed to keep his

180

sailboat, which he adored. While he was in prison he begged me to look after it for him. I was never much interested in sailing, so at weekends, during the last three years of his life, he used to go with friends to sail on the Balaton. Or sometimes he went alone. It was after one of these lone sailing jaunts that he didn't return when I expected him. I waited. I just sat at home waiting for hours. I agonized. All night. The next day someone rang me up. His boat had capsized, he had drowned.' I slipped noiselessly into the seat next to her. 'I've always had my doubts about what happened.'

'Do you mean that he may have been killed?'

'I think the authorities still considered him a "trouble-maker".' Teréz looked at me, sighed and gave me a faint, friendly smile. 'I'll never know anything for certain.'

I asked her how she had been coping all these years since her husband's death.

'They've been twenty busy years — I've had to keep busy in order to earn my living. I've been a secretary at the Egyptian and Swiss embassies, and I've done translation work for Corvina, the state publishing firm. I'm retired now, but I still do part-time work, as much as I'm allowed to. My pension isn't very large. It is possible for a woman to survive on her own. Lonely, but possible.'

'Have you never considered returning to Austria?'

'For what? It's too late for that. I've lived here for forty years. I'll never be genuinely Hungarian, but I'll stay here now for the rest of my life.'

'I nodded. 'Yes, you have memories here. . .'

'Actually,' she said, tilting her head slightly towards me, 'you haven't really got a home, either. Have you?' She gazed steadily at me with her clear blue eyes.

I was surprised by her words. We had been discussing her life, and suddenly my own had become the topic of conversation.

'It's true, I've always been in a cocoon of one sort or another, never quite managing to blend inconspicuously into my surroundings,' I replied.

'I think we have something in common,' Teréz said. 'But I've decided that it doesn't matter where you were born, where you live or what others consider you to be. As long as you find contentment. And that's something that can be found anywhere. It just depends on the person who is looking for it.'

'Yes,' I hesitated, 'I agree with that, but I think there's another factor involved. Since I've been here I've discovered something about myself. I've always fancied myself as a cosmopolitan, a "citizen of the world", a free agent who can be anywhere and at the same time nowhere. And that is still largely true. I don't believe in plastering yourself, physically, mentally or emotionally, to any one spot on the globe.

'But these last weeks I've found, to my own astonishment, that I've learnt to treasure a feeling which is diametrically opposed to this view. The feeling of returning to the womb, the only place where your existence is never questioned but accepted as inevitable. For me, it's come as a startling reassurance that no matter where I live, how far I go or for how long, no matter what language I speak or what habits I pick up from foreign parts, there will always be somewhere a cluster of relatives, a tribe, which considers me an undeniable part of itself. I may feel that the world is mine, but there is only one corner of it where I needn't account for myself, or struggle for a place in the superstructure.'

I stood up and looked once again out of the window. It was impossible to resist the city below us. I saw the green dome of Parliament and further upriver, Margaret Island, the *Ile de la Cité* of Budapest. I noticed that the traffic was building up on the Chain Bridge. For the first time, I studied the lines of the bridge itself, the long, elegant sweep of the 'chain' in the middle.

I thought of a story I had once heard, about a Hungarian writer who was visiting London. The day before his return home he was sitting by the window of a café with a friend, just sipping tea and looking out at the street. The friend asked him whether there was something special he wished to take back with him, some little item peculiar to London. 'Yes,' he said, *'that.'* He pointed to a bobby strolling by outside.

If that bobby could symbolize the spirit of London for a Hungarian writer, then, I decided, what I would like to take home with me is the vision of this bridge. For it occurred to me that my entire trip to Hungary was an attempt to build a bridge of my own, some kind of construction which would allow me to pass from one side of my life to the other, from childhood to adulthood, from East to West, from my inherited background to the life which I have chosen to lead in London.

And it seemed fitting to picture my bridge as being one long chain. Each encounter, each conversation, each discovery (no matter how infinitesimal) was another link in the chain. And one day it would all be spread out before me to examine and test.

But I knew, also, that I would have to tread carefully. I had a feeling that my construction might not necessarily last a lifetime.

In fact, it was more like a paper bridge, delicate and lightly assembled. And something which is made of paper must be taken out once in a while and checked, handled gently. It may require another bit of glue here or there. The greatest danger is neglect. If you forget about it, one day you will find it in pieces, and then what was the point of building it in the first place?

Teréz was standing next to me now, speaking softly. 'I like to come here sometimes on a cold winter's afternoon, when there's no one else about. Just for half an hour or so. I look at a few pictures, then gaze out this window and when I've had my fill of the panorama, go home again. At such times this is the most peaceful place to be. And a lot warmer than my house.'

We took the bus home. As we walked back to my mother's house, Teréz told me, sadly, how the street had changed since the forties and fifties.

'There used to be open green spaces between some of the houses. Now they've put up dull blocks of flats there. And it used to be so quiet around here. No huge lorries.'

'Do you still have many friends in the neighbourhood?'

'Hardly any. Some have died, some have gone abroad. And then there are those who were forced to leave Budapest during the *kitelepités* and have never come back since.'

Later I went to Mári and Dódi's flat to phone my husband at his office in London. I could dial directly from their place; their number is on one of Budapest's more efficient exchanges.

How odd to hear his secretary's voice come on the line. And then Robin's.

'What's been happening over there?' he bellowed.

'It's all right, you needn't shout this time, I can hear you.'

'Good, good. How's Adam?'

'Having a smashing time.'

'Great. And what have you been up to?'

'Oh,' I paused. 'Actually, if you really want to know, I've been building a bridge. Of paper.'

'What? Hold on a second, someone's just come in.' He discussed some files with a colleague. I heard rustling and I thought of his open-plan office with its scurrying articled clerks and hot-drink vending machines. It seemed at least as far away as Neptune. He turned back to the receiver. 'Now, what were you saying, something about a bridge?'

I realized that I couldn't begin to explain, not on the telephone to Neptune, with people coming in to talk about files and the office boys dropping letters into the in-tray and the secretary bringing a cup of tea and a doughnut.

'I'll tell you another time,' I said. 'It can wait.'

My mother's friend Cica, which means Kitten (I have already gone into the nation's habit of choosing nicknames from within the animal kingdom), is small and blonde and has the air of a *femme de monde*. I don't use the phrase lightly. The Parisian influence has been great on Cica. Her sang-froid is remarkable and her conversation, which is *sans gêne*, and even occasionally *outré*, is truly in the tradition of the *grandes dames* of Paris.

Copies of *France Soir* and *Paris Match* are strewn all over her bright, cluttered flat. We were sitting there, sipping the odd cocktails which she had mixed for us. She got up to play an old Edith Piaf record.

'You're going to ruin that machine one of these days,' said Attila, her son, following her and pulling her away just as she was about to experiment with the dials and buttons.

'It's my machine, you know,' she said, pretending to be cross and blowing smoke into his face.

'That doesn't mean you can use it.'

'True.' She sat down and crossed her legs. 'Let's drink to Piaf.' She raised her glass. Then the music started. 'What the hell is that?' she demanded.

'The Moody Blues.'

Cica shrugged and watched out of the corner of her eye as Attila did some fancy dancing around the room. He is fortyish, a bachelor, and isn't in the least embarrassed by people sipping drinks and watching him prance all over the carpet.

For a long time Cica has been trying to convince Attila that he should find a wife. But he always has some excuse. For several years he said he couldn't possibly get married while his grandmother was alive. 'But why?' Cica would ask. 'She needs to be looked after. I have to give her my undivided attention,' Attila would say, probably while packing his suitcase for another foreign trip (he travelled a great deal as a member of a national sports team). At last his grandmother died. Again Cica wanted to know when he would marry. 'When you snuff it, too,' he replied.

When she was young Cica wanted to be a professional dancer, but her parents didn't approve of this manifestation of the French artistic spirit, so she became a pharmacist instead. But the bohemian Franco-Hungarian tradition was not so easily abandoned. Perhaps the Magyar poets and artists no longer feel that sublime attraction to Paris, but every summer Cica goes on a pilgrimage to her cousin on the Cote d'Azur. She has spent her life as a pharmacist on the Széchenyi Embankment, but she has secretly been roaming all the while along the hills of Montmartre, through the Bois de Boulogne, up and down the Champs Elysée.

Attila's stepfather is an overworked lecturer in mechanical engineering. He sat next to me, chain-smoking and discussing in a tired, monotonous voice the mountain of work which was heaped on his shoulders. I didn't think he had much of the French influence in him until I realized that, in fact, he looked rather like one of those old, droopy Citröens.

Attila was still twisting and high-stepping in the middle of the room. I had to admit he had a good sense of rhythm. But no modesty, no modesty whatsoever. He flicked his wrists and jerked his jaw and all the time he was grinning the sickly grin of a man who believes he has accomplished a magnificent feat by reaching the age of forty without being hooked into matrimony.

Of course, all this is not in the least surprising. Frankly, it would take an extraordinary sort of woman to want to marry Attila. For a start, she'd have to have amazing patience just to put up with his shameless, frequent bouts of dancing. But that's not all. It's difficult to have a serious conversation with him because of the expression which is always rampant on his face. It's the look you would expect to see on the face of a clown who is perturbed at having been caught backstage with only half his make-up on.

I have known him for a long time. He has been to London on several occasions with the Hungarian fencing team. The team would usually stay at the house of one of their English counterparts and have a ball. According to Attila, every morning a different ravishing girl would bring the morning tea to their bedrooms. I suppose that's his idea of a pretty good time. Just as well he's never got married.

Whenever he was in London he'd do the rounds of the record shops and discotheques. Once he took me to Tiffany's. He's the sort of person who requires a lot of space when he's dancing, but the floor was so crowded that he couldn't give full vent to his irrepressible movements. So he prowled about morosely like a caged animal. Eventually I danced with someone else and Attila never forgave me. He wouldn't call a taxi to take me home. We walked.

Not many of the people I know in Hungary are able to come to London or have a particular reason for doing so. Those who come are mostly involved in sports, the arts or commerce. Or they have a relative or friend who can send them the all-important 'letter of invitation' which makes it easier to get a visa because the visitor isn't allowed to take any money out of Hungary. Most things tend to boil down to money. With a letter of invitation a person can travel every other year to the West. Without one, for those who must buy convertible currency, it's only once every three years. And then the amount they're allowed to take with them is so ridiculously small that they're forced into black market transactions. Somebody has a friend who knows somebody else who has a few dollars or Deutschmarks hidden away. . . It's a way of life.

There are people, like Pista's wife Judith, who are inexplicably drawn to England. But, on the whole, it isn't the sort of country a Hungarian would choose to visit. The Anglo-Saxon temperament and style of life are so removed from basic Magyar instincts. Perhaps it can be summed up as the difference between a static island people and a nomadic tribe which has swept across a continent, bared itself to attacks from the East and the West, and finally, in a shrewd attempt at self-preservation, rejected heathenism in favour of Christianity.

All this may have happened a thousand years ago, but the factors which forge a nationality can't be so easily discarded. The decisive element has remained intact: the Magyar 'tribe' is still as vulnerable as ever, and those characteristics of shrewdness, watchfulness, suspicion and self-protection are just as crucial to survival. And what could contrast more with the undertones, the impartiality and coolness of the English?

Those Hungarians lucky enough to get visas to the West and a little bit of money, therefore, will more often be drawn to Austria, Germany, Switzerland, France, Italy. These countries are nearer in spirit as well as geographically. And in any case, an island is less accessible, its very inaccessibility giving it another layer of remoteness and mystery.

For these reasons I'm often astonished at the number of Hungarians who actually live in England, who have made their homes there and become completely at one with their surroundings. I don't know whether it is a certain 'type' of Hungarian who is drawn to the English life, or whether being there for years and years alters their natures somewhat. One thing is obvious, though — a kind of Englishness seeps into them, almost invariably. They assume native characteristics, such as detachment, discretion, a liking for euphemisms, and a rejection of that highly Hungarian tendency to maintain tightly knit families and communities.

New York has Yorkville, 'Little Hungary', which I have already described in some detail. A self-contained, self-catering ghetto. It may have diminished in recent years, but it is still a cohesive community. In London there is no such cohesion. The Hungarians are there, but the glue is missing. For some reason, the Hungarians, unlike the Poles, have allowed the amorphous, homogeneous quality of London to get the better of their clannish inclinations. Instead of revolving in one big whirlpool, they move in countless little eddies, all different and independent.

There is an eddy of Hungarian doctors and dentists, an eddy of writers, a small-time crooks' eddy and an eddy of arty folk. Of course not all eddies go strictly by occupation, and a lot of people aren't in any eddy at all. Looking at the picture as a whole, it's very much a case of 'every Magyar for himself'.

As usual, my family didn't conform to the general rule. When I lived with my parents in Bayswater, we had a Hungarian doctor, a Hungarian dentist, a Hungarian accountant and there was a constant ebb and flow of Hungarians from all over the world (and even sometimes from Hungary) through our flat. In New York this is *de rigueur*, in London it's a feat.

When we stayed in Brighton it was at the home of a Hungarian art restorer. When we had afternoon tea at a gentlemen's club it was with that professional Hungarian, George Mikes. We heard all about the problems of attracting respectable lodgers during the Swinging Sixties from an elderly Hungarian couple who ran a boarding house in Earls Court. We heard about the difficulties of opening a restaurant during the recessive seventies from Jenő *bácsi*, who owned the *Paprika* in Shepherd's Bush. And so it went on. I suppose my family was initiated into London life by its Hungarian inhabitants.

Perhaps if there is one overriding feature of the Magyars, it's resourcefulness. They're not chameleons, they can't make themselves inconspicuous. But if they get knocked down, you can bet your life that somehow, somewhere, they're going to pop right up again and carry on with the business of life.

Eleven

The rain beat down on the corrugated iron roof above our heads. It was a bad day at Bánk. Fleur was sleeping under a fluffy blanket on the bed. Adam was trudging around outside in the mud, and the rest of us were sitting at the dining table in various degrees of dampness.

Laci and Klári had insisted that we spend a day with them at their tiny *vikend* house in the country, although the summer season had by now well and truly passed.

'There's still a lot of harvesting to be done,' Laci had said. 'You just have to see our little garden to believe it! We have plum trees, cherry trees, raspberries, rhubarb, cabbages, green peppers, redcurrants, grapes, celery, carrots, parsley, marrows, beans, tomatoes. . .' My stomach was getting bloated just hearing about them. He went on. 'And our flowers have been so prolific this year. Giant daisies, carnations, tulips, roses, dahlias, sunflowers . . .'

It had all sounded too good to be true. I had pictured us basking in the glory of this splendid garden, lazily picking a plum here and nibbling on a grape there, like ancient, hedonistic Romans. Instead we shivered inside the house, which is really about the size of a one-car garage.

'We can't keep any sort of heating here,' Big Klári said, 'we're not connected to gas or electricity supplies.' She laughed lightly. 'But who is cold, anyway? I'm never cold.'

My theory is that women with very large breasts don't feel the cold because they act as a sort of buffer zone, keeping the chest warm. Personally, I have to rely on gas or electricity.

We were taken on a spongy tour of the front and back gardens. Every inch of Laci's plot had been meticulously cultivated and bore the signs of unstinted devotion. Laci beamed out into the distance.

188

'Look at those hills,' he sighed. 'Just breathe in this lovely country fragrance.'

Behind his back Adam kicked a curly purple cabbage, sending a sprinkling of raindrops into the air. 'Let's go for a walk,' he said.

We squelched our way out to the road. There was only a slight drizzle now, and it was easier to keep warm when on the move. I glanced back at Laci's house. Except for the roof, it is made of varnished pine, and can pass for the hut of some simple, lone mountaineer.

It is in the middle of a kind of 'settlement' of a couple of hundred such *vikend* houses. The area has only been descended upon relatively recently by inhabitants of Budapest searching for a private morsel of countryside. It is an hour's drive from the capital, in the gentle, hilly region leading towards the Czech frontier.

The houses are almost all single storey and very small. Some are hardly bigger than garden sheds. I have a feeling some were put together with a do-it-yourself construction kit. And their shapes are extraordinary, like upside-down ice cream cones, shoe boxes, old-fashioned lampshades. It was like strolling through a New Town for eccentric dwarfs.

But the place was empty. Most of the dwellings were obviously closed up until the following spring. And there was no sound, only the brushing of Adam's Wellington boots against the pavement. The colony is on a hillside, and slowly we descended down towards the village.

There were bow-legged peasant women wearing the traditional ten layers of stiff skirts standing out almost horizontally so that they looked like contestants in *Come Dancing*. They wore Babushka headscarves and had big, hard hands. There were peasant boys driving carts loaded with black and yellow spotted pigs. I liked their muscular arms and coarse hair and dark eyes. I liked, also, the way they held their horses' reins so lightly between their fingers, and the way their shoulders swayed with the rhythm of the wheels on the old cobbles.

It soon became noticeable that there was something going on in the village. All was not quite in order. What had happened? The women were standing in front of houses, here and there, in small knots, whispering earnestly to each other. Old men were hesitating in doorways, looking up and down the street. Even the hens seemed to be congregating excitedly. It appeared that normal activities had ceased for some reason.

I approached a grizzled inhabitant and asked him whether there was trouble in the village.

'Trouble? Yes, there certainly is.' He nodded vigorously, then stared at a group of people across the street.

I waited. Then I inquired as to the nature of the trouble. I felt a bit like an intruder, a gate-crasher at some private family function. Perhaps it wasn't my business. But I'm nosey.

He studied me and I could see he suspected my motives. But maybe his mother once told him he should always be polite to ladies, even strange ones with peculiar accents. For after a moment he shrugged and said simply, 'It's Béla, the keeper of the local museum. His body has just been found hanging in the staircase there.' The old man shook his head. 'Who knows why he did it?' Then he continued to stare across the street.

I remembered having read that Hungary has one of the highest suicide rates of any country in the world. Statistics have never had much effect on me, just figures on a page. But they do have a tendency sometimes to creep up on you and jab you in the ribs, should you ignore them. I have already mentioned the divorce statistics, which meant little to me until I started tallying all the people in Hungary I know who have been or are probably going to get divorced. Likewise, I didn't reflect on the terribly high percentage of the population that is turning to alcoholism until I was accosted by a drunken professor in the café opposite one of Budapest's universities.

So why is Hungary so good at getting to the top of the league tables for things that are so bad? It's a volatile nationality, certainly, but not more so than a lot of others, and much less, I think, than the Italians or the Iranians, for example. And currently Hungary is more economically stable than it has been at any time since the late nineteenth century, so it can't be put down to a shaky economy.

I thought about this for a long time. My only conclusion is that mental depression and emotional fatigue, as expressed through suicide, divorce and alcoholism, can be created by a sense of stagnation. And Hungary is a country which is stagnating. Things are not too bad, indeed if they were, people would be too angry or too busy to think about getting divorced or boozing. But neither does there seem to be much hope of the social and political situation improving or developing favourably. And it's precisely when things look like staying the same for ever, when life is one interminable road without surprises, that a person can fall prey to

190

apathy and depression.

And then, just to get that final sting into the story, he might do something awful, like put a noose around his neck.

My godmother Margit has a curious hobby: she collects people. She is retired now, a widow in her late sixties. She is a frequent traveller to foreign countries where she exercises her rare talent for meeting people and fondly adding them to her collection. Margit is plumpish and has a short crop of white hair. When she grins and blinks at you and hugs herself coyly like a little girl, you can be sure she is about to show you the latest photographs of her people and recount her latest adventures abroad.

'While I was admiring Michelangelo's frescoes in the Sistine Chapel one day, I heard a soft voice beside me. I turned around and met the eyes of a handsome young priest. He was so kind. We walked around the church together, discussing art and religion. We discovered that we had a great affinity. He spoke only Italian, and my knowledge of that language is rather limited. Yet we understood each other so well. Ah. . . what a friendship. We still write to each other. . .'

Then she might easily take out a picture of herself surrounded by a huge family of diminutive Japanese. 'How I adore orientals! Just look at them. So neat and tidy and perfect. My friend Mrs Yamaguchi, whom I met in Paris last year while shopping for a scarf at Lafayette, presented me with an exquisite kimono. I can't put it on, of course, my hips won't fit in. The family promised to visit me some time soon and then I plan to give them a tablecloth which I've embroidered myself. This is what true friendship is about, my dear. Exchanging. We exchange our fondness for each other and our little tokens of lifelong affection.'

Margit is especially friendly with a family in the north of England and often sends them unexpected presents from Hungary. There is also a Swiss divorcée from Holland who has become a close friend, and a German couple she got to know rather well during a tour of the Tower of London.

Many years ago she stayed with us in our Bayswater flat. That's when I joined her collection. We often went to pubs together to drink white wine and discuss life. You can't be one of Margit's people without indulging in a lot of frank intellectual interchange. I enjoyed these occasions, because I always ended up feeling more mature than I really was, and a bit tipsy as well. We covered all the major 'women's topics' — marriage, men, childbearing, underwear.

When Margit was young she was quite an ordinary person. But I don't think that position suited her. She got a modest job as an assistant set designer at the film studio and there she came into contact with many un-ordinary people — writers, actors, directors. She grew to like them and their way of life very much, and it wasn't long before she started to collect them.

She had a pleasant house with a garden in Buda. It was peaceful there, away from the crowds and noise of the city. In time it became a popular retreat for the film world's élite. Margit was always inviting people to stay — a film actress one day, a novelist the next. Eventually she got to know them all, and they all knew her, and she was permanently ingrained in the whole scene.

Sometimes I feel she could be on intimate terms with absolutely anybody she chose. Muhammed Ali, Mrs Thatcher, Deng Xiaoping. Anybody. No one can resist her charms.

And old friendships never fade away with Margit. Although on very rare occasions they are instantly severed, like an umbilical cord: 'He was such a charming man. My dear, when he smiled you felt on top of the world. I knew him for several years. We met one summer in the Tyrol and began a regular correspondence. Then I started to send him small gifts. He was very interested in antiques, and I thought he might appreciate a piece of old Herend porcelain from time to time. He lived in Vienna. I was planning a trip there and wrote to tell him so. It would be so nice to meet again, I said. But I got a short, brusque letter back. "I'm afraid this relationship is getting too much for me," it said, "you will not find me at home." Well, I had never been so deeply shocked in my life. What could he have meant! Of course I never heard from him again. And all that beautiful Herend has been lost forever.'

Fortunately, few people so completely misinterpret Margit's intentions. She's just a woman with an endless capacity for absorbing the human species in all its shapes and forms. And she realizes that it's impossible to have any sort of hobby without some financial outlay.

'As your godmother,' she told me one day, 'I feel some responsibility for your education. Shall I take you to Szentendre, that fascinating centre of the arts, and acquaint you with current cultural activities in Hungary?'

Thus I found myself sitting on a train, staring out at the dreary outskirts of the capital, the clumsy, lazy industrial landscape dotted with crumbling factories and with only the distant hills of Óbuda to soften the view. Then for a long time we passed through a stretch of high-rise council blocks. The sides of some of the buildings had been painted with dull colours, but it seemed a futile exercise. There is only one colour in such an environment: drab. Blue is drab, pink is drab, green is drab.

At last we saw the little hill with its cluster of old streets and houses which is Szentendre. The centre of the village is a few minutes' walk from the train station. You pass quiet cobbled alleyways with views of crooked tiled roofs and church steeples, you cross an old hump-backed bridge and there you are. Everywhere I looked I saw tiny museums and art galleries and exhibitions. We climbed the hill and at its pinnacle found a group of yellow houses with chipped and peeling walls perched together like a congregation of giant moulting canaries.

'First of all we must go to the Margit Kovács Museum,' said Margit. 'She was the country's greatest exponent of ceramic art. And, incidentally, a good friend of mine during her later years.'

The museum is housed in a lovely, sparkling white house surrounded by flowers and trees. Its immaculate condition indicates that the state, which now owns the collection of ceramic figures, murals and vessels, is keen on making the most of this national treasure. As with the sumptuous National Gallery, no amount of money is too great to lavish on an asset which attracts international attention and, by doing so, adds to the country's prestige. It is only the private citizen who must live in dilapidated buildings because the state is unwilling to maintain them.

Margit Kovács's art is primitive and folklorish. There are dreaming shepherds and weeping fishermen's wives, peasants and weddings and feasts, tableaux symbolizing wickedness and saintliness and wisdom and just about everything else that can be symbolized with potter's clay. It is all marvellously expressive, but what has remained most vividly with me are the faces, and especially the eyes. They are very big and flat and unreal, the sort of eyes that startle you in the dark and make you shudder.

One of her works portrayed two women, one old and the other older, interlocked in each other's sorrow and loneliness. We studied this for a while. 'The artist never married,' said Margit. 'She was alone until the end of her life, except for her aged mother, with whom she lived. There were problems between them yet they depended on each other.' We walked on and she added, 'Margit always looked upon her artistic creations as her children. She told me once that they kept her from going mad.'

Madness seemed far from Szentendre and from us as we squinted in the sunlight angled against the canary-buildings and an endless clutter of windows tilted slightly off-balance. The village was serenity itself, and had an air of unquestionable equilibrium.

'Come, let's visit my friend Ilona,' urged Margit, taking my arm. 'She has a café nearby. The fare is superb, and the woman herself is unique.'

The café is called Nostalgia and its style is charmingly *du vieux temps*. We were served tea by a dainty little waitress in a frilly white apron.

Margit said to her in her most dulcet tone, 'I would like to see Ilona, please. Can you tell her Margit is here?'

We sipped our tea and watched some curious-looking people coming and leaving. There were quite a few young men carrying things of various shapes and sizes. I asked Margit about this. She leaned towards me and smiled conspiratorially.

'They are doubtless artists or musicians or poets. Ilona is something of a patroness of the arts. There is a lovely courtyard behind the café where concerts and poetry readings are held on summer evenings. She encourages new talent. Young, unknown songwriters are given their first chance to perform here. It's a hub of creativity.' Then she gasped and stood up. 'Ilona! How well you look!'

I saw a large woman with a good-natured face and the most colossal breasts imaginable.

'It's good of you to come,' she was saying, embracing Margit. 'And who is this?'

'My god-daughter from London.'

'London! The home of Dickens and Oscar Wilde and Shakespeare. This is most exciting. Have some more tea and try the cakes. No, better still, come upstairs and have some of my chicken soup. I've just made it.'

We followed her out into the stone-walled courtyard and up a staircase to her private rooms. There were bare wooden floors and the place seemed in a hopeless muddle, as though she'd just moved in. Photographs were piled onto tables, books and pictures were arranged in an ad hoc manner and in the middle of the floor was a tape recorder surrounded by scores of cassettes.

'I've just been listening to some great stuff we recorded at one of our concerts last summer,' she called from the kitchen as she stirred the soup. 'A fellow called Tibor who composes his own music. There are some photos of him on the floor.' I heard a rattling of crockery as she set the table for us. 'Tibi is a real natural. Sincere and morose, you know the sort of thing.'

I glanced at his pictures. It's true, there was a pockmarked frankness about his face. He had thin lips and long, unruly hair. The *sine qua non*, I suppose.

'Soup's on the table!' We all sat down to eat. 'I really enjoyed making this,' said Ilona. 'It's excellent. Why should I be modest?'

At that moment a short young man in jeans came in carrying a painting under his arm. 'Hi, Ilona,' he muttered.

'Hi, Tamás. Have a bowl of soup.'

'No, thanks.'

'What have you brought me?'

Tamás held up the canvas and revealed an oily, abstract creation in various shades of brown, black and beige. The motley scene was vaguely reminiscent of a window ledge after the pigeons have been at it.

Ilona studied it while she ate her soup. Then she nodded her head and announced, 'I like it. I don't know what it is, but it's great.'

A wide smile came over the artist's face. 'Shall I leave it with you, then?'

'Mmm. By all means.' She waved towards the chaotic sitting-room. 'Put it anywhere.' She turned to us. 'How are you doing? Like some more carrots in your soup?'

I asked her about the cultural life of Szentendre.

'There's an exciting little community of about fifty artists, sculptors, writers and poets who live and work here. There are activities going on all year long, you see, not just for the tourists and day-trippers in the summer.'

'How much freedom are you given to run your private enterprise, Nostalgia?'

'I'm in complete control. I can decorate it as I want, improve the premises or add onto them, invite any performer I want. It's very nice being a *maszek* in Szentendre, because our local authority is sympathetic and understanding and even progressive. The officials support the village's cultural life, they encourage young artists. We all get on well together.' She smiled at me. 'Does that answer your question? Now, let me pop downstairs and get us some coffee and cakes.' She rose to her feet, breasts bouncing, and said she would be right back.

Margit clutched my hand vigorously and beamed. 'Isn't she incredible? What a woman. What energy.'

We waited in the kitchen for a while, then I wandered into the sitting-room and browsed around among the pictures and *objets d'art*. Ilona was taking a long time. A few people came looking for her, and some photographers arrived to take shots of the picturesque courtyard for a magazine. I leafed through old books. I looked out the curtainless window at the houses across the lane. Still no Ilona.

'One time,' Margit informed me, 'I came to see her and we were just sitting quietly together having a drink, when she suddenly stood up and said she had to go and speak to someone. "I'll only be a minute," she said. I waited and waited. After an hour and a half I decided to go home.' She shrugged. 'That's just the sort of person she is. But you can't get cross with Ilona. You have to accept her as she is — one of the true irrepressible bohemians.'

I've nothing against bohemians, even irrepressible ones, but I didn't think we had to die of boredom waiting for one. I was just contemplating what to do when the door opened. A girl of about seven came in, glanced at us, and sat down in an armchair. She proceeded to take some paper and coloured pens out of a school satchel.

'I think I shall do a study in grey this afternoon,' she said.

She had one of those dead-pan faces, high Hungarian cheekbones and perfect composure. Already she was concentrating on her drawing, obviously no longer aware that we were even in the room.

Margit was bristling with curiosity. 'You're Ilona's daughter, aren't you?'

She didn't raise her eyes. 'Yes, the middle one.'

'Of course,' said Margit. 'There are three of you, I remember now. Ilona has told me about you children. You're all very talented.'

'Yes.' It was quiet but for the scratching of her pen on the paper.

'Are you going to be an artist like your Mum's friends?' I asked.

She gazed at me coolly. 'Definitely not.'

'Oh. What are you going to be, then?'

'A hairdresser.'

'Oh.' We seemed to have run out of conversation. Margit was

beginning to look nervous.

'What time does our train leave?' I asked.

'Soon. And we've got to get to the station first.' She glanced at her watch. 'Where's your Mummy?' she asked the hairdresser/artist.

She shrugged. 'I couldn't say.'

At that moment Ilona burst into the room, a cherub in tow. 'Forgive me, girls,' she said breathlessly. 'I remembered I had to pick up my youngest from nursery school. Someone else usually does it for me. I forgot which school she goes to, so I've been to three or four trying to find her.'

Margit was open-mouthed with amazement. Then she shrieked with laughter. 'Oh, Ilona,' she cried gleefully, 'that's you all over!'

The patroness flung her arms with mock helplessness into the air.

I stood up. I thought we ought to take our leave before she disappeared again, or else we might really miss the train. I stretched out my hand.

Ilona protested. 'But girls, you haven't tried my coffee yet. It's the best in Szentendre. Let's go down to the café. Don't worry about the train. My driver will take you back to Budapest.' She led the way down to the courtyard, where the photographers were still snapping away under their arc lights. 'As it happens,' she continued, 'I must be in the capital myself later on, so we can all go together.'

Nostalgia was filling up with groups of ardent young people, solitary old ladies, wanderers and sightseers. Cigarette smoke and the fragrance of strong coffee wafted into all corners of the café, curling around a bust of Aphrodite and meandering out to the street. The waitress in the frilly apron was bringing a tray full of cakes out from the kitchen. We sat with Ilona at a small table, quietly discussing the new season of plays in Budapest. No one came up to Ilona or called out to her. Yet everyone knew that she was there and who she was. In an unspoken, unobtrusive way, she dominated the scene.

When we rose to leave she was suddenly the centre of attention in a more apparent fashion. People were greeting her, nodding heads, raising hands. She pecked a dozen cheeks, gave vent to some hoarse, spontaneous laughter, and blew out the door.

She was about to get in the car when she froze, clutched her head and said, 'Damn! What's the matter with me? I've forgotten the kids.'

She went back to fetch the cherub, the hairdresser and an older boy who looked with dismay at the densely packed car. 'Will there be room for my etchings?' he asked.

The driver didn't say a word during the entire trip. He was small, dark and compact. Rather like a bowling ball. Ilona held court in the back, encircled by her children, all of whom seemed as though they ought to be at least twice her age. They were the 'straight men' in her perennial comic act, dignified and phlegmatic. While she was a spinning top in perpetual motion, sparks flying, so that you were wary of getting too close. And yet her very transience was unpredictable.

Ilona and Szentendre. They are one and the same to me now. Like the crack of a whip and the whip itself, when the sound becomes the object, the object the sound.

Mária is an aged, retired actress. She has known my mother since the old days, they had worked together often. In Hungary Mária's name is as well known as that of the big Hollywood stars. Neither Bette Davis nor Katherine Hepburn are more famous or admired.

Her two sons emigrated to the U.S. in 1956. They had children and grandchildren, over the years they became Americanized, they drove Chevrolets and had barbecues and holidays in Miami Beach. Mária visited them from time to time. She found herself the matriarch of a huge family with a seemingly endless outcrop of American kids.

We had met a few times in New York, during these visits to her family. Once, when I was seventeen, she had come to see us in our house in Westchester. I was then dying to become an actresss, so after dinner I had done some audition pieces for her. She had watched me silently, sternly, her eyes big and intense. When I had reached the dramatic climax she had nodded vigorously with approval. She had been solicitous and full of advice. I never became an actress. But I always remembered her encouragement.

Now for the first time I was going to visit her in her flat in the Castle district of Buda, up in the hills, on one of the old narrow streets so full of the past. She lives in a large house painted yellow with boxes of geraniums in the windows. Once the entire building had been hers, but it was confiscated some time after 1948 and she was allowed to live in only two rooms of it, as a paying tenant of the state.

Laci and Big Klári took me to see her. They had warned me that she'd grown hard of hearing. The door was opened to us by Mária's 'lady's companion', a good-humoured spinster, who showed us into the richly furnished sitting-room. Mária was in an armchair, her grey hair thick and loose about her shoulders, her back erect. She looked unchanged since the last time I saw her, over ten years before.

'Who's that?' she thundered at us in her familiar booming voice.

The companion explained in a loud voice who we were.

'Well, why didn't you say so?' Mária stood up with the help of a walking stick and stepped forward to greet me. I realized then that she must be nearly blind, for she seemed to look somewhere past my eyes, not into them.

She asked me about myself. 'How wise of you to have married rather than become an actress,' she said. 'Believe me, a career is worthless! To be loved, that is all that counts.'

'I'm a journalist now,' I told her. She didn't hear me.

'It's ghastly to be old and alone,' she went on. 'I can hardly see any more. You're just a blot to me, my girl.'

'But you still look well and youthful,' I told her.

'Ha! That's just because the skin on my face is so smooth and clear. There's not a line on it. But I'll tell you something.' She paused, then declared even more loudly, 'I'd rather my face was as wrinkled as an old peasant's arse, if only I could get my sight back.'

The companion came in, bringing us a tray of espresso and delicious vanilla cream cakes from an excellent patisserie nearby. Mária changed the subject. 'Have you taken any lovers yet?' she asked casually.

'Well,' I squirmed and laughed with embarrassment, 'not really . . .'

'Why not?' she demanded. 'Men do, all the time. Why shouldn't we? Just make sure they're rich, that's all.'

Laci and Klári exchanged quick glances and Laci, who had gone slightly pink, cleared his throat. 'Excuse me, Mária *néni*,' he began with an apologetic smile. 'But not all men do such things. I, for example, have never — '

'Oh, don't make me laugh!' roared Mária like a disbelieving lioness, tossing back her head. Her eyes, although unseeing, were marvellously alive. Her whole face was riveting. The three of us watched her in silence. Her mood seemed to change again.

'A career isn't important,' she said, staring vacantly into the room, but I supposed the words were meant for me. 'Just think about having someone to grow old with. It's terrible to face the end without anybody, take my word for it. Actresses —' she hissed the word impatiently. 'What do they count for? People forget the roles they play. I myself can't remember all those big parts I had, my famous lines, my acting partners. They're gone. They mean nothing to anyone any more. What have I got left?'

I waved my hand at the myriad of framed family photographs of all sizes, on the walls and on gleaming mahogany tabletops. 'But surely,' I said, 'you have a large family, four generations.'

She rapped her stick sharply on the floor in between her feet. 'They're all in America!'

'You've never thought of joining them?' I asked.

Mária shook her head. 'How could I? This is my home, here. I've been there many times, my sons are always sending me the air fare. But don't ask me about America. It's still a mystery to me. All I know is that my older son has a travel agency and the younger one is in the insurance business. They have nice houses and cars and charming children who now have their own children whose names I can't pronounce. The whole thing wears me out, quite frankly, just thinking about it. But I miss them, just the same.'

Klári leaned forward and patted Mária's hand. 'You must come to our house in Bánk, when the weather's nice, you'll love the flowers and the fresh air.'

'I don't often leave the flat now,' Mária said. 'I used to take great pleasure in strolling down the street to the Fishermen's Bastion and sitting on a bench there. I liked the breeze from the river. But so many people would recognize me. The admiring public would be all around me, singing my praises. Soon the bench would get overcrowded. Then I'd have to get up and there'd be no peace until I was safely back home again.

'Now my only consolation is the radio. I'd watch the television, too, if only I could see the blasted picture. I had a friend who used to visit me often, until she got her own television set. Now she sits at home watching it and I haven't seen her for ages.'

In a corner, surrounded by lush, hanging plants, an old grandfather clock was ticking away. It reminded me that it was getting late and I should be leaving.

I rose and touched Mária gently on the arm. She was still sitting as straight as a general, with a secret reserve of power despite her failing senses. She spoke again, almost as if to herself.

'Do you remember my Mother Superior in *Abelard and*

Heloise? It was my most famous role. All the performances were sold out, months in advance. And at the end of each performance I was the one to receive the biggest ovation.'

'It was a triumph,' I said.

'A triumph,' she repeated. She paused. 'I don't go to the theatre any more. The young actresses today can't be compared with my generation.' There was distaste on her lips. 'They're just like dolls, pretty to look at, with nice figures. But we were more than that. We were alive! My God, our very skirts were on fire!'

I kissed her soft, powdered cheeks. 'I was glad I could see you again.'

She pulled my face close to hers. 'Remember all that I've told you,' she said. 'Learn from it. That's the most I can do for you.'

We walked back to the Lada. The yellow house with the geraniums looked so festive and gay, I thought, looking back at it as we drove away down the street.

I must admit that I am on intimate terms with only one Hungarian count. I shall call him Count X. That has a good ring to it.

Count X was once a high-ranking officer in the Hungarian army. He was also a gifted equestrian. In those days he was a slim, elegant man with a decidedly noble look to him. Now he is elderly, still slim, but with a grandfatherly conviviality.

At the communist take-over in 1948, when the aristocrats were hounded and terrorized, if not executed, Count X was thrown into prison. No reasons were given, no charges made. Oppressors don't require justification. He was sentenced to fifteen years and resigned himself to it with nothing in his possession but a copy of the *Pocket Oxford Dictionary*, 1937 edition. He read it from cover to cover, and thus learned to read and write in English.

He was set free after two years, although of course he wasn't officially allowed to return to his home in Budapest. But through some extraordinary administrative error, he was mixed up with another person of similar name, a butcher or an electrician or something. So that poor plebeian was forced to pack his bags and move out to the depths of the wilderness, while X remained incognito in the capital and resumed his old life.

X is a pragmatist. He is without bitterness or anger or sadness. He is very good-humoured, however. And after all, you have to laugh at a society which first stabs its noblemen in the back and then, a few decades later, scours the country for them because they've become *en vogue*. In defence of my compatriots I will add only that the inspiration for the former came chiefly from 'Uncle Joe' Stalin, and I guess when he told someone to stab, they bloody well stabbed.

I once asked X about his years in prison. 'What sort of people were in there with you? Were there many prisoners?'

'We were about 4,000 in all. And every kind of person you can imagine. The communists weren't choosy. In my cell there were four of us. We became good friends.'

'Tell me about them.'

X put his hands into the pockets of a well-tailored English sports jacket and grinned. 'When I was put into the cell there was only one other man there. A quiet, melancholy fellow. He had written some poems which didn't go down well with the authorities. He recited them to me in a whisper. We discussed them. Then we spoke about Blake and Keats and Byron. He knew a lot about English poetry. He was the sort of person who is very sensitive to his environment and I wondered how long he would last in that prison. It was bitterly cold, we had little to eat, they gave us practically nothing to occupy ourselves with.

'One day they brought a third man into our cell. He was quite different. He wept a lot, and moaned with his head in his hands. We tried to console him. "What is it, my friend? What has happened?" we asked. "I've nothing any more," he wailed. "They've taken all my possessions away from me. And my piano! My beloved piano. I'll never see it again. Oh, what can I do, what can I do?" This went on for days. We tried everything to cheer him up, but it was impossible. The loss of his piano seemed insupportable.

'Then at last our fourth cell-mate arrived. Calm and composed and good-natured. I can still see him, leaning casually against the cell wall, arms folded, surveying us philosophically. Just to have him there with us raised our spirits. The piano man was still in a rather bad state, though, and one day he cried out miserably, "It's all very well for you to stand there like that, watching us so coolly with your arms folded, as if you were at a cocktail party! I'll bet they didn't take all your worldly possessions away from you."

' "Yes, I'm afraid they did," he answered, a faint smile appearing on his face. "What did they take?" the piano man demanded. "Everything — my twenty-seven castles and my 180,000 hectares of land." We stared open-mouthed at him and he laughed. "We haven't been properly introduced. My name is Pál Esterhazy. Who are you?" The piano was never mentioned again.'

X is a very knowledgeable person and is especially versed in Hungarian history. He was somewhat taken aback to learn that I hadn't yet seen the Crown of St Stephen on display at the National Museum.

'But that's scandalous,' he said. 'You must see it, it's your duty as a Magyar. Besides, it's rather a nice crown. Let me take you there.'

It can only be viewed on certain days of the week. It is in a special room of its own at the museum, a room with walls of red velvet and with theatrical lighting and a sober-looking guard in each corner. In the middle of the room is a rectangular glass case containing the crown and other items of the coronation regalia. It is roped off, and viewers must pass in a regulated manner along a strip of carpet, from the front of the case to the side and then round the back and out through another door. It's a bit like going to see a great statesman or film star lying in state in his plush coffin.

We edged our way slowly around the beautiful, glittering objects. The golden crown is encrusted with gems and contains cloisonné enamel plates made in the imperial goldsmiths' workshop of Constantinople. It has an upper part of two crossed stripes which also have enamelled plates, pearls and almandines. What I like best about it is the golden cross at the top, perched at a cocky angle as if to suggest that the whole thing isn't as awesome as all that.

'According to tradition, Pope Sylvester II sent this crown to Vajk, son of Prince Géza, for his coronation in the year 1000. Vajk had become a Christian and was the first king of Hungary under the name of István, or Stephen.' X was speaking quietly. We were alone in the room except for the guards who stared at us in their boredom. 'The Pope's gesture was meant as a warning to the new king: the feuding tribes of Hungary would have to conform to the conditions set by Christian Europe or perish. So the original system of clans and tribes was replaced by that of feudalism.'

'How odd that they should equate feudalism with Christianity,' I remarked.

'But you must understand, the only people in Europe at that time who could provide a contrast to the Christians were the Barbarians. Feudalism, at least, provided order, a structured society. That was preferable to the free-for-all indulged in by bellicose tribal chiefs, whose predatory campaigns caused Europe at first to tremble, and then to learn Magyar tactics and eventually counter them with superior feudal war techniques.'

And so we chatted about serfs, landowners and freemen, and the large estates they lived on, called *latifundia*, and King Stephen's German wife who came to Hungary with a cortège of knights and priests, and his canonization in 1083. X knows about all of these things.

'One of Stephen's greatest virtues,' he said, 'was that he welcomed strangers with open arms, so tradesmen and craftsmen from all over flocked to the newly developing cities of Hungary. And they, in turn, helped the cities to prosper. He told his son Imre: "Weak is the land of one language." '

Before we left the room, I looked back once more at the crown, at its jewels sparkling under the spotlights. It is the symbol of a nation and its sad, turbulent history. So much drama has been packed into these thousand years. Too much. And too little democracy. But those Hungarians, you have to hand it to them, they keep bouncing back, keep slipping out in front of you through revolving doors. They must have something.

I remembered having read a few years ago about the return of St Stephen's Crown to Hungary, after having been in the possession of the United States government since 1945. After the war, the U.S. didn't want the priceless relic to fall into the wrong hands, i.e. the Russians. A lot of things were falling into their hands at that time. So it was kept secretly somewhere in America, awaiting the day when Hungary would be, what? Free, autonomous, lifted out of Eastern Europe and put somewhere safe and cosy like Australia, I don't know. Of course, even Americans face up to reality sooner or later. And so one day they just handed the crown back with a touching ceremony. And that was that. I'm glad they gave it back. Because now X can go to see it and ruminate on the past. And it can give him pleasure.

We wandered out of the museum and down the grand steps where Petőfi stood and roused the masses during the War of Independence. At the bottom my friend the Count and I parted company. He was going to meet friends at the Zserbó, and I was going home. Juszti was cooking a special lunch in my honour and my mother had told me that, crown or no crown, I'd better not be late for it.

In my adolescence there were certain images which I naturally associated with the state of being Hungarian. There was the gypsy with his colourful clothes and violin, of course, because I nearly always saw one when I went to a Hungarian restaurant on Second Avenue. There were the sights and fragrances of Magyar cooking. There were bits of music — Bartók, Liszt, Lehár — which had floated around me so many times through my mother's piano playing that they had worked their way into every crevice of my brain and snuggled down for good.

But beyond these I harboured a hazy, atavistic vision of Hungary itself. Budapest, I knew, was no more indicative of the nation as a whole than New York was of America. So what was it like? A vast, sublime plain, an endless prairie; in a word — the *puszta*. It's a Hungarian word which means bare, bleak, but it also refers to the lowlands of Hungary, in particular the region to the east around the city of Debrecen.

It is known as Hortobágy, and Petőfi, who was born and bred there, called it 'the brow of God'. He wrote many poems about it, but the best known is called 'Alföld' (Lowlands), in which he declares that while he admires the Carpathians, he does not love them.

> My world and home are the lowlands,
> The Alföld, the open sea.
> I look on the plains of this infinite
> And the prisoned eagle of my soul is free. . .
>
> How beautiful the Alföld — for me at least.
> Here was my cradle, here my birth,
> Here put me in a shroud, and here
> Let cover me a soft mound of earth.

Another writer who was besotted with the *puszta* and wrote a great deal about it was Zsigmond Móricz. He wasn't a native of Hortobágy, but visited it several times between 1923 and 1942, the year of his death. He even made a national cause out of it, struggling to make its problems more widely recognized, chiefly, the poverty of its inhabitants and the devastating droughts which recurred each summer.

Through some strange process of osmosis or, as I mentioned earlier, an atavistic sense, my conception was of a flat, dusty land, populated by those gruff but engaging characters, the *puszta*'s famous herdsmen. The *csikós* is the cowboy, the *juhász* the shepherd. They wore long shaggy coats and moustaches slightly shorter. The cowboys had bright red whips and, if they were in the mood, could do amazing stunts on their horses like the men who rode with Attila and Genghis. Great stuff.

Needless to say, Hungary, for the most part, is not a plain at all, nor is it arid. But the *puszta*, Hortobágy, does still exist and superficially is more or less unchanged. The essential difference is that now it is a national park, a conservation area. It is dotted with museums celebrating its way of life, or at least, the way which existed in past centuries and was still very much in evidence during Móricz's days. That was before modern technology crept along, even into Petőfi's cradle.

Sitting in the back of Géza's oft-dented Mercedes on our way to Hortobágy, my mind hurried ahead to the part of the country which had for so long roused my imagination. Gizi was chattering gaily in front of me, but I wasn't listening. Instead I heard Móricz's words:

I once walked over from Kisujszállás to Karcag. I shall never forget that walk, for on the way I seemed to absorb the huge Hungarian Plain. It is impossible to describe the glorious feeling of seeing nothing all day but the sky and the lowlands on which no tree ever grows. People from mountainous regions find this hard to appreciate, but for the lowlanders it is ecstasy to perceive this wonderful, enormous world.

It was a damp, dull day. It had been drizzling since we left Budapest and I was worried that I would indeed see nothing, not even the sky and the lowlands on which no tree ever grows.

'Did you know,' asked Géza, 'that Petőfi walked all the way from Debrecen to the capital, when he was a poor, unknown poet?'

'Why did he do that?' I wasn't really concentrating.

'Why? To bring his poems to the publishers, of course.'

'Couldn't he just post them?'

He threw an odd glance at me in the rear-view mirror. Then Gizi took up the story of Petőfi's life.

'He was quite a lady's man, you know,' she said. 'He had a pretty wife who was also very patient and tolerant. I suppose she'd have to be, with him. Goodness, men are all the same.'

'What do you mean by that?' asked Géza.

Some sort of minor argument ensued, but I heard little of it because I thought again about what Móricz had written after one of his trips to the *puszta*:

206

It is awe-inspiring to stand in the centre and look around, to see the infinity of time long since past and the cheerlessness which, far from being depressing, gives a tremendous lift to the heart. The sky is a clear, flawless blue, no cloud in sight. The soul must simply unite with this sky that seems like a lord above us and enters us through every pore of our skin.

I twisted my head so that I could look straight up at the sky. There were plenty of clouds in sight. In fact, there was precious little else. I was becoming almost morose, contemplating my rotten luck. When would I get a chance to come this way again? I just had to stand in the centre and look at the infinity, I *had* to. I had to find a *juhász* somewhere with a shaggy coat and a moustache. I had to pass roaming herds of cattle and sheep and goats and swine. At this rate, the only thing to unite with my soul and enter every pore of my skin would be rain. I get enough of that in London.

'Do you think we'll see some of the herdsmen in their traditional clothes?' I inquired meekly, feeling like one of those elderly, rich American widows always on the look-out for a 'typical' sight to bring back to the folks in Duluth, or wherever.

'I'm afraid not,' said Géza. 'Nowadays the old costumes and methods are only for the tourists during the height of the summer season. The rest of the time they go around in jeans and lorries.'

'Oh,' I was crestfallen.

'Sorry. Thought you knew.'

'Yes, but I still harboured a little secret hope. . .'

'Never mind!' Gizi chirped. 'We'll have lunch in a real old-style *csárda*, where you can order the dish the herdsmen on the *puszta* have been eating since the nineteenth century.'

'What's that?' I asked, the thought of food filling me with fresh hope.

'*Bogrács gulyás*. Delicious. It tastes a lot better than ordinary goulash, because it's cooked in the local way, in a great pot over an open fire. The herdsmen used to make it outdoors, on the open plain, while they were tending the livestock.'

It was still too early to eat, so we stopped at a small, round museum with a thatched roof. There was no one inside and the glass door was locked, so we stood in the drizzle with our faces against the glass. Presently a short, wiry fellow with a silver tooth came along, said hello to us and unlocked the door. He wore blue jeans and matching jacket with studs on it.

He turned the lights on inside the immaculately clean and modern museum. I then expected him to disappear and carry on with whatever he'd been doing before. Instead, he picked up an old-fashioned schoolteacher's pointer and proceeded to explain in minute detail a blown-up chart of the Hortobágy on the wall. I understood virtually nothing of his dissertation, on account of his local accent.

But there was a table with stacks of brochures and leaflets, and I chose the English language ones, so I could read all about it. Thus I learned about the swamp of Kunkápolnás with its variety of reeds, bulrush, cat's-tail and sweetgrass, and about the summer life of the fish ponds. This sort of literature is always riddled with misspellings and odd expressions, which would add to their charm, except for the fact that you tend to start using them too.

But after the grandeur of Móricz's sentiments, it was quite refreshing to think of the *puszta* in down-to-earth scientific terms. According to my leaflet, the area's avifauna consists of 160 species, and during migration over 20,000 birds assemble there. Wind-screen woods were planted long ago to protect them from harsh weather conditions.

The red-footed falcon, long-eared owl, lesser shrike, ruddy shelduck and whooper swan all sounded such sympathetic creatures. Also the insects — different species of locusts and the dear steppe-tarantula. I read about the mammals to be found there, the weasel and field mouse, the steppe polecat and something with the enchanting name of 'eastern urchin'. But I saw none of this wildlife.

We drove on and soon arrived at the famous bridge with nine arches. According to local custom, if a pair of sweethearts kiss underneath one of these arches it's supposed to bring them good luck. Gizi dragged Géza down there for a kiss.

'But we're already married,' he protested. 'What more do you want?' Then he became cross because his feet sank into some sludge.

There are two more museums near the bridge and we went to see them. They have some of the black, wooden carriages and carts in which the people of the *puszta* used to transport their things. They have some genuine old local furniture and a few dummy herdsmen geared up in the traditional clothing — those sheepskin coats, hard black hats, embroidered felt jackets, boots — even down to the spindly pipes in their mouths.

Then we had lunch at the *csárda* across the street. We sat underneath a huge bull's skull and I watched as a fly crept curiously inside one gaping eye socket and out of the other. We ordered *bograćs gulyás*. The neighbouring tables were mostly full of Germans and Austrians. I think the waiter was the only other Hungarian there, and he was rather sullen.

We each received our goulash in a scalding metal pot with a handle, like a sort of ancient kettle. The stuff was hot, spicy and greasy. My anglicized stomach became queasy almost immediately. But I didn't want to hurt anyone's feelings, least of all the waiter's. He seemed unhappy enough already. So I spooned it in. The fly was exploring inside the cavity where the bull's nostrils once were. I was feeling decidedly wonky now.

Gizi said she had a good idea. It was well worth having a brief look into some of the stores of downtown Debrecen, she said, because you never knew what good buys you might find. Those provincial cities often contained goodies which were not available in Budapest, where anything worth buying was snapped up right away.

It seemed to me that the sky was possibly clearing up. Perhaps by tea-time the clouds would be gone and the full extent of the *puszta*'s beauty would be revealed to me. Perhaps, if I was really lucky, I could witness a lowlands sunset, which is said to be extraordinarily impressive. About just such a sunset on Hortobágy Móricz once wrote:

It would surpass the imagination of any painter. It is as though there were a fire somewhere, a blaze to which there is no end. The flames are flaring up and crowding into each other, the lava breaks through, a whole world is collapsing into glowing embers smouldering and eventually petering out towards the mountains around Eger.

We drove straight to the main shopping street of Debrecen, which was quite ordinary. There was one large department store and a few smaller establishments which Gizi wanted to inspect. Géza went with her, either to help carry back the shopping, or to make sure Gizi herself didn't get carried away by her fervour and spend all the money, I'm not sure.

The goulash was wreaking havoc with my insides. I lay down in the back seat of the car, prepared for a long wait. I went to sleep.

I woke up much later to the sound of bags and parcels being loaded into the boot. Gizi told me she'd found some lovely Scottish plaid material with which to make kilts for herself and Merci, slinky trousers, a hat, shoes, and other things.

'Are you better now?' she asked with a look of concern on her face. The doctor in her had got the better of the shopper. 'You're very pale.'

'I'd like a cup of tea,' I croaked.

'Of course,' said Gizi. 'That's just the thing. Géza! We must go to the Golden Bull Hotel straight away. We'll get some tea there.'

Soon I was beginning to feel myself again. It was an uninteresting smoky café, and the clientele wasn't exactly *distingué*. But the tea was all right. My thoughts returned to Petőfi, Móricz, the herdsmen and the inimitable landscape of Hortobágy.

'What shall we see next?' I asked.

Gizi said her feet were aching terribly and whatever we saw, it would have to be from a sitting position.

Géza said there was a forest nearby which we could drive through. It had great natural beauty.

Gizi mentioned the famous Debrecen College, founded in 1564.

Géza wondered whether the richly adorned County Hall with its many statues would be of interest to me.

I assured them that I would like to see it all. But in particular, I said, I longed for that magnificent *puszta* sunset. The blaze to which there is no end, the world collapsing into glowing embers.

We finished our tea and paid the bill. We stood up. I stretched my arms and legs. 'Oh, that's better,' I said. We left the café of the Golden Bull Hotel.

But meanwhile it had turned completely dark outside. It was too late to see anything. The sun, unbeknown to us, had already set.

We drove back to Budapest on the narrow, unlit highway, nearly knocking down two pedestrians and three bicyclists before we got there.

At home I found my mother downstairs, alone, looking through what appeared to be stacks of old newspapers and letters.

'How is your knee?' I asked.

'They're taking the plaster off tomorrow.'

'Well, that should be a big relief. What are you reading?'

'I found my bundles of fan mail from the thirties and forties in one of these drawers under the bookshelves. I destroyed many of them during the war; I couldn't keep them all. But these were special to me, so I held onto them.'

I picked one up from the wooden bench next to my mother. The envelope and paper were a very faint pinkish colour. It was dated 30 January 1943 and had been posted from someplace called Balassagyarmat. It began, 'Deeply Respected *Művésznő!*'

It informed my mother that a local fan club had just been set up in her honour. It ended with a request for an autographed photo and was signed 'Judith Schümmer, Club President'.

There was a series of letters from an anonymous admirer, a doctor, who kept hoping to fix up a rendezvous and was disappointed each time my mother refused.

'Even the Nazis went through this mail when they ransacked the house in '44. God knows what they expected to find,' my mother said. She began to tie the bundles up again with old ribbons.

'And what's in this?' I asked, picking up a yellowed newspaper dated 22 December 1948.

'Let me see.' She turned to the middle of it and showed me a short article, printed in italics and headed with her name and a head-and-shoulders drawing of her. It was a resumé of her life and career to date, mentioning her stage performances, concerts, the Hangli, the fifteen Hungarian films she had played in. Then it gave a 'how the famous people live' type of description of her life on Budakeszi Avenue:

> She doesn't smoke or drink. Her main passion is her garden, which she has filled with old-fashioned flowers and grasses, and where she and her father spend much time ardently gardening. She is very fond of animals and the current star of the household's four-legged members is a dachshund which, by virtue of his wisdom, answers to the name of Doktor. Her husband, our excellent colleague Péter Halász, says she is the strictest critic of his work.

Next to the newspapers were some old, pale blue school notebooks from my mother's days at a boarding school in Kaposvár, and later at a convent in the Austrian village of Zwettl. Some of the notebooks were half-empty, others were entirely covered in a very neat, even handwriting. Exercises in Latin, German, religious studies. All had been carefully put away and cherished for half a century. Yet to me they didn't look at all old, but fresh and crisp, as if awaiting their schoolgirl owner to take them up at any moment and continue the good work.

Gently I returned the notebooks to their neat pile. My mother leaned over her bad knee and stroked it. I heard her give out a low, tired sigh. Suddenly I was filled with sadness. There she sat, no longer young, with her leg in plaster, holding a few aged pieces of paper in her hand. Letters, notebooks, newspapers. What were they worth now?

And again I wanted to tell her — the past is a mirage. A mirage. You want to reach it, grasp it, comprehend it. But you can't. Because it isn't there any more.

Yet how could I blame my mother when I had come to that house trying to do exactly the same thing?

I helped put all her things away, back into the darkness of the drawers. Then she took my arm and slowly we went upstairs together.

Twelve

I am speaking to Gabriel Ronay in London, in the sitting-room of his house in Highgate. I have just been introduced to his children — three slim, pert girls of thirteen, triplets. They have gone upstairs now, to do their homework. But through the ceiling I can hear them playing some pop music and, every once in a while, giggling amongst themselves. Gabriel's eyes drift upwards and he frowns. He hesitates, as though he might go up and tell them to get on with it. But he thinks better of it, shrugs, and turns his attention to me.

'You must understand,' he begins, 'that I have never considered myself to be a refugee. I was in a rather special position after the 1956 revolution, having been one of its student leaders. I was flown to this country by the British. I saw the refugees, in their thousands, at the transit camps. I'll never forget their desperate, lost faces. I was profoundly grateful not to have to be among them. But let me go back to the beginning, to the days of the uprising itself.

'I was then twenty-four, studying at the Institute of Slavonic Studies, Budapest University. I involved myself in various activities when the violence broke out, such as helping to organize the general strike by 30,000 workers at the Csepel Island industrial complex. That was on the evening of 23 October. Later, I made repeated trips to the Austrian frontier in an attempt to get messages through to the United Nations, so that they would know what was happening in Hungary. I did this with the aid of the Indian Ambassador in Budapest and his counterpart in Vienna. They acted as mediators, passing our messages on. It was a risky business. Eventually the authorities found out. When I learned that they were after me, I decided it was time to leave.

'I fled across the border into Austria. There was the usual sort of stuff to contend with, Russian tanks, shooting, ambushes.' He speaks quietly and nonchalantly as he sits in his armchair in this most English of sitting-rooms. The phone rings and before he can answer it, one of his daughters darts into the room and picks it up. It's a school friend. They have a brief, animated conversation about some project or other, then the triplet flashes us a smile, tosses a ponytail over her shoulder and leaves the room.

'To continue,' says Gabriel, unruffled. 'I made my way to a youth hostel in Vienna. There, along with many other students, I was closely questioned by the British authorities. I had to explain why I wanted to come to England, why I needed political asylum. They were careful about whom they accepted. I believe we were all vetted by British intelligence. Fortunately, I was able to prove my bona fide standing and passed the screening. I became one of a group of thirty students to be flown here on a collective passport, under the auspices of London University.'

'You spoke fluent French and German, but no English. So why did you choose to come here?' I ask.

'It's true I could have gone anywhere in the world to study. While I was staying at the hostel, representatives of learned institutions from many countries came to invite us. It was appealing to consider Canada, the U.S., Australia and other distant, exotic places. But what I craved more than anything at that time was to live in a true "working democracy". And although I wasn't blind to the warts, I saw in England a country with the kind of parliamentary system which I respected and could live under.

'Also, I wanted to get as far away as possible from 1956 and its horrors. I was invited with some other students to 'take tea' at the British Council's office in Vienna. We had genteel little sausages and cucumber sandwiches. And I realized that the English were as far removed from my previous life as anything I could imagine.

''56 was really my starting point. It thrust me into awareness, it was the beginning of my *Weltanschauung*. Everything in my present life has sprung, directly or indirectly, from that event.'

Gabriel offers me a glass of sherry. I get up and have a look at the books which cover one wall of the room. He is a historian, an author and a journalist. I'm not quite sure in which order he considers himself to be these things, but it would be apparent to anyone who runs an eye along his books that their owner is of scholarly inclinations. I am curious to know in which subject he obtained his degree from Edinburgh University.

'Philology', he replies. 'Some time after I completed my studies my father wrote me a letter in which he urged me to return home.

"It's time to come back to where you belong," he said. He sent me other letters, all saying the same thing. Then one day an unsigned postcard arrived. It said simply, "Disregard all my previous correspondence." I learned later that the authorities had been putting pressure on him to get me to return to Hungary. It dawned on them that because of the revolution they had lost an awful lot of highly educated young people, and now they wanted them back. The "People's Republic" needed them.

'Needless to say, I had no intentions whatsoever of going back. I loathed what was going on in my country. I had grown up during the war, during the years of Stalinism, and I despised it all.'

'You haven't been at all homesick over the years? You feel no sense of affinity with Hungary any more?' For some reason I want to see whether I can stir up a bit of emotion, some nationalistic fervour. Gabriel is being far too English.

'I am one of those Hungarians who were born in the Romanian part of Transylvania. I still feel strongly about my birthplace and definitely consider myself Hungarian; I would be a phoney if I tried to pass myself off as an Englishman. And I am still concerned with the issues which affect Transylvania. I have written lately about the repression of the Hungarian minority there. But I have found myself naturally inclined towards what Goethe described as *Wahlverwandschaft. . .*'

'I didn't quite catch that word,' I mutter ashamedly. Must swot up on Goethe, I tell myself.

'Let me explain. It means to have "elective affinity", to embrace the style of life, the ambience, the political beliefs which suit you, rather than blindly accepting and devoting yourself to those of the country in which you were born. In other words, to choose some things and reject others, according to your conscience. There is no such thing as "my country right or wrong".

'Many facets of the English way of life — the whole approach, the humour, the reserve, the standards — are totally alien to what my family stood for. Yet these things have always seemed so natural to me. When I was a child my father used to say I was like the "cold-blooded English", because I didn't wear my emotions on my sleeve like Hungarians do. I kept things to myself.'

'So I assume it didn't take long for you to feel at home here?'

'Not at all. And when I am abroad, I feel very English indeed.'

'I also felt immediately at home in London, when I moved here. Although perhaps for different reasons to yours. You fit in so well because the English mentality and manners are so natural to you. I

215

can't say they are natural to me. Amongst a gathering of Oxbridge graduates, I still feel like a gawky American high-school kid. And occasionally, so I'm told, my outbursts are of a decidedly temperamental Magyar nature. I have tried my hand at *Englishness*, at the casual toss of an under-statement here and a euphemism there, at the modest, mild-mannered and self-deprecating look, but without much success. So, what-the-hell, I don't pretend to be anything but what I am. And that's why I fit into London. It's a city which never pushes you into pretensions. Anyone from anywhere can live here and remain true to his own nature. All it demands in return is an equal measure of tolerance from you.'

Gabriel tells me about the books which he has had published here, works which have added considerably to the historical knowledge of this country. 'I believe that through my work I have made a place for myself here, and been accepted,' he says. 'I've done a great deal of intricate research, which has led to the revelations about English and Central European history contained in my book, *The Tartar Khan's Englishman*, and in my latest work, as yet unpublished.'

As befits any historian worth his salt, he is not afraid of arousing controversy, which is precisely what his historical discoveries do. And like a true English intellectual, in order to defend himself against attacks, he plunges with enormous relish into lengthy letters to the Editor of *The Times*, battles with sceptical academics and other unbelievers. And he always emerges looking good, because, unlike most academics and historians, he has had many years of journalistic training behind him and knows how to deal a deadly verbal blow.

So of what do these revelations consist?

'I unearthed certain documents with the help of which I was able to piece together the life story of the chief envoy at the court of Genghis Khan, a ruthless man who destroyed over half a dozen nations in Europe with his "negotiations". I discovered that he was an Englishman, a former Catholic priest who had been recruited by Tartar spies, and whose aim was to convert England to Islam.

'Now, in my latest book, I explain my theory, supported by documentary evidence, of what really happened to Edward and Edmund Aetheling, the sons of Edmund Ironside, who were the original models for the famous "princes in the Tower".'

'The princes allegedly murdered by Richard III?'

'Precisely. Of course, Shakespeare was using literary licence in the play. He based the incident on something which had occurred long before Richard, in the eleventh century.'

Suddenly the house is quiet. No more music is wafting through the ceiling. It is as if we are alone. Gabriel pours a spot more sherry. He has awakened my curiosity, but now sits in silence, contemplating his drink.

'Well?' I ask at last. 'What happened in the eleventh century?'

'Are you interested? I'll make the story short. The brothers, heirs to the throne, were to be put to death by King Knut of Denmark. But they were saved and managed to escape. Eventually they ended up in Hungary, and settled there. Forty years later Edward returned to England as rightful successor to the throne. But within twenty-four hours he was assassinated. All this led to the succession of King Harold, the Norman Invasion, and thus to the present link with the ancient Anglo-Norman ruling house and the end of the Saxon connection. So, you see, it was a decisive turning point in history.'

I shake my head slowly, reflecting on the fate of poor Edward Aetheling, the English prince who had spent part of his life in my country.

'Unfortunately,' says Gabriel, 'I had hoped to do some research crucial to my book in Hungary, but was thwarted by the Hungarian authorities last year. It was my first attempt to go back since '56. I was led to believe that I would be granted a visa without any problems, but at the last minute official co-operation was withdrawn without explanation. I was shocked. After all, I had thought I was *persona grata* there. *The Tartar Khan's Englishman* had even been reviewed with much enthusiasm in the Hungarian press. So why the abrupt change of mind?

'Some pathetic little bureaucrat's decision in the Foreign Ministry had made it extremely difficult for me to complete my book. Naturally I wasn't going to let it rest. I was determined to kick up a row that would make things damned unpleasant for the comrades. They had violated the Helsinki agreement, that was clear. Why should they get away with it?'

'But what could you, an individual, do about it?'

'A lot. That's why I chose to live in this place. I gained the full support of the British Council and the Foreign Office (which promptly withdrew permission for four Hungarian writers and journalists to come here under the official cultural exchange programme), not to mention the Society of Authors and the National Union of Journalists. By the time I was through, cultural and public relations between the two countries were not what they had been.

'But the whole thing has had a sad outcome. My feelings towards Hungary have been permanently soured. It's put paid to any link I had with it. The umbilical cord has snapped. You asked before about homesickness. How can anyone be homesick for a country in which such unjust, arbitrary actions can so easily be taken? No, any homesickness I may have had has been killed off. I now have a purely uncommitted, neutral relationship with Hungary.'

'Does your family feel the same way?'

'The trip last year was to have been a big family affair. My wife, who is English, and the girls were all very excited about it. In fact my children are most interested in their father's background. But now, I'm afraid, their heritage is closed to them. I will certainly never attempt to go to Hungary again. As for the children, when they are adults and able to make their own decisions, it will be up to them.'

As if on cue, the triplets enter with a little girlish fanfare. But now there are four of them. A friend has arrived for supper. She is also slight and ponytailish.

'Hello,' says Gabriel. 'Who are you?'

'I'm Becky. Can we watch *Top of the Pops?*' The sisters exchange looks and chuckles. They all edge hopefully towards the portable black-and-white set in a corner.

Gabriel glances at me questioningly.

'I don't mind,' I offer magnanimously, realizing that my time is about to be up shortly, anyway. They switch the set on and we are all immediately drowned by 'new wave' music.

'Please turn the volume down, girls,' says Gabriel, the very model of fatherly restraint.

When we can hear each other again we resume our conversation.

'The reason I'm here, as you know,' I tell him, 'is because we have both escaped from the Hungarian Revolution, although, unlike myself, you've never actually held refugee status. There is also the great difference that you escaped as an adult, whereas I was a mere child. But there is an underlying bond between us, because 1956 decided our fates for us, albeit not in the same fashion. Its personal significance for us, therefore, is plain. But what was the importance of the revolution as far as the rest of the world is concerned?'

'It was a pivotal point in history, rather like the murder of

Edward Aetheling. It was a milestone, because it destroyed an image of monolithic communism in Europe and ended the belief that those peoples born and brought up under communist dictatorship would go on accepting it, putting up with it forever. At last Russian imperialism was shown to be the brutal and ruthless force that it is. The impact of the uprising on the West was unlike that of any other previous event. For the first time the crude colonial exploitation of the subject nations of Eastern Europe were visibly made plain; the West could no longer pretend suppression didn't exist.

'The uprising, although doomed, did ensure a higher standard of living for Hungarians thereafter, as well as a measure of internal independence. But the price was unacceptably high — 35,000 young people were killed during the revolution. In terms of a small nation such as Hungary, that figure is appalling. Undoubtedly it made its impression on the world. For example, the British Communist Party never recovered from 1956, but resignations from the Party were massive worldwide. Internationally known left-wing and liberal figures were outraged. Camus said: "The subjugated and enslaved Hungary did more for the cause of freedom and justice than any other people in the world during the last twenty years." John F. Kennedy said: "October 23, 1956 is a day that will live forever in the annals of free men and free nations. It was a day of courage, conscience, and triumph. No other day since history began has shown more clearly the eternal unquenchability of man's desire to be free, whatever the odds against success, whatever the sacrifice required." So, to answer your question, the impact of the revolution on the rest of the world was great, its importance inestimable. A country rose against a tyrant and shook it off, for a while. But the effects of this action were more dramatic and significant than the revolutionaires themselves had intended. And afterwards, the educated élite who had escaped were at last able to convince the West that defectors from the East weren't the rascals and misfits which their oppressors made them out to be.'

I ask what were the moments he remembered most vividly from the revolution. Tanks being blasted by Molotov cocktails? Schoolchildren firing sub-machine guns? Or perhaps he was there when the revolutionaries took revenge on the despised A.V.O.s, some of whom were rounded up and shot or lynched?

'Yes, I saw all those things, and once or twice I nearly lost my life, too. But one scene has stayed with me more sharply than the rest, a scene which was not violent but intense, and full of irony and pathos. It was when a large number of powerful Russian "advisers" and their families, who had been living in the capital, were loaded together with their belongings onto a paddle-steamer on the Danube. It had been chartered by the Red Cross for the purpose of expelling these hated representatives of suppression and exploitation. I stood on the quay amidst a crowd of Hungarians, watching the Russians as they queued to get on the boat, struggling for places, losing a lot of their belongings in the process. I wrote an article about this, the only time I ever wrote about my experiences during the revolution.'

His article ends with these lines:

It was tea-time when the last of the fleeing Russians was eased into the bulging boat. Crammed like sardines, they stood on the deck and looked at the city, not in our direction and the shot-up houses beyond, but towards Buda and the smart villas that had been their homes in the days of power and influence. Perhaps they were taking their leave.

The crowd on the upper quay was awaiting their departure in utter silence. There were no catcalls, there was nothing to gloat about. The Soviet advisers were leaving but the memories of terror and humiliation were staying with us. The people on the ship's deck and the people on the quay looked at each other but saw only the past.

The paddle-steamer moved off the quay and we watched for a while the dirty waves it churned up. Then we dispersed.

Gabriel and I sit for a while without speaking. We finish our sherry. On the floor in front of the television the girls are sprawled out, their chins in the palms of their hands, their long hair tumbling down their backs nearly to their waists. They are engrossed in the performance of some rising star of the rock world. They haven't been listening to us. Their minds are not on such weighty matters. For an instant my mind shoots back to the time when I was a mere slip of a schoolgirl, listening to records and watching *Star Trek* before supper, hoping no one would find out I hadn't yet done my maths homework. I sigh, feeling old.

Meanwhile, Gabriel stifles a yawn.

'You're tired,' I say, standing up. 'I'm sorry, I've kept you too long.'

'Forgive me.' He rises, too. 'I've been doing the night shift recently at *The Times*. From time to time my job as foreign news sub-editor and copy-taster requires me to work rather ungodly hours.'

We shake hands, I thank him, we say good-bye. I am almost through the front door when one of the triplets comes running after me.

'Excuse me!'

I turn around.

'Excuse me, miss. Are these your gloves?'

They are my gloves. As usual, I have left them behind. I smile at the girl and thank her. She grins back.

Delightful child, I think to myself as I get into my car and drive off.

Thirteen

Adam and I stood together in the front garden in Budapest, watching a gypsy cut down an apple tree. My grandfather had planted it long ago but for several years now it had been neglected, no one took much notice of it, and so it had grown sickly. My mother decided it must be cut down. There is an amiable, dark-skinned gypsy who does odd jobs around the neighbourhood, so she sent for him. He was delighted to do it. He stuffed his pockets with apples from the tree, handed one to Adam, and started to hack away with his axe.

It was the last full day of our trip. The following morning we would be boarding our plane for London. The four weeks had marched by so quickly. As with a parade, I had tried to see and remember, to experience as fully as I could everything which passed before me. The colours were dazzling, the 'displays' exciting to watch. But inevitably, my head began to spin with it all, my vision became blurred. And so perhaps it was time to go home.

In my mind's eye I saw London. Whenever I am away from it for any length of time I begin to ache for that fat, grey, lazy metropolis. It would be good to be back again, I thought. That reminded me that I hadn't yet packed. I took hold of Adam's hand. He was still munching on his apple. We started to walk towards the house. Then I heard someone call my name.

It was a woman I couldn't recognize. She was coming in my direction from Imre and Mária's house next door. She stepped lightly over the rocks and weeds dividing their garden from ours. When she was near I saw that she was older than I had thought. Her slim figure and loose, long hair had made me think she was in her twenties. But she was fortyish.

'Hello,' she said, 'I'm Kati. I'm visiting my parents from America. I arrived yesterday and heard that you were here, too.'

'Kati! I didn't know you were coming to Budapest.'

'Impulsive decision. Never mind, I hear you're leaving tomorrow. This is our only chance to meet. Come and have coffee.'

The mongrels started yelping and leaping at our approach. Imre, who had been tending the roses at the back of the garden in his Guatamalan cap, came to calm them down.

Kati and I went into the kitchen. The sun shone in through the open side-door and from where I sat I had a good view of my mother's house, the pine and chestnut trees and the little falling apple tree. A breath of cool October air came in, swept once around my legs and expired.

It was an instant I knew I would never want to relinquish. October. . .it is a month unlike the rest, when anything can happen, when life is on the verge of death. The sun may shine but you cannot ignore the chill of approaching destruction; it is easy to linger in hope, but the winter soon puts an end to it. In short, it is a month rife with dreams and delusions. It is followed by November, with whose voracity we are all familiar.

Kati smoothed back her hair and studied me. 'Do you remember the last time we were together?' she asked. 'It was in October '56. You and your brother were sitting on my lap in a big armchair in the sitting-room; we were reading a Barbar book. You used to come over and visit me. I'd read you stories or we'd play games. You were nice kids. By the end of November, we had all left the country.'

'Did you ever regret your decision?'

'No, because I've always been happy. The state of my nationality has been somewhat confusing, I must confess. But perhaps more to other people than to myself. Anyway, it isn't really such a bad thing to be 'displaced', as long as you're happy.

'There's only one place where I feel truly at home, and that's Paris. Which is odd, considering it's where I have spent least of my life. But I've always had an instinctive affinity with it and I speak French more naturally than Hungarian or English. I've lived in the U.S. more or less continuously since '56, but I still feel myself to be a guest there, even in my own house.

'In Paris people take me to be a Parisian, because I'm like someone in her element. Yet I am not in any way French. I am a citizen of long standing in the U.S., where I'm always being mistaken for a visitor. And here in Budapest,' she smiled and shrugged, 'here I have the oddest sensation of all. When I'm in my parents' house I feel totally at home, as if I had never left it. It is a natural, comfortable place for me. Yet the minute I step out onto the street I feel like a foreigner in a strange country.'

'Have you no friends or acquaintances here any more?'

She shook her head. 'They've all left. They're spread out all over the world. But that doesn't matter. I come to see my parents, I usually bring my son and I show him the old house, the city, he picks up a few Hungarian words, he learns something about the country and his mother's background. We have a very pleasant time.'

'Doesn't your husband ever come with you?'

'He rarely visits Europe at all. You know the Americans, they can be quite insular, even nowadays. Besides, he's usually too busy with his job, he's a professor of philosophy.'

We sat without speaking for a while, on either side of the wooden kitchen table. I could see that Kati was engrossed by the novelty of the situation. Here we were again, same people, same place, a generation later. We had Adam by our feet. We both watched him crawling under the table after some little trinket, and heard his cry of delight once he had retrieved it. He seemed to have become a kind of timeless and unspoken bridge between Kati and me, and I wondered whether she, too, felt this.

I was overcome by a curiosity about the past. 'What were we like as children?' I asked.

She thought for a moment. 'Well, your brother rather fancied himself as my suitor. He would call to me over the fence when he saw me coming home, and ask me where I'd been. He was protective towards you. Once when you were here you pulled your skirt right up around your waist and I told you it wasn't ladylike. Your brother put an arm around your shoulder and said, "We're leaving. We shan't stay here if you're going to insult us." And both of you were always up to some mischief. This house was your refuge. You ran across the garden to escape punishment at home. Goodness, how you two would make us laugh.'

I told Kati that I would have to go and pack now, because relatives and friends would be dropping in soon to say farewell, so I wouldn't get a chance to do it later. She said she understood. We kissed each other's cheeks. Adam wouldn't put down the little toy he'd been playing with and Kati said he should keep it, it was just a silly thing her own son had left here during a holiday some years before.

When Adam and I reached our own garden we turned back and waved to her.

'Good-bye!' she called to us. 'Have a good journey home.

Maybe we'll meet again somewhere, you can never tell.'

That last evening in Budapest was a rich and ebullient affair. I hadn't realized how many new friends I had made, or how much closer I had become to the old ones. All of a sudden people were coming to see me, filling up the house, bringing me gifts. The dining table became a forest of bottles for me to take back to London — Russian champagne, homemade *pálinka, tokaji aszú*. And with them came drinking instructions: to be knocked back first thing in the morning, or sipped slowly last thing at night, or drunk to the accompaniment of Liszt's Hungarian Fantasia.

Everyone had a few sage last words, everyone wanted promises. Certainly I'll be back one day, yes, soon, and I won't forget any of you or Sándor Petőfi or the Homeland. A part of me will always remain, I promise.

Anna Éber brought me one of her small pastel chalk pictures. It was all turquoise and white, a Balaton scene in which the sky and the water merge together, punctuated only by two seagulls and a distant sailboat. This was an unexpected prize for me. It would always remind me of her and her studio and the boundless compassion which emanates from all her work.

Of Adam, they all agreed that he was eminently *életrevaló*, an expression which has no real English equivalent, but means 'suited to life'. I suppose it is a polite way of saying 'very energetic, exhausting and frequently naughty'. He got a toy dog from Sanyi and Manci, who arrived in a taxi and were most excited about meeting him at last.

'I knew he would look like your father,' Manci told me as she bent down to hug him. 'Can't you see it, Sanyi? The dark hair, the dark eyes!' Sanyi looked down at them and smiled and nodded. The plaster was gone from his chin and there was no sign of the unfortunate shaving cut. He seemed unsteady on his feet so I put a hand under his arm. It was just as well, for Little Pali appeared from somewhere and the two boys chased each other around the room knocking into poor Sanyi's legs. He winced slightly, but I think it may have been more from amusement than agitation.

Ervin and his wife arrived. He had fashioned a pretty little necklace for me down in his dungeon and now he hung it around my neck.

'I'm sure you can buy much better ones abroad,' he said. 'But this is just a token. Remember me to your father. Tell him I still think often of those days we spent as prisoners together and that I haven't forgotten. . .well, I haven't forgotten anything.'

When Pista and Judith arrived the jokes and anecdotes began to explode around us like fireworks. Drinks were poured, old stories dredged up, the young men grouped together over the dining table and exchanged a few pornographic laughs.

Gizi and Géza came. She was smartly dressed and had her frizzy wig on. She went into a lengthy conversation with my mother about orthopaedics. Meanwhile Géza stood quietly to one side and seemed somehow lost without being enclosed by his family or his Mercedes. I thought of the evening we drove up to the Fishermen's Bastion, soon after my arrival, of the sight once again after so many years of the sparkling, silent city below us. This silence, I had felt, was reflected in eyes, and I couldn't quite understand how or why, nor do I think I shall ever understand. For tomorrow I would be going away and leaving this reality behind me and, from the moment I am gone, it will begin its slow transmogrification into unreality. And I will be like a cosmonaut, travelling through space and through time, looking back at a world growing ever smaller and hazier, but perhaps also becoming all the more precious for that.

Géza's mother was there, too, an unhealthy woman with swollen limbs. And others came, distant relations whom I had barely heard of, let alone met. But *why* were they all coming? Surely it was too late now, there could be no hope of getting to know them very well. What was the point?

I began to understand the point, gradually. For many of them I was a link between them and the West. I could see by now that the West was less of a geographical definition than an abstract conception. And as a visiting fraction of it, I was an object of considerable curiosity. This was their last chance to get a bit nearer the conception, to one of its tangible products.

Laci and Big Klári and Little Klári and Csaba arrived together in the shiny red Lada. Was it my imagination, or did Csaba seem rather less oppressed than usual? His pink cheeks began to glow when he spotted the knot of men standing and joking together, and he quickly disappeared into their midst.

Little Klári came close to me and whispered with girlish glee, 'Guess what? We've found a place to live. A little maisonette which we can rent for one year from a couple who are going abroad. The house is new, in fact it's still being built. But who minds living on a building site? At least we can get married now!'

Laci gave me an enormous hug. 'How's our little English lady?'

I tried feebly to wriggle away. 'I'm not an English lady, really,' I said.

'Well, then,' someone else called out, 'what are you? A Magyar?'

'Yes, yes,' I said, 'a Magyar.' There was laughter, merriment, jokes, music, Adam and Little Pali were still chasing around the house, in and out of the kitchen, bumping into Juszti, who was just wheeling out a great plateful of her own freshly-made pastries.

'There are some chestnut cakes here, and marzipan ones, if anybody is interested,' she announced to the room in general.

When you get a band of Hungarians together you can be certain of a few things: there will be more than enough to eat and drink, someone is going to start singing, there will be bursts of noise and laughter, and the evening will begin to wind its way around your skull like a snake, numbing your senses. Then it becomes increasingly difficult to take anything else in, you want to be alone and go to bed. But you are also aware that it is your fate to be there and this knowledge immobilizes you. In a way, you are possessed by these people. It's as simple as that. So you stay put, you tell yourself you're having a ball, until at last you feel the snake letting go. And then, in a peculiar way, you're sad that it's all over. You've got used to the old snake.

In the morning I made a few last-minute phone calls to say good-bye to people; mercifully the line was in tolerable working order. For the last time I heard the friendly thunder of the actor Sándor's voice and I envisaged him in his glamorous one-room flat, striding about in a silk dressing-gown.

I spoke to Bandi, the ex-dentist and psychiatrist.

'We didn't really get a chance to talk,' he said.

'No, the time passed so quickly.'

'Maybe one day in America,' he sounded jovial and optimistic, 'or who knows? We might bump into each other anywhere. It's not a very big world, is it?'

Then I called Attila, the fencer, whose voice was distant and impatient.

'You women always phone at the wrong time,' he said, 'I'm just having a bath.'

'Sorry. It's nothing important. I'll ring back in about ten years.'

Next I spoke to Margit, and that conversation went on for a bit. I glanced at my watch.

'Do write to me from London,' she was saying in a breathy, eager voice. 'We must keep in touch. And if there's ever anything you want from Hungary, let me know. Don't hesitate.'

By now the telephone line was growing sick. Following its admirable and sustained effort, it was giving way to crackling and buzzing. I signed off hastily before it died out altogether, and joined the others at the breakfast table.

'Have a nice cup of tea,' Big Pali said, pouring a dash of milk into my cup before filling it up with Earl Grey. 'Sugar? One lump or two?'

A month ago he'd been a Huszár. Now he was an English country gentleman.

I turned to Juszti, who was placing two jars of homemade jam on the table.

'Have you ever been on an airplane?' I asked.

She shook her head vigorously and laughed. 'Goodness, no. I couldn't possibly do *that*.' She looked pensive. 'No. I haven't been anywhere at all, really, by any form of transport.'

It occurred to me that there are millions of people in the world who have never travelled across a frontier, never been in a plane.

No sooner had I finished breakfast than we heard the sound of the Zsiguli rolling into the driveway. Presently, Dódi and Mári came in. Dódi was rubbing his hands together and his moustache twitched with anticipation. Mári wore that look of barely suppressed emotion with which I had become familiar.

'Shall we put your suitcases into the car?' she asked.

'Please. I'll be ready in a minute. I just want to see if I've left anything upstairs.' I knew there was nothing there, but I felt I had to run up those steps one more time. It isn't the sort of house you can take your leave of lightly or hurriedly. I went into the bedroom where Adam and I had slept for a month. Emptied of our belongings it seemed unlike a bedroom at all. It was like a room you might wander into during a dream - still and silent, but curiously full of presence.

I heard someone come in behind me. It was my mother.

'What are you thinking about?' she asked.

I was embarrassed. As I said once before, I'm not a sentimental person. I'm a cynic. Cosmopolitan. Worldly-wise. So what was I doing blowing my nose and wiping my eyes into an old paper handkerchief? Once again, I'd been caught out and felt silly and childish, like the moment four weeks earlier when my plane landed at Ferihegy Airport and I didn't know what had taken hold of me.

The answer was plain. I would finally have to admit something to myself: a refugee will always be a refugee, and with only one refuge - his own sensibility. It was useless to search for 'roots'. The roots of an emigrant do not grow downwards into the soil of any particular place, neither the old country nor the new. They grow inwards, deeper and deeper into himself, and they become knotted and intertwined. And he carries them everywhere he goes. So, contrary to popular belief, he hasn't 'left them behind' at all. Maybe once in a while he can use his X-ray vision to examine them, or he might want to dispose of them altogether. But that would call for major surgery. And who likes operations? So more likely than not, he'll just accept them as part of himself.

I had come to Hungary in search of answers. But there were no answers, because it had been a mistake to ask the questions in the first place. If you want figures, I can say that Hungary has ten million people and two million live in Budapest and among them half a million own cars. But how is it possible to frame the question 'Do you still love the country of your birth?' It's like asking someone whether they still love their mother. Of course they do. They may feel like screaming at her from time to time, they may not want to go round for Sunday lunch every week, but they love her. Each country, like each mother, is unique. And it is uniqueness which inspires love within those for whom it exists.

As it happens, Hungary is not a difficult country to love. It is resourceful, its people have great humour despite the series of unhappy predicaments the country has found itself in throughout the centuries. Its smallness makes it vulnerable. It hasn't the size and might of Poland, for example. Unlike Poland, it is no longer on the verge of furious eruption. It has found other, quieter methods of existence. One day it might produce its own Lech Walesa, but for the time being there is no desperate need for one. Hungary has accepted its vulnerability, it has made compromises.

The Hungarian language is equally inspiring of love. It is lyrical, expressive, rich. It is designed for poets and romantics. But it is impossible to translate; the finest poetry turns into mundane words and rhymes. Its isolation has made it inaccessible to others.

I embraced my mother, said good-bye and went downstairs where Mári and Dódi were waiting, Adam in hand, to leave for the airport. It was brilliantly sunny outside but, as usual, the sun could not find its way into the sitting-room. Tall trees shaded the windows. Juszti was standing in the doorway, wiping her eyes. She was so small and innocent.

It seemed odd to me as I stood there, looking around for the last time, that anyone could live in that house. It was not a house to me at all, but some kind of time machine, too full of distracting echoes. And more than this, it was a symbol. My mother has clung to it for a quarter of a century, as the evidence of past success and happiness. Yet for me it symbolizes the hopelessness of trying to live simultaneously in two different worlds and in two different eras. Yet I can understand why she should want to cling to it. It, too, is unique.

We drove through the gates. A final journey down Budakeszi Avenue under the chestnut trees, alongside a yellow streetcar. The dead leaves rose and then fell again in our wake. Onto the bridge, with Budapest opening itself to us.

'The Danoob River!' cried Adam, pointing at the water which glistened like ice in the sunlight.

Mári and Dódi sat in the front. I watched their heads bobbing up and down to the ruts in the road, as they did a month earlier when we were going in the opposite direction. I wanted to say something to them, I felt it was important. I might not see or speak to them again for years. But I was tired and drained and didn't know what to say.

I hardly saw the outskirts of the capital. My mind was already in London, with my husband. I imagined our conversation, our exchange of news and stories.

We arrived at the airport. Adam began to pull away and skip in his excitement. He's a seasoned traveller. He saw half of Europe in his first year. But it still excites him. I wondered whether the globe was big enough to keep these jet-age babies contented all their lives. There's something to be said for the Jusztis of the world: it will always be endlessly mysterious for them.

We stood in a close group in the terminal building.

'Do you know,' asked Dódi, 'the difference between the English and the Hungarians? The English part without saying good-bye, while the Hungarians are always saying good-bye but never part.'

I laughed politely. It's true, Hungarian farewells seem to go on forever. But not this time. I would be very English. As soon as I had checked in my baggage I kissed them both, heaved Adam up in my arms and went through passport control. I looked back and waved briefly. Then I couldn't see them any more.

There was a delay. Through the glass doors overlooking the

230

tarmac I watched the blue and white Malév planes waiting, being loaded, taxi-ing down the runway. On the information board flight numbers and destinations kept scurrying into new positions. Warsaw, Leningrad, Prague, London. Just outside, on the other side of the glass, soldiers with truncheons, pistols in brown holsters, and walkie-talkies in their hands were walking by in single file. There was the sound of an ambulance somewhere in the distance, then the noise of another plane taking off.

At last we boarded.

'Morning Madam. Lovely day, isn't it?' said the steward.

I settled down with *The Times* and the *Guardian*. As soon as we had taken off, two stewardesses rolled a trolley full of drinks down the aisle.

The captain introduced himself in a modest, jolly sort of way.

'Our flight time will be two hours, twenty minutes,' he announced.

London really isn't so far away, I thought to myself as I sipped a sherry on this little piece of England flying through the sky. Only two hours, twenty minutes and twenty-five years.

Throughout my life, airplane trips have heralded new eras for me, they have meant *beginnings*. The first time I flew was on 29 December 1956. My family had been staying at the Korneuburg refugee camp in Vienna, but we were transported to Munich and flown from there on a U.S.A.F. plane to Camp Kilmer in New Jersey to be processed as immigrants. It was a massive airlift scheme, which became known as 'Operation Mercy'. The seats on the plane were facing backwards, an ironical reflection of the occasion. Some of the passengers, perhaps, have been looking in that direction ever since.

On the 25 July 1970, I flew from New York to London. A second emigration, as it turned out. Then it was by jumbo jet and my gaze was most definitely straight ahead, on the future. That's the best way to begin an era.

The friendly steward bent down and grinned at Adam.

'How'd you like to meet the captain, old chap?' he asked.

'Go on,' I told my son, 'He might let you wear his cap.'

They walked hand in hand towards the cockpit. I sat alone by the window. I thought about Hungary. How close had I come to it? Closer, I think, than many outsiders. Yes, I believe it was a good beginning. And I suppose I will continue to meet people at cocktail parties now and then for whom 'Hungarian' means little else besides Bull's Blood and Béla Lugósi. What can I say to them?

CZECHOSLOVAKIA

AUSTRIA

Lake Fertő

SOPRON ●

Fertőd ●

GYŐR ●

River Danube

Zebegény ●

Bánk ●

BUDAPEST

H

U

N

Balatonfüred
Tihany ●
●

Lake Balaton

Gölle ●

KAPOSVÁR ●

River Danube

PÉCS ●

YUGOSLAVIA